GUIDE
TO ANALYSIS
OF LANGUAGE
TRANSCRIPTS

Second Edition

Kristine S. Retherford, Ph.D.

THINKING PUBLICATIONS
EAU CLAIRE, WISCONSIN

© 1987, 1993 by Thinking Publications, *A Division of McKinley Companies, Inc.*
Thinking Publications grants limited rights to individual professionals to reproduce and distribute pages that indicate duplication is permissible. Pages can be used for student instruction only and must include Thinking Publications' copyright notice. All rights are reserved for pages without the permission-to-reprint notice. No part of these pages may be reproduced in any form, electronic or mechanical, including photocopy, recording, or any information storage and retrieval system without permission in writing from the publisher.

Published 1987. Second Edition 1993

02   01   00   99   98   16   15   14   13   12

Library of Congress Cataloging-in-Publication Data

Retherford, Kristine S.
    Guide to analysis of language transcripts / by Kristine S. Retherford. —2nd ed.
        p.   cm.
    Previous ed. published under: Stickler, Kristine Retherford.
    Includes bibliographical references.
    ISBN 0-930599-87-X
    1. Children—Language—Evaluation.   I. Title.
RJ496.L35S84 1993
401' .9—dc20   93-19445
                                                                            CIP

Cover Design: Kris Madsen
Printed in the United States of America

THINKING PUBLICATIONS®
A Division of McKinley Companies, Inc.
424 Galloway Street • Eau Claire, WI 54703
1-800-225-GROW(4769) • FAX 1-800-828-8885
E-Mail:custserv@ThinkingPublications.com
www.ThinkingPublications.com

DEDICATION

To Emily Katherine

TABLE OF CONTENTS

TABLES

CREDITS

Table 2.9   Rules for Counting Number of Words from *Certain Language Skills in Children* by M. Templin, 1957, Minneapolis, MN: University of Minnesota Press. © 1957 by University of Minnesota Press; © renewed 1985 by Mildred C. Templin. Reprinted by permission.

Table 2.10   Calculating Vocabulary Diversity Using Type-Token Ratio (N = 480) from *Certain Language Skills in Children* by M. Templin, 1957, Minneapolis, MN: University of Minnesota Press. © 1957 by University of Minnesota Press; © renewed 1985 by Mildred C. Templin. Reprinted by permission.

Table 3.1   Rules for Assigning Morphemes to Utterances from *A First Language: The Early Stages* by R. Brown, 1973, Cambridge, MA: Harvard University Press. © 1973 by the President and Fellows of Harvard College. Reprinted by permission.

Table 3.2   Predicted MLU Ranges and Linguistic Stages of Children within One Predicted Standard Deviation of Predicted Mean from "The Relation Between Age and Mean Length of Utterance in Morphemes" by J. Miller and R. Chapman, 1981, *Journal of Speech and Hearing Research, 24*(2). © 1981 by the American Speech-Language-Hearing Association. Reprinted by permission.

Table 3.3   Brown's (1973) Target MLU in Morphemes and Upper Bound Lengths for Each Stage from *A First Language: The Early Stages* by R. Brown, 1973, Cambridge, MA: Harvard University Press. © 1973 by the President and Fellows of Harvard College. Reprinted by permission.

Table 4.1   A Profile of Pragmatic Characteristics of the Child with Specific Language Impairment from "Pragmatic Characteristics of the Child with Specific Language Impairment: An Interactionist Perspective" by H. Craig, in T. Gallagher (Ed.), *Pragmatics of Language*, 1991, San Diego, CA: Singular Publishing Group. © 1991 by Singular Publishing Group. Reprinted by permission.

LIST OF COMPLETED ANALYSIS FORMS

PREFACE

Guide to Analysis of Language Transcripts evolved from the frustration experienced when attempting to teach undergraduate and graduate student clinicians to analyze language production in children. While many procedures are available, most failed to meet my needs as an instructor; they lacked explicit directions and offered limited interpretation of results. The procedures included in this *Guide* attempt to improve existing procedures by providing explicit directions, guided practice, and principles for interpretation of results.

Guide takes readers from the data collection stage through the organization and analysis of data to the early stages of remediation planning. The selection of procedures to include for semantic analysis was influenced by my familiarity with an elaborate set of semantic categories for describing children's productions varying from approximately two to five morphemes in length. Procedures for analyzing productions of children in the one-word period were included, as was a procedure for analyzing vocabulary diversity. Of the many syntactic analysis procedures available, Jon Miller's procedures for assigning structural stage were selected for inclusion in this *Guide*, with modifications as deemed appropriate. The selection of procedures for analyzing pragmatic aspects of language production was very difficult. Sets of procedures for describing the functions of utterances were included, as were procedures for analyzing turn taking and appropriateness judgments. Overall, the semantic, syntactic, and pragmatic procedures described in *Guide* provide an organized, systematic approach to the analysis of language production.

The procedures consolidated in this *Guide* have been applied to transcripts of the language of preschool children for demonstration purposes. An understanding of the variability in the productions of normally developing children is essential before accurate diagnosis of with language delays and/or disorders can occur; the relevance of the procedures must be learned by first applying them to transcripts such as the ones included in *Guide*. A companion textbook to *Guide, Guide Applied: Production Characteristics of Language Impaired Children* (1992), applies each of the procedures presented in *Guide* to transcripts of children with language impairments.

To ease readability, masculine pronouns are occasionally used in *Guide* to refer to "the child." In no way does the use of masculine pronouns imply that only boys' language is analyzed; neither does the use of masculine pronouns imply a lessening of importance of the female gender. Masculine pronouns, which are to be interpreted generically in *Guide,* were used whenever confusion would occur from the use of nonsexist plural pronouns.

I am grateful to many individuals for their assistance in the preparation of *Guide to Analysis of Language Transcripts.* My students provided inspiration; for their criticism of and confusion over existing procedures, I offer thanks. Nancy McKinley contributed many hours of careful editing; her attention to detail is greatly appreciated. My reviewers, Marc Fey, Vicki Lord Larson, Linda Maro, and Susan Schultz, offered insightful suggestions; I am grateful for their input. Vivian Joubert provided expert technical advise; I appreciate her explanations. Florence Clickner endured endless revisions; I am particularly grateful for her enthusiasm and cheerfulness. Dan provided understanding and encouragement; I shall always be grateful.

The revisions to *Guide to Analysis of Language Transcripts* have been in the works almost from the time the first edition was in print. Some revisions have evolved from class discussions and serve to clarify ambiguity. Other revisions have grown out of suggestions offered by instructors who use *Guide* and add information or additional interpretation. To both of these groups of individuals I extend my gratitude. Marietta Plummer and Michele Roddick contributed many hours of analysis and completed transcript rechecks for *Guide.* I am grateful for their persistence. Sharon Fredericks provided reliability checks and made suggestions for the glossary. I am grateful for her assistance. Florence Clickner again endured the revisions and format modifications with cheerfulness and enthusiasm. I appreciate her endurance. Linda Schreiber contributed endless hours of careful editing and insightful discussion. I appreciate her attention to detail.

And Jessica Stickler and Krista Curtis, as 4-year-olds, provided priceless examples of rich sentence elaboration. These utterances were central to my in-class discussions long before the first edition of *Guide*. And now these examples have found their way into the glossary of this edition. I am grateful for their willingness to talk about anything and everything. In spite of the fact that these two are almost teenagers now, I will always remember their fourth summer when I use one of their utterances as an example. My all-time favorites describe the search for "jellies what have holes for your toes." Thanks, Jess and Krista.

ABOUT THE AUTHOR

Kristine S. Retherford, Ph.D. is Professor in the Department of Communication Disorders at the University of Wisconsin—Eau Claire. She is also Director of Clinical Programs in Communication Disorders and oversees operations in the Center for Communication Disorders. In that capacity, she coordinates undergraduate and graduate clinical experiences off-campus and in the Center for Communication Disorders. In the Center for Communication Disorders, she supervises undergraduate and graduate students working with preschool children with language delays. Dr. Retherford frequently presents at inservices and workshops on language analysis and on intervention with infants and toddlers.

CHAPTER 1
General Production Analysis Considerations

Identification of children with language delays and/or disorders is one of the goals of the speech-language clinician. To identify such children, an evaluation battery must include the two major processes of language performance, language comprehension and language production, plus the interaction of these two processes in ongoing conversation. Numerous formal assessment procedures that have statistically documented validity and reliability measures with diverse sample populations are available for the evaluation of comprehension abilities. Among these are the *Peabody Picture Vocabulary Test* (Dunn and Dunn, 1981), the *Boehm Test of Basic Concepts—Revised* (Boehm, 1986), the *Test for Auditory Comprehension of Language—Revised* (Carrow-Woolfolk, 1985), the *Miller-Yoder Language Comprehension Test* (Miller and Yoder, 1984), the *Preschool Language Scale—3* (Zimmerman, Steiner, and Pond, 1992), and the *Test of Early Language Development* (Hresko, Reid, and Hammill, 1981). While many of these formal procedures also include cursory measures of language production, few result in a thorough description of production abilities. In addition, formal procedures for the analysis of communicative interaction are relatively few in number, the exceptions being the *Test of Pragmatic Skills* (Shulman, 1985), the *Let's Talk Inventory for Adolescents* (Wiig, 1982), and the *Let's Talk Inventory for Children* (Bray and Wiig, 1985).

Analysis of language production relies primarily on comparison of various aspects of production with data obtained from the language of normally developing children. But determining the appropriate linguistic behaviors to compare to normative data may be difficult, and comparison

under conditions identical to those in which the data were collected may be impossible. In addition, efficient management of the data leading to synthesis for development of remediation goals and objectives is cumbersome. The goal of *Guide to Analysis of Language Transcripts* is to provide guidelines for identification of various aspects of language production, analysis of the developmental level of the identified structures, and interpretation of the results of these analyses. Summaries of the data relevant to each of the analysis procedures are provided and methods for comparing analysis data to normative data are described. In addition, once each component of language production is analyzed, strategies for synthesis of data as the foundation for remediation are discussed. With practice, the task of analyzing language transcripts becomes easier and more efficient. Practice in making the necessary judgments is provided for each of the analysis procedures described within *Guide*.

There are many sets of procedures available for the analysis of specific aspects of language production. Commercially available procedures typically are designed to analyze one aspect of language production. For example, the *Developmental Sentence Score* (DSS) described by Lee (1974) provides a procedure for analyzing subject + verb complete utterances on the basis of the developmental level of eight grammatical categories. These include indefinite and personal pronouns, primary and secondary verbs, negation, conjunctions, interrogative reversals, and wh-questions. Although some of the categories analyzed would be considered semantic, the major intent is to provide a syntactic analysis of language production. The *Language Assessment, Remediation, and Screening Procedure* (LARSP) developed and described by

Crystal, Fletcher, and Garman (1976, 1991) provides for analysis of sentences, clauses, phrases, and word types. Again, some semantic information can be gleaned from this analysis procedure, but the primary result is analysis of syntax production. For analyzing semantic production abilities, the *Environmental Language Inventory* (MacDonald, 1978) provides a format for analysis of a child's use of "semantic-grammatical" rules. A variety of semantic relations are identified and scored as used in the language transcript. Although syntactic and pragmatic analyses are suggested, procedures are not specified.

In addition to the commercially available procedures, procedures described in the literature may make reference to syntactic and semantic aspects of language production, but no guidelines for the integration of these two components are described. For example, the *Assigning Structural Stage* procedure described within Miller (1981) includes identification of the developmental level of a variety of grammatical forms for syntactic analysis. Miller also identifies a variety of semantic analysis procedures, and Chapman (1981) summarizes a variety of pragmatic taxonomies. Application of syntactic, semantic, and pragmatic analyses to the same language transcript is not provided. The procedures described in *Guide to Analysis of Language Transcripts* have been developed to be used together to analyze semantic, syntactic, and pragmatic aspects of the same language transcript.

COMPUTER-BASED ANALYSIS PROCEDURES

One might ask, "Why should I learn to analyze language transcripts when computers can do the work?" It is true that a variety of microcomputer software programs has been developed for analysis of language transcripts. However, available programs differ in the types of analyses performed and the ease with which the coding procedures are learned and the analyses are accomplished. For example, *Lingquest 1: Language Sample Analysis* (Mordecai, Palin, and Palmer, 1982) offers three major types of analyses. First, the grammatical form analysis provides a frequency-of-use to opportunities-for-use comparison of eight major categories of grammatical forms including nouns, verbs, modifiers, prepositions, conjunctions, negations, interjections, and wh-question words. Error analysis and pattern identification can be accomplished. Second, the lexical analysis results in a frequency-of-use to opportunities-for-use comparison of vocabulary plus a measure of vocabulary diversity (a type-token ratio [TTR]). A mean length of utterance (MLU) in words can be obtained as well as an MLU in morphemes. Third, the structure analysis also provides frequency-of-use to opportunities-for-use comparison of a variety of phrase types, sentence types, and question types. Utterances to be analyzed must be transcribed with coding to identify structures to be analyzed. In addition, an expanded version of the utterance must be transcribed. This process may be difficult and time consuming. No tutorial is included with this program. Resulting summaries are valuable; however, frequency-of-occurrence data and error pattern identification can only be interpreted with a working knowledge of developmental data. No developmental stage information is provided.

Systematic Analysis of Language Transcripts (SALT), developed by Miller and Chapman (1983, 1991), is one of the most flexible and complicated software programs available. As with *Lingquest 1*, three types of analyses can be performed. First, word and morphemic analyses can be accomplished resulting in MLU, TTR, and omission summaries. Second, structural analyses are possible with verb element, question form, and negative form summaries. Third, utterance analyses can be performed, resulting in, among other things, preceding and following utterance-match summaries. In addition, numerous other options can be selected and/or created by the user. Because of its sophistication, considerable practice is necessary to master the program. However, a tutorial program is included to facilitate coding. Again, interpretation of results is dependent on the user's knowledge and experience and/or a comparison of the results to developmental norms. A reference database has been developed but is not included in the program.

A third software program for the analysis of language transcripts is the *Computerized Language Sample Analysis (CLSA)* developed by Weiner (1984). This program results in summaries of the frequency of occurrence and accuracy of use for 14 grammatical categories. Analysis of nouns, verbs, sentence types, length of utterance, and word usage can be accomplished. In addition, more detailed analyses can be selected. Schwartz (1985), in his review of *CLSA,* contended that familiarity with language analysis is crucial for the interpretation of information resulting from these analyses. Weiner (1984) has provided a tutorial to assist in learning to code utterances and to use this program. An updated version of this program is available under the title *Parrot Easy Language Sample Analysis* (Weiner, 1988).

A more recent language sample analysis program has been developed by Pye (1987). The *Pye Analysis of Language (PAL)* permits morphologic, syntactic, and phonologic analysis using procedures described by Ingram (1981). In addition, it is possible to create other analyses by manually coding the transcript. It is important to keep in mind that the program requires knowledge of DOS and DOS commands for coding and analysis.

The Computerized Language Profiling Version 6.1 (CP) developed by Long and Fey (1989) contains several analysis systems including many previously described procedures for hand analysis. Among these are *LARSP* (Crystal, Fletcher, and Garman, 1976, 1991), *PRISM+* (Crystal, 1982), and *DSS* found within *DSA* (Lee, 1974). Pragmatic and phonological analyses are possible as well. Depending on the type of analysis performed, complex manual coding is necessary and time consuming. Only the *DSS* and *Conversational Acts Profile* found within *CP* contain normative data for interpretation.

Although the development of microcomputer software programs represents a major advance in resources available to the speech-language clinician, without a thorough understanding of what each program accomplishes or does not accomplish, a knowledgeable development of remediation programming is impossible. In his review of existing software, Schwartz (1985) contended that microcomputer software programs for the analysis of language

production "are only as accurate as the coded transcriptions on which they are based" (p. 39). In other words, accurate analyses can be obtained only if the language sample is representative of the child's production abilities, has been transcribed correctly, and has been coded appropriately. Obviously, these same criteria apply to manual procedures as well. The time-saving advantage of microcomputer software comes with the frequency-of-use summaries. Responsibility for interpretation of the results obtained from either software programs or manual procedures continues to be dependent upon the knowledge and abilities of the clinician. The procedures described in *Guide* can aid in understanding what computer analyses accomplish and can assist in the interpretation of results of computer analyses.

In addition to being dependent upon user skill for coding and interpretation, there are a number of analyses that microcomputer software programs cannot accomplish. First, software programs currently available are not capable of accomplishing semantic role analyses that rely on nonlinguistic context for making these judgments. Second, with the exception of the conversational context search provided by *SALT*, no existing program can perform an analysis of pragmatic aspects of language production including speech act analysis, topic maintenance analysis, or appropriateness judgments. Third, existing programs are incapable of analyzing nonverbal variables, such as eye gaze, gestures, and/or intonation, that may influence interpretation of an utterance. Finally, microcomputer software programs available at this time do not provide analysis of stylistic variations in speakers that may influence listeners' judgments of the speaker.

Thus, judicious use of microcomputer software programs for the analysis of language production can save time in tallying the frequency of occurrence of specific structures. In addition, software programs can permit the clinician to accumulate sufficient data so that, over time, local norms for specific behaviors could be developed. *Guide to Analysis of Language Transcripts* can facilitate use of microcomputer software programs by familiarizing the beginning speech-language clinician with a set of structures to be identified and coded for computer analysis and summary. The practice provided in *Guide* facilitates more accurate coding of target structures and assists in the interpretation of results of computer analyses. In addition, the procedures delineated in *Guide* can provide analysis of structures and/or aspects of language production currently not available through microcomputer analysis. Finally, appropriate development of remediation goals and objectives from computer analyses may be enhanced through the use of *Guide*.

TARGET POPULATION

Guide to Analysis of Language Transcripts has been designed to provide analysis procedures for use with language transcripts obtained from children at the one-word level through Stage V++ (Miller and Chapman's [1981] extension of Brown's [1973] original five stages) of linguistic production or encompassing the chronological ages of 12 months through 6 years for normally developing children. Some procedures are appropriate for use with children older than 6 years of age; however, the major focus is on analysis of semantic, syntactic, and pragmatic aspects of language production during Brown's stages of linguistic development and minimally beyond. Within each chapter are procedures appropriate for use within a more limited age range than 1 to 6 years, and guidelines are provided for determining which procedures to use with a particular child.

A word needs to be said about the use of language production measures to identify children with language delays and/or disorders. The procedures described in *Guide to Analysis of Language Transcripts*, when combined with other information about a child (i.e., chronological age, cognitive level, comprehension level), can identify a child whose productive language level differs from that expected on the basis of chronological age or cognitive level. Whether such children are language delayed or language disordered may not be clinically relevant. Various criteria have been used to determine language delays and language disorders, including performance two standard deviations below the mean (Bloom and Lahey, 1978), performance below the 10th percentile (Lee, 1974; Rizzo and Stephens, 1981), or delays greater than six months (Crystal, Fletcher, and Garman, 1976). For purposes of this *Guide*, the child whose

productive language is at least one production stage below expectations or one standard deviation below the mean (whenever available) based on chronological age or cognitive level, whichever is lower, or whose language behaviors are penalizing to him as a conversational participant, will be considered a candidate for language intervention. Language production measures alone cannot be used to determine the existence of a language problem. It is not this author's intent to resolve the debate regarding the definition of language delay and/or disorder; it is to make it clear that *Guide* adheres to a developmental perspective in that once a level of language performance has been determined, and the decision is made that a child is a candidate for intervention, the accomplishments of the next developmental level can be taught during intervention.

USE OF *GUIDE* IN LEARNING LANGUAGE TRANSCRIPT ANALYSIS

Guide to Analysis of Language Transcripts was developed to provide a comprehensive set of analysis procedures encompassing semantic, syntactic, and pragmatic aspects of language production. *Guide* differs from other sources previously available in that it provides a set of procedures for analyzing all three components of language. Each analysis procedure is demonstrated using sample transcripts. Blank analysis forms and summary sheets are provided, and practice in making crucial judgments is incorporated into the discussion of each procedure. The inclusion of practice sections for each procedure should increase accuracy in identifying and coding targeted structures and should increase the reliability of the resulting analyses. No other source currently available includes an integration of procedures for analysis of semantic, syntactic, and pragmatic aspects of language production, or includes a framework for gaining experience making judgments before applying the analysis procedures to sample transcripts. Additional transcripts also are provided for continued practice.

In the analysis of a single child's language production, the developmentally appropriate procedures from each chapter should be applied to thoroughly describe the child's production abilities. In some cases, the developmental level of the child would preclude the use of syntactic analysis procedures but, typically, analysis should proceed from semantic to syntactic to pragmatic analysis. For example, some form of semantic analysis will be performed for all language transcripts. Depending upon the child's age and/or developmental level, that semantic analysis may be an analysis of the meanings expressed in one-word utterances, analysis of semantic roles and relations expressed in multi-word utterances up to approximately four words in length, and/or analysis of vocabulary diversity using the Type-Token Ratio. If a child's MLU is over 1.0 morphemes, analysis of syntactic aspects of the transcript must be performed. Such analysis may be cursory in that very few target structures are present; however, analysis is necessary to document emergence of early structures. The child whose MLU exceeds 6.0 morphemes may be at a level beyond which the structures analyzed with procedures in *Guide* can be documented. However, unless the structures described here are present in the child's production, and the highest level for each is observed, that conclusion cannot be drawn. In all cases, some form of pragmatic analysis must be performed. Again, depending upon the child's age or developmental level, such analysis may be limited to the function of one-word utterances or may be as extensive as a conversational acts analysis with measures of appropriateness. In nearly every case, thorough analysis of language transcripts involves semantic, syntactic, and pragmatic analysis. Clinical experience has demonstrated the effectiveness of proceeding with analyses in the order mentioned above. This order is consistent with the ordering of chapters in *Guide*. Decision rules regarding which of the three sets of procedures (i.e., semantic, syntactic, pragmatic) to use with any particular child are discussed in each chapter. An interpretation of the results of each analysis procedure is incorporated into the discussion of that procedure. These can be used as the foundation for intervention.

Guide to Analysis of Language Transcripts is intended for use in teaching undergraduate and graduate students in communication disorders clinical training programs to obtain quality language production transcripts and to analyze the semantic, syntactic, and pragmatic aspects of those transcripts. The terminology used assumes minimal clinical background, and the extensiveness of the practice sections are designed to provide the clinician-in-training with introductory exposure to the types of judgments necessary for successful analysis of language transcripts. *Guide* also may be helpful to the practicing speech-language clinician who is looking for a comprehensive set of procedures for analyzing all three components of the language production system. While the use of practice items may not be necessary for those familiar with similar analysis procedures, an examination of the practice sections is encouraged because many of the judgments to be made have not been clear in previous demonstrations of procedures. Documentation of the clinical validity of procedures is not provided, as such documentation currently does not exist. However, use of these procedures has proved successful in identifying children with language production deficits evaluated in a university setting, and successful intervention programs have been based on the results of the described procedures. *Guide* should be used as a manual to learn each of the analysis procedures presented. Clinical use of the procedures should be supplemented with readings on the theoretical foundation of each procedure; sources are provided for that purpose.

OBTAINING LANGUAGE SAMPLES

The first step in analyzing language production transcripts is to obtain samples of the child's productive language. When collected appropriately, the language sample may be the best picture of the child's production abilities. In fact, Gallagher (1983) contends that "spontaneous language sampling is the centerpiece of child language assessment" (p. 2). However, the communicative interaction often is contrived to such an extent that the resulting sample is anything but representative of the child's usual productive language.

The term *representative* has been used in various ways in the literature. Miller (1981) supports the notion that a representative sample is one that is reliable and valid. McLean and Snyder-McLean (1978) suggest that a representative sample reflects the child's optimal performance. And Gallagher (1983) reports that throughout the years, a sample has been considered to be representative if it portrays the child's usual performance. In *Guide*, the term *representative* has been used to describe a child's usual productive language abilities, including performance that may be somewhat below or somewhat above usual abilities.

Nature of the Interaction

Miller (1981) contends that a number of aspects of the communication interaction affect sample representativeness, and that each aspect can be controlled to ensure representativeness. The first variable, nature of the interaction, refers to with whom the child is interacting and to whether the other participant asks questions or engages in conversation during interactive play. Miller supports the notion of obtaining a number of language samples with the child interacting with a variety of people, including the speech-language clinician, a parent, and a sibling or peer. While the general assumption has been that a child will produce language that is most representative when interacting with his mother, studies comparing mother-child and clinician-child interaction have been inconclusive. Olswang and Carpenter (1978) found that the only variable of 21 lexical, grammatical, and semantic measures that was significantly different in the two interactions was the total number of utterances. Children produced significantly more utterances when interacting with their mothers than they did with familiar clinicians, but other length and complexity measures were not significantly different. Other studies comparing mother-child interactions obtained at home and clinician-child interactions obtained in the clinic have found that some children produce longer utterances with the clinician, other children produce longer utterances with the mother, and still other children produce utterances of equal length with each conversational co-participant (Scott and Taylor, 1978; Kramer, James, and

Saxman, 1979). Gallagher (1983) suggests that the numerous research design differences between these studies may have contributed to the differences in results.

Studies comparing fathers to mothers as interactive partners also are fraught with inconsistencies in conclusions. Gallagher's (1983) sampling of relevant studies found some that indicated no significant differences between the interactive style of mothers and fathers (Smith and Daglish, 1977; Golinkoff and Ames, 1979; Wilkinson, Hiebert, and Rembold, 1981). Gallagher also found studies supporting the contention that fathers' language to children was different from the language mothers used with children. She supports the contention that the "most facilitating communication partner" may be one or the other of the parents, or neither. None of the studies cited by Gallagher compared fathers interacting with children to clinicians interacting with the same children.

Peer and/or sibling interaction may result in some language differences; however, the exact differences are not easy to predict. For example, some studies document length and complexity adjustments when children are interacting with a younger child (Shatz and Gelman, 1973; Sachs and Devin, 1976). Other studies emphasize differences in conversational acts, including more responses to adults' questions (Martlew, Connolly, and McCleod, 1978) and more repetitions, attention holders, and directives with peers than with adults (Wilkinson, Hiebert, and Rembold, 1981). Gallagher (1983) has concluded that "child-child communicative behavior" has not been described sufficiently with regard to a single variable to predict the effects on communicative interaction (p. 9).

Overall, results of various studies comparing children interacting with various conversational partners reveal a variety of differences. Although it may be possible to predict that a range of possible differences will occur, apparently it is not possible to predict which differences will occur with a particular child and a particular conversational co-participant. Therefore, instead of pairing the child with only one conversational co-participant to obtain a language sample, it is prudent to obtain samples with the child interacting with various partners. Differences in samples add to the picture of the child's overall communication abilities.

Miller (1981) includes conversational act variables, such as questioning and responding, as aspects of the nature of the interaction. He suggests that in attempting to obtain a representative sample, clinicians should keep question asking to a minimum. The assumption is that children will produce larger and more complex utterances when spontaneously conversing than when responding to questions. However, in a study in which children were asked to retell a story as they acted it out with toys, to tell what they were doing while playing with toys, and to respond to questions about toys as they played with them, Stalnaker and Craighead (1982) found inconclusive results. General group trends followed the order mentioned above for language complexity, but these authors concluded that none of the methods of language sampling was superior to the others.

Overall, it is apparent that a conversation in which one partner only asks questions and the other responds is not a natural interaction. As conversational partners, clinicians should make efforts to reduce the number of questions asked and to permit the child to take the lead in the interaction. However, complete absence of questions on the part of the clinician would be impossible to attain and may not result in a representative sampling of the child's productive abilities.

Setting

The second variable that Miller (1981) indicates may affect sample representativeness is setting. Miller specifies a number of possible alternatives to the therapy room and asserts that using more than one setting is optimal. He suggests that samples could be obtained in a variety of locations at home, at school, in a residential facility, or at a clinic; and although he contends that "representative samples can be collected almost anywhere," differences may arise in the language of the child because of the setting (p. 11). For example, the differences found in the mother-child versus clinician-child studies previously mentioned (Scott and Taylor, 1978; Kramer, James, and Saxman, 1979) may have been due primarily to the differences in

setting. The mother-child samples were obtained in the home and the clinician-child samples were obtained in the clinic. In two other studies, the effects of two settings on the language use of 3- to 4-year-old children were compared (Dore, 1978; Hall and Cole, 1978). Results indicated that a supermarket setting did not elicit more complex language than the classroom and that differences, again, were related more to the interactive style of participants than the setting (Dore, 1978).

While it may not be possible to predict which setting will result in more complex language for a particular child, obtaining samples in more than one setting is optimal. The resulting differences, if any, add to the description of the child's communication abilities.

Materials

The third variable that Miller (1981) suggests may affect sample representativeness is the materials that are present. He reports that children with language disorders talk more about new and unique toys, but Nisswandt (1983) reports the opposite for language-normal children. Various other authors have found that different types of materials result in different language behaviors. Longhurst and File (1977) examined the effect of single-object pictures, multi-object pictures, toys, and no materials present on the language complexity of 4- to 5-year-old children. While group data supported increases in complexity in the order above, individual data indicated that increases in complexity could occur in any ordering of the stimulus conditions. Cook-Gumperz and Corsaro (1977) reported differences in the communication demands placed on 3- and 4-year-old children with three different sets of materials: playhouse, sandbox, and adult-directed arts and crafts activity. Results indicated language differences across conditions, with very few initiative turns in the arts and crafts activity, adherence to role-play conventions in the playhouse, and unpredictable fantasy interactions in the sandbox. Cook-Gumperz and Corsaro concluded that the sandbox was the most difficult of the three settings in terms of interactive demands and resulted in an increased use of repetition and expansion, semantic typing, and verbal descriptions of behaviors.

Once again, different materials may result in differences in language frequency and complexity. The differences, however, appear not to be predictable for children. Therefore, it is wise to provide a variety of developmentally appropriate materials and to encourage the child to interact with as many materials as possible. Differences, again, will contribute to the overall picture of the child's communication abilities.

Sample Size

Another variable that Miller (1981) indicates will affect sample representativeness is sample size. He contends that sample size can be determined in two ways. The first is to obtain a specific number of utterances from the child (or transcribe that number from a sample containing a larger number). For example, various authors have suggested numbers of utterances ranging from 50–200 for the sample to be representative (Lee, 1974; Tyack and Gottsleben, 1974; Crystal, Fletcher, and Garman, 1976, 1991; Miller, 1981). The other alternative is to obtain utterances during a particular period of time, for example, 30 minutes, regardless of how many utterances occur during that time frame. This 30-minute period is likely to result in 100–200 utterances for children functioning at a 24-month level or older (Miller, 1981). Longer periods of time will be necessary to obtain 100 utterances from children younger than 2 years of age, and it may be prudent to supplement a sample with diary accounts from parents. The obvious conclusion may be that the more utterances, the better, but in an effort to be realistic, practical, and efficient, 100 utterances gathered under various conditions typically results in a respectably diverse sample.

Method of Recording

The final two variables that Miller (1981) contends will affect sample representativeness are really variables affecting the overall quality of the resulting transcription. The first of these is the method of recording. The optimum is videotape recording, because it permits the clinician either to interact freely with the child or to watch undistracted as others interact with the child. Transcription from videotape recordings is considered to be the most reliable

method and permits detailed delineation of changes in nonverbal context.

The second method of recording is audio tape recording. Again, the clinician is free to interact with the child, but making notes about the child's activities during the taping is important for providing the nonverbal context for transcription. In addition, audio tape recorders are readily available in most clinical settings, and battery-operated recorders can be taken anywhere the sample is being collected.

The third method of recording suggested by Miller (1981) is on-line transcription. This method of recording is useful in settings where audio and/or videotape recording is not practical. This author has found on-line transcription to be particularly useful in recording a child's productions on field trips or other outings away from the clinical setting. The major criticism of on-line transcription is that it results in transcriptions that under-represent or over-represent the child's actual productions. However, Miller (1981) reports a high reliability for MLU computations based on on-line transcriptions and transcriptions from tape recordings. The key to obtaining reliable on-line transcriptions may be to use one of the procedures suggested by Miller: time sampling. Using this procedure, the clinician transcribes for a few minutes, then rests for a few minutes before continuing with transcribing. This method maximizes attention during transcription. The alternative, writing down everything the child says, can be cumbersome and exhausting. As in audio tape recording, nonverbal context notes should be made to complete the transcription process.

Regardless of the method of recording the interaction, quality transcripts can be obtained. Each method has its own problems and advantages, and each relies on accurate representation of the child's productions for valid and reliable transcripts.

Specification of Context

The final variable affecting the quality of the obtained language transcript is the specification of context. This includes the utterances of the other conversational co-participant as well as the nonverbal or situational context. The utterances preceding and following a child's utterances may dramatically affect the interpretation of the child's utterance. In addition, the objects that are present and the events that are taking place as the child produces an utterance greatly influence interpretation of the child's utterance. It will become obvious in the chapters which follow that semantic and pragmatic analyses require the specification of nonverbal context; it also is very helpful with syntactic analysis. Overall, a quality transcription must include a detailed account of both the linguistic and nonlinguistic context.

Guidelines for Interaction

The preceding discussion highlights numerous variables that are important to consider when obtaining representative language samples and producing quality transcripts. The following guidelines for interacting with a child to obtain a representative sample of the child's productive language are offered as a synthesis of the preceding discussion. Guidelines 1–3 should be adhered to in sequence to establish the conversational interaction. Guidelines 4–9 are general guidelines to be followed throughout the interaction.

1. Begin with parallel play and parallel talk. With a young child at the one-word stage, imitate his verbalizations and use many animal sounds and vehicle noises. With a child older than 2 years, talk about what you are doing as you play and use role-playing dialogue (e.g., "I'm gonna make my guy drive. Here's the tractor for him. 'Wow, what a big tractor. I'm gonna go fast!' ").

2. Move into interactive conversation. With the young child, use some routine questions (e.g., "What's a doggie say?") and elicit finger plays (e.g., "Let's play Patty Cake"). With the older child, invite him to participate in play (e.g., "Hey, you be the gas station guy. I'll bring my car in. It needs fixing"). Continue in role-playing dialogue, unless establishing rules for play. Encourage the child to participate in plans for play, including what toy people/animals will be doing (e.g., "Hey, how about having a picnic?").

3. Continue the child's topic. If he is role playing, stay in role. If he shifts out of role,

follow his lead. Respond to questions, acknowledge comments, solicit more information about a topic.

4. Attempt to restrict your use of questions to approximately one question for every four speaking turns. Eliminating use of questions is unnatural, but too many questions may reduce the length of the child's utterances. The often-suggested "Tell me about this" can also break down the conversation and result in descriptive strings from the child. Instead, carry on a conversation with the child at the child's level.

5. Give the child options that are presented as alternative questions (e.g., "Should we play gas station or have a picnic?"). While children under 3 years of age may not comprehend the alternate question form (Beilin, 1975), pointing to each option provides contextual support for the choice prior to full comprehension of the question form. By using alternate question forms, the shy or uncooperative child does not have the option of saying no, but can feel in control by choosing one of your options.

6. Use utterances that are, on the average, slightly longer than the child's utterances. Keep the number of utterances per speaking turn to approximately the same number as the child's.

7. Learn to be comfortable with pauses in the conversation. If you are too quick to take a speaking turn in order to fill a pause, you deny the child the opportunity to take a turn. In addition, the child may come to expect you to fill pauses and thus feel no obligation toward continuing the conversation. If a pause becomes too long (longer than eight seconds), continue with parallel play and parallel talk until the child moves back into interactive conversation.

8. Have a variety of materials available to keep the child's motivation high, but do not move abruptly from activity to activity. Offer the child the option of changing activities and follow his interests. A diverse combination of materials might include role-playing toys like cars, trucks, and people, farm sets, and kitchen sets as

well as manipulative materials like clay, paints, paper, pens, markers, and items for making a snack.

9. Do not be afraid to be silly and have fun. Many a shy child has been brought into the interaction by asking silly, obvious questions (e.g., "Those are great shoes. Can I wear them?") or by making silly comments (e.g., "There's a mouse in your pocket!"). Enjoy the child and he will enjoy the interaction.

TRANSCRIBING LANGUAGE SAMPLES

The next step in obtaining a language transcript for analysis is to transcribe the interaction recorded. Table 1.1 summarizes a number of conventions that are helpful in transcribing language samples obtained from videotape recordings, audio tape recordings,

and on-line interactions. Adult and child utterances can be transcribed in English orthography except when utterances are unintelligible or the child's approximation deviates substantially from expectations. Conventions for specifying the nonlinguistic or situational context are described, since this information is crucial for each of the analysis procedures delineated in *Guide*. When transcription from videotapes is not possible, audio tape recordings or on-line transcriptions may be used. However, it is important to make context notes during the interaction so that the situational context may be specified in the transcript. A sample transcript has been provided (see pages 16–31) to demonstrate transcription conventions. In addition, a blank transcript form is provided in Appendix A and three more transcripts are available in Appendix B.

TABLE 1.1

CONVENTIONS FOR TRANSCRIPTION OF CHILD LANGUAGE SAMPLES
(Adapted from Bloom and Lahey, 1978)

1. All speech produced by the child and to the child (or within the child's auditory field) is fully transcribed in standard English orthography. Words that appear to function as one word for the child (e.g., lookit, alldone, goodnight) are transcribed as one word. Whenever possible, unintelligible utterances are transcribed using the International Phonetic Alphabet (IPA). Utterances produced by the child are transcribed in the right-hand column of the page, and utterances produced by other speakers are transcribed in the left-hand column. Information about the situational context appears in the middle column and is enclosed in parentheses. Individuals are identified within the situational context by an initial (e.g., M for Mommy, D for Daddy, J for Jane, etc.).

	(M takes toy from boy and offers	
	it to J)	
Lookit this/		
	(J takes toy)	
		puppy/

2. Names within utterances are capitalized. The initial letter of a child utterance is not. The initial letter of an adult utterance typically is capitalized.

Continued on next page

TABLE 1.1—*Continued*

3. An action or event that occurs simultaneously with an adult or child utterance appears on the same line as that utterance.

	(D banging cars together)	boom/
A new car/	(M handing car to D)	

4. When an utterance precedes or follows an action or event, the utterance appears on the preceding or succeeding line.

	(D eats cracker)	
		all gone/
		more cracker/
	(D reaches for bag)	

5. Different verb tenses are used in describing situational context: present progressive tense for simultaneous action, when the action is performed by the speaker; simple present tense for actions or events that precede or follow an utterance, or for simultaneous action that is not performed by the speaker.

6. Utterances that succeed each other with no change in situational context are transcribed on the same line.

Are you still hungry?	(M opening bag;	
	D reaches for bag)	
		more/more/cracker/
	(D reaching inside bag)	more cracker/

If there is any change in situational context, put the utterances on different lines.

	(D reaches for bag)	
		more/
	(D sticks hand in bag)	
		more/
	(D pulling cracker out)	cracker/

When in doubt about the situational context, use separate lines.

Continued on next page

11

TABLE 1.1—*Continued*

PUNCTUATION

7. The punctuation for an utterance boundary is a slash (/). The boundary is determined by length of pause before the next utterance and apparent terminal contour. Pauses greater than two seconds prior to the next utterance typically mark utterance boundaries, with or without rising or falling terminal contour. Specification of pauses of any length to mark utterance boundaries is viewed as secondary to other criteria.

8. Utterances by adult or child may be followed by an exclamation mark. When a child utterance is exclamatory, it should be followed by both an exclamation mark and a slash.

	(D takes wheel off car)	
		there!/all done/

9. Adult questions are indicated by question marks. For child utterances, one of two procedures is used. For wh-questions, a question mark and a slash are used.

	(D looking in bag)	where's da cracker?/

When a child utterance seems to be a question because of its rising intonation, it is marked with a rising arrow (↑) instead of a question mark and followed by a slash.

	(D shaking empty bag)	no more in there↑/

Even for a "well-formed" yes/no question (i.e., one with subject-verb inversion), the arrow to indicate rising intonation is more informative than a simple question mark.

	(D meeting K at door)	do you have cookies↑/

10. A pause of less than two seconds within an utterance is indicated by a dot (·).

	(D trying to fit wheel on car)	put · this one on/

11. A long pause either between speakers or between utterances of the same speaker is indicated by three horizontal dots in the context column. This convention is used only if the situational context remains the same.

	(D trying to get wheel on)	wheel go there/
	• • •	
	(D succeeds)	
		there!/

Continued on next page

TABLE 1.1—*Continued*

If the situational context changes, a long pause is indicated by three vertical dots in the context column.

	(D playing with blocks)	make a tower/
	•	
	•	
	•	
	(D running to bathroom)	potty/go potty/

12. A colon is used to indicate that an utterance or word is drawn out.

	(D trying to fit large peg into	no:/
	small hole)	

13. A curving (⌣) arrow is used when there seems to be an utterance boundary but the utterance is drawn out, such as when the child is counting or listing.

	(D pointing to raisins)	one⌣/
		two⌣/
		three⌣/

14. Stress marks indicate strongly emphasized words.

Do you want this´ one?	(M giving D a blue crayon)	
		no!/
	(D reaching for red crayon)	that´ one/

15. An utterance may be followed by a falling arrow (↓) when it is important to emphasize the fact that the utterance has falling terminal contour.

	(D looking in box;	cow↑/
	pulls out cow)	
		cow↓/

Continued on next page

TABLE 1.1—*Continued*

16. When the child or other speaker suddenly interrupts his own utterance leaving the utterance unfinished, a line (_____) indicates the abrupt stop.

Do you want some _____ /		
	(D picks up cup and spills milk)	

17. When the child or other speaker interrupts his own utterance to change or correct it, a "self-correct" symbol (s/c) is used.

Those are your s/c my cookies/		
		more cookie s/c cracker/

18. An unintelligible utterance or portion of an utterance is indicated by three Xs (XXX). Whenever possible, a phonetic transcription is used instead, and if possible, a gloss is provided in brackets.

	(D reaching for bag)	XXX/
	(D pointing to sky)	/ʌpə/ [airplane]

19. The following abbreviations may be used to indicate the manner in which the utterance was produced:

(lf) = laugh	(wh) = whisper
(cr) = cry	(wm) = whimper
(wn) = whine	(yl) = yell
(gr) = grunt	(sg) = sing

The abbreviation should follow the utterance in parentheses.

	(D holding finger to mouth)	she's sleeping/ (wh)

NUMBERING LANGUAGE TRANSCRIPTS

The final step in preparing language transcripts for analysis is to number the child's utterances. Each fully intelligible child utterance to be analyzed should be assigned an utterance number. If an utterance is repeated with no intervening activity or utterance by the other speaker, the utterance is considered a repetition and does not receive an utterance number. In addition, totally or partially unintelligible utterances should not be assigned an utterance number. Finally, incomplete utterances resulting from self-interruptions or overlapping speakers are not assigned utterance numbers. The alternative would be to number all child utterances and exclude repetitions, unintelligible utterances, and incomplete utterances from analysis. The convention of not numbering these utterances has been selected to aid in managing the process of coding individual utterances and computing percentages. Obviously, there will be times when a repetition or incomplete utterance is erroneously assigned a number. Coding schemes described in this volume permit designation of utterances as such. When a numbered utterance is designated a repetition or incomplete utterance, it should not be included in analyses. Additional utterances should replace repetitions or incomplete utterances if additional sequential utterances are available following the original 100 utterances. If replacement utterances are not available, percentage and mean computations must be adjusted to reflect the number eliminated from 100 utterances.

All analysis procedures described in *Guide to Analysis of Language Transcripts* are based on 100 child utterances. As previously reported, there is considerable variability in the literature regarding the number of utterances recommended for analysis. While it may be difficult to obtain 100 utterances from children less than 2 years of age (Miller, 1981), for the purposes of the analysis procedures described in this volume, a minimum of 100 utterances collected under a variety of conditions has been judged necessary to capture the variability in performance present in spontaneous language. Utterance numbers have been handwritten on the sample transcript to demonstrate the conventions for numbering described here.

One final word about transcription of samples of children's productive language: Transcription is a time-consuming task which becomes easier and faster with practice. The validity of the analysis procedures applied to language transcripts is contingent upon the quality of the transcriptions. Therefore, an investment of time and energy in transcribing and numbering the utterances is necessary to ensure that quality transcripts are being used for analysis. The remaining three chapters present how to apply various analysis procedures following accurate transcription.

A sample transcript of a 28-month-old child (Bridget) appears on pages 16–31. Review the transcript to study the conventions for transcription described in Table 1.1. Bridget's transcript will be analyzed in Chapters 2, 3, and 4. For demonstration purposes and to aid in counting, each child utterance has been placed on a separate line.

Name of Child ___Bridget___   CA ___28 months___

Type of Situation ___free play in living room___   Date ___3-12___

Length of Tape ___1 hr, 20 min___   Length of Transcript ___100 utterances___   Time of Day ___1:30 pm___

Materials Present ___circus set, dolls, doll buggy, tea set, kitchen set, toy telephone___

People Present ___M = Mother; B = Bridget (Bill, the camera operator, is also present)___

ADULT	CONTEXT	CHILD	
	(B trying to put lion on bar by tail)	/wʊp/ [whoops]	1
What happen to the lion?			
		fall down/	2
Did he get hurt?			
		no/	3
	(B looks at M)		
		yes/	4
He did?			
What happened to him?			
What happened to him?			
	(B reaches to lion;		
	pointing to tail of lion)	hurt his tail there/	5
		see↑/	6
Uh huh/			
	(B looking back)	XXX/ (lf)	
		what else?/	7
What else?			
How about ____ /			
Yes/			
	(B taking giraffe from box)	giraffe/	8
What is that?			
		giraffe/	9
That's right/			

© 1993 Thinking Publications *Duplication permitted for educational use only.*

ADULT	CONTEXT	CHILD	
	(B giving giraffe to M)	here/	*10*
What's that?			
		put upside down/	*11*
Put him upside down too?			
		yeah/	*12*
Okay/			
	(B reaching for giraffe and	bar/	*13*
	pointing to bar)		
		here/	*14*
Up there/			
You do it/			
	(B tossing giraffe to M)	Mommy you do it/	*15*
Don't you want to do it honey?	(M holding out giraffe;		
	B looks in box)		
You make him stand up here/			
You wanna see if he can go like	(M placing giraffe and B watches		
this maybe/	M holding box)		
Oh/			
	(B looking)	what else?/	*16*
What else?			
Find something/			
	(B reaching in box)	lookie in the box/	*17*
	(B pulls out two toys)		
The monkey's right here/			
		XXX/	
The monkey's right here/			
	(B looks where M points)		
		that's not enough/	*18*
	(B looks back in box)		

© 1993 Thinking Publications *Duplication permitted for educational use only.*

ADULT	CONTEXT	CHILD	
		what else?/	*19*
Find something/			
Where did you put the	(B pulls toys out of the box and		
elephant this morning?	sets them on the floor)		
Where did you put the			
elephant this morning?			
You were playing with him/			
		he's not here/	*20*
Where is he?			
	(B scans the floor with her eyes)		
Where did you put him?			
		I don't know/	*21*
What?			
	(B pushes toys on the floor)		
Where did you put him?			
		find him/	*22*
Find him?			
		where it is?/	*23*
		where that elephant go?/	*24*
I don't know/			
Did you put him in with _____ /			
oh what's that?			
	(M points to a toy on other side of		
	room, B looks)		
What's that over there?			
		the elephant/	*25*
Will you get it?			
	(B stands up)		
	(B walks over and gets the elephant,		

© **1993 Thinking Publications** *Duplication permitted for educational use only.*

ADULT	CONTEXT	CHILD	
	brings it back to M)		
		stand up/	*26*
	(B holding legs of elephant)	legs/	*27*
		stand up/	*28*
Oh I think he might be too heavy/			
	(B stoops, stands up, stoops again		
	to stand up elephant)		
Let's put another one of these	(M pulling box around B and		
up here/	over to her)		
Let's put another one of these			
up here/			
	(B stands and M pulls ladder		
	from box)		
How does this work?			
		huh↑/	*29*
Do you know how this works?			
	(M attaches ladder)		
Like this?			
		yeah/	*30*
Oh okay/			
Put him up on top/	(B stoops)		
Is he too big?			
Up here/			
Put him up there/			
	(B sitting on floor holding toy)	you do it upside down/	*31*
Oh:/	(B puts elephant on ladder)		
	(B pointing)	there's a elephant/ (lf)	*32*
There's another one/			
Do you want to put him up there too?			

© **1993 Thinking Publications** *Duplication permitted for educational use only.*

ADULT	CONTEXT	CHILD	
		no it's heavy/	*33*
	(B wipes nose on shirt sleeve)		
Oh it's heavy/			
Okay/			
Is he too heavy?	(M pointing to toy on floor)		
		yeah/	*34*
He's just a baby one/			
	(B looking around floor)	where's another one?/	*35*
How about the circus man?			
	(B turns and kicks toy structure)		
Woo: what happened here?	(M catching toy structure)		
What happened?			
		I kick im/ (lf)	*36*
You kicked him?			
		yeah/	*37*
You know what you need?			
	(M turns and brings back tissue)		
You need a Kleenex/			
	(B reaching for tissue)	gimme/	*38*
Can I help you?			
	(B wipes nose and gives tissue back to M; M wipes B's nose)		
Look/			
	(B turns head away)		
		/ɪk/	*39*
Let me see that/			
	(B looking at hand)	/aʊɪ/ [owie]	*40*
Okay/			
		/aʊɪ/ [owie]	*41*

© 1993 Thinking Publications *Duplication permitted for educational use only.*

ADULT	CONTEXT	CHILD	
What happened?			
Did you fall down?			
	(B looks at M;		
	holding her own hand)	yeah/	*42*
Oh:/			
How does it feel?			
		pretty better/	*43*
It feels better/			
	(B kisses finger)		
Okay/			
Can I kiss it too?			
	(B extends finger so M can kiss it)		
Okay/			
	(B extends arms and pulls toy		
	structure back into lap; M rebuilds		
	structure)		
You wanna put 'em back up again?			
Let's put 'em back up again/			
You gonna make them fall down again?			
	(B watching M)	he fall/ (lf)	*44*
Why did you kick him?			
	(B elevates body and returns to sit)		
		I kick him/	*45*
/ɔː/			
	(B leans forward and with a wave of		
	her hands, knocks the toy over)		
		fall down · boom/	*46*
Is that funny?			
		yeah/ (lf)	*47*

ADULT	CONTEXT	CHILD	
You think so?			
		yeah/	*48*
Are you done playing with this?			
Should we do something else?			
		yeah/	*49*
You want to take this man for a ride in the buggy?			
	(M pulls buggy over)		
You want to take him for a ride in the stroller?			
Hm?			
	(B pulling buggy)	/sokə/ [stroller]	*50*
	(M stands bed up and moves other toys away; points to bed)		
Can you bring him over here and put him in bed?			
		yeah/	*51*
Okay/			
	(B places man in bed)		
		go to sleep/	*52*
		shh/	*53*
shh/			
Did you give him a kiss and tell him good night?			
	(B bending over bed)	goodnight/	*54*
There he is/			
	(B points to bed and whispers to M)		
Is he tired? (wh)	(Both whispering to one another)	yeah/ (wh)	*55*
	(B squeals as she turns man over)		

© **1993 Thinking Publications** *Duplication permitted for educational use only.*

ADULT	CONTEXT	CHILD	
	(B lifts man out of bed)		
Oh, you woke him up/			
	(B puts man in bed, touches nose		
	with finger; M puts finger to her face)		
shh/			
What else should we do?			
What else should we do?			
	(B picks man up; M leans over her)		
		I wake him up/ (yl)	*56*
How about having some coffee?			
	(B puts man in bed)		
Should we go get some coffee?			
Will you go get me a cup of coffee	(M pushing aside toys)		
please in your kitchen?			
Can you go get me a cup of coffee			
in your kitchen?			
	(M goes to kitchen)		
I want some coffee/			
Can I have some coffee?			
	(B stands up and walks to kitchen)		
		allright/	*57*
Oh I'll have some milk too/			
What's that?			
		cow/	*58*
Who makes the milk?			
		huh↑/	*59*
Who makes the milk?			
Wooo/			
The dishes are dirty/			

ADULT	CONTEXT	CHILD	
	(B picking up a ball and turning	there's a ball↑/	*60*
	toward camera)		
Yeah but I want to have some coffee/			
	(B walking with ball and milk	d · d · d · there's a ball/	*61*
	carton in hand)		
		there's a ball/	
Okay come on/			
Let's have some coffee/			
Come on/			
Come on Bridget/			
Can I have a cup of coffee please?			
Here's the milk/			
Get me a cup of coffee/			
	(B moves hands in air and walks		
	back to cabinet)		
You have one too/			
Okay?			
	(B stooping at cabinet, pulling	this yours/	*62*
	out a cup)		
Okay here's mine/			
	(M extends arm)		
Thank you/			
Can I get a plate too?			
	(B holds teapot in position to pour		
	into cup, hands cup to M)		
Thank you very much/			
		welcome/	*63*
Can I have a plate please?			
	(B reaching for a plate)	okay/	*64*

© **1993 Thinking Publications** *Duplication permitted for educational use only.*

ADULT	CONTEXT	CHILD	
I want to eat something too/			
		here's yours/	*65*
This is mine?			
What about yours?			
Do you want some too?			
	(B puts pot down on cabinet,		
	moves dishes around)		
		/wʌzət/else?/ [what else?]	*66*
		else/	*67*
		else/	
		else/	
Bridget?			
You mean those?			
The other ones are over there/			
	(B walking, banging pot and cup	huh↑/	*68*
	together)		
Huh · uh oh/			
You're going to give some coffee			
to Bill and Kay?			
Is that what you're going to do?			
	(B walking back to M)	yeah/	*69*
Let's sit down and have some			
first okay?			
You sit down okay?			
Sit down/			
	(B sits down)		
Tastes good/			
How does yours taste?			
		more↑/	*70*

© 1993 Thinking Publications *Duplication permitted for educational use only.*

ADULT	CONTEXT	CHILD	
How does yours ₛ/ᴄ yes please/			
	(B pours from pot to M's cup)		
Thank you/			
You want some more?			
	(B standing up, extending arm	Bill/	*71*
	toward camera)		
		take 'em Bill/	*72*
I think Bill's full/			
		take 'em Bill/	*73*
I don't think he's hungry/			
	(B sitting down)	huh↑/	*74*
I don't think he's hungry/			
But I'd like some more please/			
	(M places her cup on floor in front of		
	B; B pours from her cup to M's cup)		
How does yours taste?			
		taste good/	*75*
Does it taste good?			
	(B hitting her cup against her foot)	yeah/	*76*
What else?			
Does it taste delicious too?			
		yeah/	*77*
Could I have some cookies please?			
Could I have some cookies please?			
	(B shaking head back and forth)	no cookies/	*78*
Hm?			
		allgone/	*79*
Are they?			
		yeah/	*80*

© 1993 **Thinking Publications** *Duplication permitted for educational use only.*

ADULT	CONTEXT	CHILD	
Who ate them?			
Who ate them?			
Who ate the cookies?			
		somebody ate the cookies/	*81*
Who ate them?			
	(B claps pot and cup together,		
	takes drink from cup)		
Can I have a piece of toast please?			
	(B shakes head, drops pot and cup)		
There's some in there/			
	(M points to cabinet)		
See it?			
	(B looks toward cabinet)		
Get me some toast please/			
	(B crawls to cabinet)		
		XXX/	
	(B withdraws something from		
	cabinet, looks toward M)		
Uh huh/			
		okay/	*82*
	(B stands and walks to M)		
		way up here/	*83*
		plate/	*84*
A plate/			
Oh/			
Oh you're going to give me			
toast on a plate/			
	(M extends plate)		
Can I have one piece please?			

ADULT	CONTEXT	CHILD
	(B turns her plate over M's plate)	
Thank you/		
	(M tastes "toast")	
Tastes good/		
		yeah/ *85*
Could I have some peanut butter on it?		
	(B waves her plate near M's "toast")	
Will you put some peanut butter		
on it?		
	(B drops plate)	
Please?		
Here put some peanut butter		
on my toast/		
	(B takes "toast" from M)	
	(B puts hand in mouth, then in	
	back of her)	
Oh you ate mine/		
You ate mine/		
	(B giggles)	
	(B points to mouth)	
Oh give me that/		
	(B points to mouth again)	
		ate mine/ *86*
Oh/		
I'm going to eat up your tummy/		
	(B walks toward M, extends	
	her tummy)	
A rum rum rum/		
	(B backs off and returns)	

© 1993 Thinking Publications *Duplication permitted for educational use only.*

ADULT	CONTEXT	CHILD	
A rum rum rum/			
	(B holding M's head to tummy,	look at it/	*87*
	talking to camera)		
I see it/			
		look at it/	*88*
A rum rum rum/			
		look it Bill/	*89*
A rum rum rum/			
		look it Bill/	*90*
A rum rum rum/			
	(B releases M's head and puts		
	hand on tummy)		
Want me to eat you all up?			
		huh↑/	*91*
Would you like me to eat you all up?			
		yeah/	*92*
Why?			
	(B walks to M's face, tummy		
	extended)		
Why?			
Why?			
Why would you like me to eat			
you up?			
Hm?			
What are you doing now?			
	(B lies on floor and holds toy)		
Hm?			
What are you doing now?			
	(B getting up)	telephone/	*93*

© 1993 Thinking Publications *Duplication permitted for educational use only.* **29**

ADULT	CONTEXT	CHILD	
Let's see here/			
		telephone/	*94*
		telephone/	
Want to talk on the telephone?			
		yeah/	*95*
I think we'll play with the other			
telephone/			
You want to talk on the phone?			
Here you sit down and I'll get it/			
	(B turns around; M stands up)		
I'll get it/			
	(B walks over to M)		
Uh oh/			
		what happened?/	*96*
Where did it go?			
		in that box/	*97*
Here it is/			
	(M picks up phone)		
I found it/			
There/			
You want to talk?			
	(M puts phone on floor)		
Why don't you call up Gramma?			
Turn around/			
	(B sits on floor)		
Call up Gramma/			
	(B picks up receiver)		
Dial first/			
	(B dials phone)		

© **1993 Thinking Publications** *Duplication permitted for educational use only.*

ADULT	CONTEXT	CHILD	
		hello/	*98*
		Gramma here/	*99*
	(B holds out phone to M)		
		you talk/	*100*

CHAPTER 2
Semantic Analysis

Semantic analysis of language transcripts provides valuable information for determining the developmental level of children with potential language delays. A variety of procedures are appropriate, including analysis of individual semantic roles (Bloom, 1973; Nelson, 1973), analysis of prevalent semantic relations (Brown, 1973), analysis of conjunctions (Clancy, Jacobsen, and Silva, 1976), and analysis of vocabulary diversity (Templin, 1957). Most of these analyses are based on data obtained from transcripts of normally developing children interacting with their mothers. While the diagnostic validity of some of these procedures has not been documented, results of systematic analysis of the semantic content of language transcripts can support other judgments regarding the presence of language delays, including syntactic and pragmatic analysis results. In addition, semantic analysis procedures yield data crucial for the development of remediation goals and objectives.

The following procedures have been selected on the basis of clinical relevance and are applicable for use with children up to 8 years of age; however, the majority of the procedures are appropriate for use with children producing utterances primarily between one and three words in length. It is at this early age that the procedures delineated in this chapter are most applicable. These procedures have been selected to work together resulting in a complete analysis of the semantic content of a child's productions, but each may be used separately to provide an analysis of a single aspect of the semantic content. Each of the procedures will be described in detail with directions and examples. All procedures will be demonstrated using the transcript of Bridget at the end of Chapter 1. Demonstration of procedures will follow the detailed description of each procedure. Blank forms for semantic analyses can be found in Appendix C. An additional completed analysis of another transcript (Sara) also can be found in Appendix C. Recall that additional unanalyzed transcripts are located in Appendix B.

When analyzing the semantic content of child language transcripts, an important distinction must be made. This is the distinction between referential and relational aspects of the child's productions. Analysis of referential and relational aspects of production yields different results. Referential analyses describe the child's use of individual words to refer to objects or classes of objects and events in the environment. Relational analyses describe the meaning relationships expressed by words in relation to aspects of objects or events in the environment, or by words in relation to other words. This distinction can be seen in the obvious difference between the child's use of a word to label (or refer to) an object in the environment (e.g., "ball") versus the child's use of a word to describe the relationship between a previous situation and a current situation (e.g., "all gone" after eating a cookie) or two object labels in combination to describe the relationship between the two objects in the environment (e.g., "Daddy ball"). This chapter examines various types of analysis procedures to describe both referential content and relational content of child language productions.

ANALYZING SEMANTIC CONTENT OF ONE-WORD UTTERANCES

The first step in analyzing the semantic content of one-word utterances is to identify the one-word utterances in the transcript. Two different procedures will be used to analyze the semantic content of the one-word utterances: a categorization of one-word utterance types described by Bloom in 1973, and a classification scheme provided by Nelson, also in 1973. While both types of analysis are appropriate for use with productions one word in length, each provides slightly different information. Each will be considered in detail before examining the differences in results.

Bloom's One-Word Utterance Types

Bloom's categorization scheme describes the three types of words that children use in their one-word utterances. The first type of word used by children in their one-word utterances is a SUBSTANTIVE word. A SUBSTANTIVE word refers to an object or event, like *ball* or *cookie* or *chair*. At times, children refer to particular objects or events, and these are called NAMING words. The child might use a NAMING word to refer to the family pet, parents, siblings, or other important people in the environment. The third type of word in Bloom's categorization scheme is a FUNCTION word. FUNCTION words refer to conditions shared by many objects or events and make reference across classes of objects or events. A word like *up* is not just a direction. It may refer to the desired relationship between a child and a parent, or it may describe the location of an object in relation to another object. A word like *more* does not just refer to an object but indicates the recurrence, or desired recurrence, of an object. The description of the child's use of these three types of one-word utterances allows examination of the role that language plays in communication for the child.

A few typical one-word utterances are provided for practice in using Bloom's categorization scheme before attempting to categorize the sample transcript. The right side of the page can be covered, each example can be categorized, and then categorizations can be checked with those provided. An explanation is included for each utterance.

(C picks up toy horse)
horsey/

SUBSTANTIVE
This utterance refers to a real or pretend object, so SUBSTANTIVE is the most appropriate category.

(C hears door opening)
Dada/

NAMING
This utterance refers to a particular person, the child's father, so it is coded, NAMING.

(C reaches for cup on table)
cup/

SUBSTANTIVE
This utterance labels an object, so SUBSTANTIVE is the most appropriate category.

(C picks up car with no wheels)
broke/

FUNCTION
This utterance does not label an object but refers to the condition of an object.

(dog barking in background) Didi/	NAMING This utterance refers to the family pet and names it. It is important to be familiar with the names of significant people and animals in the child's environment before attempting to categorize the child's utterances.
(C takes a drink from cup) juice/	SUBSTANTIVE This utterance provides a label for liquid refreshment.
(M says, "Where's that shoe?" and C says) there/	FUNCTION This utterance refers to the condition (or location) of an object. It is not a label for an object.
(C points to picture of a baby in picture book) baby/	SUBSTANTIVE This utterance provides a generic label for a person.
(C points to self in mirror) baby/	NAMING In this utterance, the child is referring to himself, not just labeling a baby. The nonlinguistic context is crucial for making judgments like this. If the child had been labeling the object, SUBSTANTIVE would have been used.
(C picks up music box and looks at M) no/	FUNCTION While it is impossible to determine the type of negation being expressed without the additional nonlinguistic context, various types of negation are coded in this way to make reference across classes of objects or events.
(C carries cup to sink while holding it out for M to fill) drink/	SUBSTANTIVE Again, the nonlinguistic context is crucial for differentiating the labeling of liquid refreshment from the description of an activity. In the second case, FUNCTION would have been used.

These examples should be helpful in completing the categorization of one-word utterances from language transcripts. At this point, the one-word utterances in the sample transcript need to be identified and the category into which each utterance fits needs to be determined. Using Bridget's transcript in Chapter 1 and the One-Word Utterances (Bloom's [1973] One-Word Utterance Types) analysis sheet in Appendix C, put each one-word utterance into the appropriate column on the analysis sheet. If a particular word occurs more than once, tally additional instances of that word next to the original recording of the word (e.g., "ball //// /" means the word occurred seven times in the transcript). A completed analysis sheet is provided on the next page.

Semantic Analysis
One-Word Utterances

Name of Child *Bridget*

Bloom's (1973) One-Word Utterance Types

Substantive	Naming	Function
giraffe / bar legs owie / stroller cow plate telephone /	Bill	whoops no yes see here / yeah ⁄⁄⁄⁄ ⁄⁄⁄⁄ ⁄⁄⁄⁄ / huh //// gimme ick goodnight allright welcome okay / else more allgone hello

Bloom's One-Word Utterance Types

_____11_____ Substantive = _____21.6_____% of Total One-Word Utterances

_____1_____ Naming = _____2.0_____% of Total One-Word Utterances

_____39_____ Function = _____76.4_____% of Total One-Word Utterances

TOTAL NUMBER OF ONE-WORD UTTERANCES _____51_____

TOTAL NUMBER OF UTTERANCES _____100_____

_____51_____ % OF TOTAL UTTERANCES

36

© **1993 Thinking Publications** *Duplication permitted for educational use only.*

Summary and Interpretation of Results Obtained Using Bloom's One-Word Utterance Types

Following the identification of each one-word utterance and the categorization of each into one of the three categories, a summary of the frequency of occurrence of each type is completed. Proceed as follows:

1. Count the number of words in each column, including additional instances of each, and put the total for each in the blank provided. Keep in mind that *good night* and *all gone* are listed as one word because they typically function as such for children this age.

2. Add all instances to obtain the total number of one-word utterances, and put that number in the blank provided. This can be double-checked by returning to the transcript and counting the one-word utterances.

3. Return to each one-word utterance type and compute the percentage of total one-word utterances accounted for by this type. This is accomplished by dividing the number of instances of the type by the total number of one-word utterances and multiplying by 100.

4. Determine the percentage of total utterances accounted for by one-word utterances. Do this by dividing the total number of one-word utterances by the total number of utterances.

In the sample transcript, there were 11 SUBSTANTIVE words, which when divided by 51 total one-word utterances, yielded .2156. After rounding this off and multiplying by 100 to convert to a percentage, this means that 21.6 percent of the one-word utterances could be categorized as SUBSTANTIVE words. (See page 36 and note where this number is filled in on the analysis form.) One instance of a NAMING word divided by 51 and multiplied by 100 yielded 2.0 percent. There were also 39 FUNCTION words, and when 39 was divided by 51 total one-word utterances, a total of 76.4 percent of the one-word utterances could be accounted for by FUNCTION words. Finally, the total number of one-word utterances (51) was divided by the total number of utterances (100), yielding 51 percent. This means that 51 percent of the total utterances were one word in length.

But look again at Bloom's FUNCTION word category on the sample analysis sheet. The most striking thing about the words listed is the preponderance of "yeahs." A look at each FUNCTION word listed reveals that there are several variations of yes/no responses and many routine responses (e.g., *hello, good night, welcome*). These responses can be called conversational devices and communication routines respectively; they will be presented in detail on pages 60–61. If these responses are eliminated, six words are left, one of which occurs twice. Those are checked on the corrected sample analysis sheet on page 38. This changes the total number of one-word utterances to 19 and the individual computations to 57.9 percent SUBSTANTIVE words (11 SUBSTANTIVE WORDS divided by 19 one-word utterances), 5.3 percent NAMING words (1 NAMING word divided by 19 one-word utterances), and 36.8 percent FUNCTION words (7 FUNCTION words divided by 19 one-word utterances). Exclusion of certain one-word utterances from the analysis may appear to be an arbitrary decision; however, an examination of Bloom's examples of FUNCTION words will indicate that this is an appropriate decision.

Now the results of the analysis can be interpreted. To begin, the percentage of total utterances accounted for by one-word utterance types must be considered. In the sample transcript, 19 percent of total utterances were one-word utterance types, allowing for the exclusion of conversational devices and communication routines. This indicates that more than half of the child's utterances with semantic content in

Semantic Analysis
One-Word Utterances

Name of Child *Bridget*

Bloom's (1973) One-Word Utterance Types

Substantive	Naming	Function
giraffe / bar legs owie / stroller cow plate telephone /	Bill	~~whoops~~ ~~no~~ ~~yes~~ see ✓ here / ✓ ~~yeah~~ ℍℍ ℍℍ ℍℍ / ~~huh~~ ℍℍ gimme ✓ ~~ick~~ ~~goodnight~~ ~~allright~~ ~~welcome~~ ~~okay~~ / else ✓ more ✓ allgone ✓ ~~hello~~

Bloom's One-Word Utterance Types

___11___ Substantive = ~~21.6~~ 57.9 % of Total One-Word Utterances

___1___ Naming = ~~2.0~~ 5.3 % of Total One-Word Utterances

~~39~~ 7 Function = ~~76.4~~ 36.8 % of Total One-Word Utterances

TOTAL NUMBER OF ONE-WORD UTTERANCES ~~51~~ 19

TOTAL NUMBER OF UTTERANCES 100

~~51~~ 19 % OF TOTAL UTTERANCES

© 1993 **Thinking Publications** *Duplication permitted for educational use only.*

this sample were longer than one word in length. At this cursory level, one might suspect that the child is beyond the one-word stage. Thus, it could be concluded that the child's lexicon exceeds 50 words (Bloom, 1973), because a child's lexicon containing less than 50 words would have a greater percentage of total utterances accounted for by one-word utterances, even after exclusions. Consequently, the analysis of one-word utterance types may not be the most important analysis regarding this particular child's semantic abilities.

However, some conclusions about the types of words used can be drawn. Note that this child used more SUBSTANTIVE words than either FUNCTION or NAMING words. Various authors have described the proportion of one-word utterances accounted for by various types of one-word utterances. Some authors contend that the first 50-word lexicon is comprised primarily of nouns, or in this categorization scheme, SUBSTANTIVE or NAMING words (McNeill, 1970; Gleitman, Gleitman, and Shipley, 1972; Huttenlocher, 1974; Benedict, 1979). Only later in the one-word stage do children add FUNCTION words. This would suggest that the child in the sample transcript is in an early stage of language production.

On the other hand, Bloom, Lightbown, and Hood (1975) described a nominal-pronominal continuum in children at the one-word utterance stage. Children whose one-word utterances refer predominately to nouns are considered to be on the nominal end of the continuum. Children whose one-word utterances refer to nouns, but in the pronominal form (e.g., *this, it, that*), and to relations between objects and events are considered to be on the pronominal end of the continuum. This apparent tendency is reported to persist into the preschool years (Horgan, 1979). From the present transcript, the conclusion might be that in this sample this child tends to be predominately nominal. In addition, when this is considered along with the percentage of total utterances accounted for by one-word utterance types (i.e., 19 percent), the conclusion that

this child has progressed beyond a simple labeling stage and is cognizant of the functional relations existing between objects and events is appropriate.

More data are necessary to substantiate this hypothesis. For example, would this same distribution occur in another transcript obtained under variations in conditions described in Chapter 1? This example points out the need for multiple samples of the child's productions. Overall, the results of this analysis indicate that examination of more diverse aspects of the child's productions is necessary to capture the child's semantic abilities.

Nelson's One-Word Utterance Types

The second categorization of one-word utterances that will be used is one that was developed by Nelson (1973) to describe the first 50-word lexicons of children approximately 18 months of age. Her data were obtained from diary accounts of the children's productions that were analyzed to provide a frequency distribution of five categories. In this analysis, the one-word utterances produced in 100-utterance language transcripts will be used. This analysis procedure may not be appropriate for language transcripts, but is being completed for the purpose of demonstrating Nelson's analysis in *Guide*. Thus, data from the sample transcripts cannot be compared directly to Nelson's data. Only diary accounts of productions of a child being assessed can be compared directly to Nelson's normative data. Miller (1981) describes a format for obtaining diary accounts from parents. The description includes directions to parents regarding the format for what to record, what context information to specify, and when to collect data. Concerns regarding accuracy of recording will always exist, but diary accounts can be very helpful in obtaining samples from children at the one-word stage.

The five categories that Nelson used to analyze one-word utterances are listed and defined in Table 2.1.

TABLE 2.1

NELSON'S ONE-WORD UTTERANCE TYPES

(Adapted from Nelson, 1973)

1. **NOMINALS**

    a. **SPECIFIC NOMINALS:** Words used to refer to particular instances of people, animals, and objects.

    b. **GENERAL NOMINALS:** Words used to refer to general instances of objects, substances (e.g., *snow*), animals, people (including pronouns), abstractions (e.g., *birthday*), letters, and numbers.

2. **ACTION WORDS:** Words used to refer to actions through description (e.g., *bye-bye, go*) and expression of attention (e.g., *look, hi*) or demand for attention (e.g., *up, out*).

3. **MODIFIERS:** Words used to refer to properties or qualities of things and events including expressions of recurrence, disappearance, attribution, location, and possession.

4. **PERSONAL-SOCIAL:** Words used to express affective states (e.g., *want, feel*) and social relationships (e.g., *please, thank you, yes, no*).

5. **FUNCTION WORDS:** Words used to fulfill grammatical functions (e.g., *what, where, is, for*).

Once again, a few one-word utterances are provided for practice before attempting to categorize the utterances in the sample transcript. As before, the right side of the page can be covered, each utterance can be categorized, and then categorizations can be checked with those provided. The explanations should clear up discrepancies. The same examples used for Bloom's categories are provided again and a few new ones are added.

(C picks up toy horse)
horsey/

GENERAL NOMINAL
This utterance refers to a real or pretend animal.

(C hears door opening)
Dada/

SPECIFIC NOMINAL
This utterance refers to a particular person.

(C reaches for cup on table)
cup/

GENERAL NOMINAL
Again, this is an example of a general instance of an object.

(C picks up car with no wheels)
broke/

MODIFIER
This utterance describes the quality of the car.

(C reaches up to M, who has entered bedroom)
up/

ACTION WORD
This utterance provides a description of an action or a request for an action. In either event it is coded ACTION WORD.

(dog barking in background)
Didi/

SPECIFIC NOMINAL
Since Didi is the family pet, this is an example of a particular instance of an animal.

(C takes a drink from cup) juice/	**GENERAL NOMINAL** This utterance refers to a substance that is general in nature.
(M says, "Where's that shoe?" and C says) there/	**MODIFIER** This utterance describes the location of something and therefore refers to a property of that object.
(C points to picture of a baby in picture book) baby/	**GENERAL NOMINAL** This utterance provides a general label for a person.
(C points to self in mirror) baby/	**SPECIFIC NOMINAL** Again, it is important to know that this child refers to himself, but no one else, as "baby" to determine that this is an example of a particular baby.
(C picks up music box and looks at M) no/	**MODIFIER** This particular utterance was used to refer to the previous prohibition of an object and therefore it was coded MODIFIER. If the context had revealed that the child was responding to a question (e.g., "Do you want to go night-night?"), the utterance would have been coded PERSONAL-SOCIAL.
(C carries cup to sink while holding it out for M to fill) drink/	**GENERAL NOMINAL or ACTION WORD** Depending on the nonlinguistic context for the next utterance, this utterance could be referring to a general substance (GENERAL NOMINAL) or to an activity (ACTION WORD). The next utterance by Mom would determine how this utterance was interpreted.
(C holds up larger half of cookie) big/	**MODIFIER** This utterance describes a property (attribute) of an object or event.
(M says, "What do you say?" as she holds out cookie and C says) please/	**PERSONAL-SOCIAL** This utterance reflects a convention used in social relationships.
(clock on wall makes buzzing sound and C looks at M) what?/	**FUNCTION WORD** This utterance fulfills a grammatical function in requesting the label for something.

The translation of utterances previously coded using Bloom's One-Word Utterance Types into Nelson's categorization scheme was fairly straightforward. The category posing the greatest difficulty was probably the FUNCTION WORD category. The types of words coded in this way, using Bloom's coding scheme, were quite different from those using Nelson's coding scheme. Bloom's FUNCTION WORDS were more closely aligned with Nelson's MODIFIERS, although some of Bloom's FUNCTION WORDS overlap with Nelson's PERSONAL-SOCIAL category and others overlap with Nelson's ACTION WORD category. Keeping that in mind, return to the one-word utterances identified and categorized for Bridget's transcript using Bloom's One-Word Utterance Types. This time, code them using Nelson's One-Word Utterance Types. Put each word in the appropriate column on the analysis sheet. Again, if a word occurs more than once in the transcript, tally additional instances next to the original. A completed analysis sheet is provided on the next page.

Summary and Interpretation of Nelson's One-Word Utterance Types Analysis

Once again, the frequency of use of each one-word utterance type needs to be summarized. Count the number of words in each column, including additional instances of each word, and put the total for each type in the blank provided. Add all instances together to obtain the total number of one-word utterances and put that number in the blank provided. Double-check this number by returning to the transcript and counting the one-word utterances. Now return to each one-word utterance type and compute the percentage of total one-word utterances accounted for by each type. Unlike Bloom's One-Word Utterance Types, Nelson specifies that yes/no responses and other routine forms are to be included. Consequently, there will be no need to recompute percentages after eliminating some one-word utterances. In the sample

transcript, there were 11 GENERAL NOMINALS, which when divided by 51 total one-word utterances and multiplied by 100, indicated that 21.6 percent of one-word utterances were categorized as GENERAL NOMINALS. One instance of SPECIFIC NOMINALS divided by 51 yielded 2 percent. Three ACTION WORDS divided by 51 total one-word utterances yielded 5.9 percent of one-word utterances. Five MODIFIERS divided by 51 yielded 9.8 percent. Twenty-five PERSONAL-SOCIAL words divided by 51 indicated that 49 percent of one-word utterances were PERSONAL-SOCIAL. With 6 FUNCTION WORDS, divided by 51, observe that 11.8 percent of one-word utterances were characterized as FUNCTION WORDS. Again, the final step is to determine the percentage of total utterances accounted for by one-word utterances: Divide 51 by 100 total utterances, then multiply by 100 to obtain 51 percent.

Unlike Bloom's categorization scheme, normative data on the frequency of occurrence of Nelson's categories are available. Table 2.2 indicates the percentage of the child's first 50 words accounted for by each of Nelson's categories. Keep in mind that Nelson's data are based on types, i.e., the first 50 words used by each child. In other words, one word might have been used in 50 percent of all word attempts, yet in Nelson's data it would contribute only 2 percent to a type category (i.e., 1 divided by 50 equals 2 percent). Data from the language sample cited in the last paragraph are based on percentage tokens (i.e., how often a word type appeared in a sample of 100 utterances). Thus, it is not possible to compare these results directly to Nelson's data. Remember, data from this analysis were obtained from a 100-utterance language sample, and Nelson's data were obtained from diary accounts of the child's first 50 words. To apply Nelson's normative data directly, a diary account of the first 50 words a child had produced would be needed. As previously mentioned, it may be very productive to obtain a diary account using Miller's (1981) procedures.

Semantic Analysis
One-Word Utterances

Name of Child ___*Bridget*___

Nelson's (1973) One-Word Utterance Types

General Nominals	Specific Nominals	Action Words	Modifiers	Personal-Social	Function Words
giraffe / bar legs owie / stroller cow plate telephone /	Bill	whoops see gimme	here / ick more allgone	no yes yeah ‖‖ ‖‖ ‖‖ / allright welcome okay / hello goodnight	huh ‖‖ else

Nelson's One-Word Utterance Types

___11___ General Nominals = ___21.6___ % of Total One-Word Utterances

___1___ Specific Nominals = ___2.0___ % of Total One-Word Utterances

___3___ Action Words = ___5.9___ % of Total One-Word Utterances

___5___ Modifiers = ___9.8___ % of Total One-Word Utterances

___25___ Personal-Social = ___49.0___ % of Total One-Word Utterances

___6___ Function Words = ___11.8___ % of Total One-Word Utterances

TOTAL NUMBER OF ONE-WORD UTTERANCES ___51___

TOTAL NUMBER OF UTTERANCES ___100___

___51___ % OF TOTAL UTTERANCES

© 1993 **Thinking Publications** *Duplication permitted for educational use only.*

TABLE 2.2
PERCENTAGE OF FIRST 50 WORDS ACCOUNTED FOR BY NELSON'S ONE-WORD UTTERANCE TYPES
(Computed from Nelson, 1973)

NOMINALS

SPECIFIC...14%

GENERAL...51%

ACTION WORDS...14%

MODIFIERS...9%

PERSONAL-SOCIAL..9%

FUNCTION WORDS..4%

So how are these data to be interpreted? Cautiously. If one erroneously compared the frequency data directly to Nelson's, the distribution would be quite different. One could conclude that the sample is too limited and diary analysis is needed. Rather, the analysis revealed that approximately half of the utterances were longer than one word in length, warranting not a diary analysis but an analysis of the semantic content of the longer utterances. In addition, the sample data can be considered in relation to a continuum similar to the nominal-pronominal continuum described by Bloom et al. (1975). Nelson refers to this continuum as a referential-expressive continuum. Children whose first 50-word lexicons consisted of a high percentage of NOMINALS were considered to be referential children. In contrast, children whose first 50-word lexicons consisted of a high percentage of PERSONAL-SOCIAL words and/or FUNCTION WORDS were considered to be expressive children. Again, these early preferences for types of words used may reflect different strategies for communicating and appear to persist beyond the one-word stage. From the sample transcript, it would be reasonable to conclude that this child is an expressive child with 61 percent of her utterances consisting of PERSONAL-SOCIAL words and FUNCTION WORDS. Overall, the best judgment from the analysis performed would be to pursue additional analyses of more diverse aspects of the semantic content of the child's productions in this sample transcript. This is due primarily to the fact that, as previously stated, Nelson's data were obtained from diary accounts and represent a first 50-word lexicon, but the data from the sample transcript represent a single, 100-utterance sampling. Therefore, the comparison just made may be likened to comparing apples to oranges. And definitive conclusions drawn from such a comparison are not appropriate. However, Nelson's categories are extremely helpful in analyzing children's first 50-word lexicons and can be useful in documenting changes in one-word utterance types over time. It is because a large number of this child's utterances in this 100-utterance sample are longer than one word that analysis of more diverse aspects of semantic content is warranted.

A word needs to be said here about the recommendation that will continue to be made regarding obtaining additional samples and about the fact that the conclusions drawn from analyses are considered to be hypotheses. Because these procedures do not result in scores or percentages unequivocally indicating the presence of delays, these procedures, and many of those which follow, must be considered as aspects of diagnostic therapy. That is, conclusions rarely can be drawn from a single sampling of the child's production. Samplings obtained under a variety of conditions over time, as in the course of diagnostic therapy, yield the most valuable results. This is not said to postpone a decision, but rather to emphasize that these procedures must be considered as part of the ongoing process of hypothesis generation and testing through obtaining additional data.

Comparison of Bloom's and Nelson's One-Word Utterance Types

Bloom's and Nelson's One-Word Utterance Types are similar in some ways and different in others. Analysis of one-word utterances using Bloom's categories revealed the previously mentioned distinction between referential and relational aspects of semantic content. Bloom's SUBSTANTIVE and NAMING categories characterize a child's use of words to refer to specific and general instances of objects, people, and events, or to referential aspects of semantic content. Her FUNCTION words capture the child's emerging ability to make note of the relations between objects and events, or the relational aspects of semantic content. In fact, Bloom contends that a child's early two-word utterances grow out of greater explicitness in noting the relations between objects and events (e.g., "more" later becomes "more juice" or "more milk" as the context requires greater explicitness and as the child sees greater efficiency in the use of the longer utterance).

On the other hand, Nelson's categories appeared to reflect a quasi-grammatical function of individual words. Her categories more closely parallel a part-of-speech classification scheme beyond the individual meaning roles expressed and include routine forms. While more referential in nature than Bloom's scheme, Nelson's scheme may capture the transition toward two-word utterances as well as Bloom's scheme does. At the stage that a child's vocabulary includes approximately 50 words, Nelson contends that nouns, or NOMINALS, account for between 50 and 65 percent of the words. The child's vocabulary might be considered predominately referential. Later, words for describing actions increase (Leonard, 1976). These more verb-like words parallel Nelson's ACTION WORDS. Then, words to describe attributes, locatives, and possessors of objects (Nelson's MODIFIERS) increase. It is about this time that two-word utterances emerge. Consequently, the transition to two-word utterances may be predicted more accurately with Nelson's categorization scheme. Overall, when using either Bloom's One-Word Utterance Types or Nelson's One-Word Utterance Types, if analysis of one-word utterances reveals less than half of the utterances to be one word in length, analysis of more diverse aspects of semantic content is warranted.

ANALYZING SEMANTIC CONTENT OF ONE- AND MULTI-WORD UTTERANCES

Two procedures will be used to analyze the semantic content of one- and multi-word utterances: semantic role analysis (Retherford, Schwartz, and Chapman, 1981) and prevalent semantic relation analysis (Brown, 1973). Both of these procedures are based on semantic coding of all utterances within a production transcript. The first procedure employs a set of categories delineated by Retherford, Schwartz, and Chapman (1981). Analysis of the frequency of occurrence of individual semantic roles within multi-term relations yields data interpretable as characteristic of children in Brown's Stage I of linguistic development versus Stage II or III. The second procedure is based on the same semantic coding of one- and multi-word utterances but results in an analysis of frequently occurring multi-term combinations. Interpretation of data is accomplished by comparing data to reported frequencies of occurrence of Brown's (1973) Prevalent Semantic Relations and expansions of prevalent semantic relations. Again, identification of combinations characteristic of children in Brown's Stage I versus Stage II is possible.

Semantic Coding of One- and Multi-Word Utterances

The semantic roles and grammatical categories described in Table 2.3 were developed to code utterances of children in Brown's (1973) Stages I–III as well as the utterances of the mothers of these same children (Retherford, Schwartz, and Chapman, 1981). Included in this categorization scheme are semantic roles which correspond to those contained within Brown's (1973) eight Prevalent Semantic Relations, as well as categories which parallel those relations he specified as occurring with low frequency. In addition, many of the categories overlap with categories delineated by Greenfield and Smith (1976) for coding one-term utterances and by Bloom (1973) and Schlesinger (1971) for coding one- and multi-word utterances.

The nonlinguistic context is crucial in determining the relational meanings expressed by children in the early stages of language acquisition. Many of the definitions that follow rely heavily on the nonlinguistic context for interpretation. Transcripts with detailed description of nonlinguistic context, as described in Chapter 1, are necessary for successful coding.

The first step in semantically coding one- and multi-word utterances is to become familiar with the definitions and examples of semantic roles and residual grammatical categories provided in Table 2.3. Not all utterances are codable using these 21 roles and categories. The content of those utterances will be explained in Table 2.4 using two remaining categories, described on pages 60–61.

TABLE 2.3
SEMANTIC ROLES AND RESIDUAL GRAMMATICAL CATEGORIES IN MOTHER AND CHILD SPEECH: WHO TUNES INTO WHOM?
(Retherford, Schwartz, and Chapman, 1981)

Semantic Roles

The following 15 semantic roles are used for coding semantic content of mother (adult) and child speech. Additional content may be coded more appropriately using one of six grammatical categories which follow these definitions or one of the conversational devices or communication routines, described in Table 2.4. Definitions of semantic roles and/or descriptions of use are provided. Examples of mother and child use follow definitions.

ACTION   A perceivable movement or activity engaged in by an agent (animate or inanimate).

Mother: Can you *hit* the ball? (M addressing C)

Child: Mom *cook* some. (C gestures toward toy stove)

LOCATIVE   The place where an object or action is located or toward which it moves.

Mother: The flower *upstairs*. (in response to C's request for a flower)

Child: Milk *in*. (C pulling cup away from M)

Child: *Doctor*. (in response to M's question of where to take a broken doll)

Child: Jason *work*. (in response to M's question of where Jason is)

AGENT   The performer (animate or inanimate) of an action. Body parts and vehicles, when used in conjunction with action verbs, are coded AGENT.

Mother: *I'll* cover you. (C pretending to sleep)

Child: *You* do it. (C holding wind-up toy out to M)

OBJECT   A person or thing (marked by the use of a noun or pronoun) that receives the force of an action.

Mother: Let's pick up your *blocks*. (M and C playing with blocks)

Child: Somebody ate the *cookies*. (M and C playing with toy tea set)

DEMONSTRATIVE   The use of demonstrative pronouns or adjectives, *this, that, these, those,* and the words *there, right there, here,* and *see* and *look* when stated for the purpose of pointing out a particular referent.

Mother: *That* Santa Claus? (M pointing to picture)

Child: *This* one. (C reaching for container)

Continued on next page

TABLE 2.3—*Continued*

RECURRENCE
A request for or comment on an additional instance or amount, the resumption of an event, or the reappearance of a person or object.

Mother: *Another* bead. (M referring to beads C is dropping in box)

Child: I *more* hat mama. (C putting second hat through rungs of fence)

POSSESSOR
A person or thing (marked by the use of a proper noun or pronoun) that an object is associated with or to which it belongs, at least temporarily.

Mother: Get *baby's* puzzle. (M walking toward puzzle)

Child: *My* fence fall down. (M and C playing with toy farm)

QUANTIFIER
A modifier which indicates amount or number of a person or object. Prearticles and indefinite pronouns such as *a piece of, lots of, any, every,* and *each* are included.

Mother: There's sure *a lot of* mommies in that bus. (referring to dolls C put in bus)

Child: *Five* fingers. (C holding puppet's hand and tapping its fingers)

EXPERIENCER
Someone or something that undergoes a given experience or mental state. This category often implies involuntary behavior on the part of the EXPERIENCER, in contrast to voluntary action performed by an AGENT. Body parts, when used in conjunction with state verbs, also are coded EXPERIENCER.

Mother: *I'd* like to see Ernie, please. (referring to puppets C is playing with)

Child: *She* feels better. (C hands baby doll to M)

Child: My *tummy* hurts. (C puts head in M's lap)

RECIPIENT
One who receives or is named as the recipient of an OBJECT (person or thing) from another.

Mother: Can you sing "Ring around the Rosie" *to her*? (M and C pretending Gramma is on toy telephone)

Child: Give *me*. (C putting beads in container)

BENEFICIARY
One who benefits from or is named as the beneficiary of a specified action.

Mother: I already dumped it out *for you*. (M dumps puzzle and hands board to C)

Child: Do it *for me*. (C hands doll with untied shoe to M)

COMITATIVE
One who accompanies or participates with an AGENT in carrying out a specified activity.

Mother: Come *with mommie*. (M standing, extending hand)

Child: A go *mommie*. (M puts C in crib and starts to walk away)

CREATED OBJECT
Something created by a specific activity, for example, a *song* by singing, a *house* by building, a *picture* by drawing.

Mother: Can you draw an *apple*? (C playing with paper and crayons)

Child: Write *tummy*. (same as above)

INSTRUMENT
Something which an AGENT uses to carry out or complete a specified action.

Mother: Don't write on the sofa *with that green pen*. (C writing on sofa)

Child: Draw *with red*. (M helping C make a greeting card)

STATE
A passive condition experienced by a person or object. This category often implies involuntary behavior on the part of the EXPERIENCER, in contrast to voluntary action performed by an AGENT.

Mother: You *want* some milk? (M and C playing with breakfast set)

Child: She *feels* better. (M kisses baby doll and hands to C)

Continued on next page

TABLE 2.3—*Continued*

Grammatical Categories

The preceding semantic roles do not exhaust the optional content of mother or child speech. Six additional categories were used to code this content for utterances not classified as conversational devices or communication routines when none of the preceding semantic roles fit. The authors felt that it was more appropriate to label these *grammatical categories* rather than semantic roles. Their description and examples follow.

ENTITY
(one-term)

Any labeling of a present person or object regardless of the occurrence or nature of action being performed on or by it. To be coded as a one-term ENTITY, the utterance must contain only one semantic role or grammatical category. The utterance may contain more than one word as in the first and third examples.

Mother: *The Piggy.* (M and C looking at picture book)

Child: *Baby.* (M and C looking in fish tank)

Child: *B.* (C pointing to letter on block)

ENTITY
(multi-term)

The use of an appropriate label for a person or object in the absence of any action on it (with the exception of showing, pointing, touching, or grasping); or someone or something which causes or is the stimulus to the internal state specified by a state verb; or any object or person which is modified by a possessive form. ENTITY is used to code a possession if it meets any of the preceding criteria. The choice of the multi-term ENTITY category is made whenever an utterance contains more than the ENTITY category. There is no substantial difference between the two categories in terms of meaning. That is, each category describes a person or object in the absence of action on it or by it. The only difference between the two categories is their occurrence in relation to other semantic roles and categories. That difference is reflected in separate tallies.

Mother: Dirty *diaper*. (M looking at diaper on floor)

Child: That's a *baby*. (C pointing to doll)

NEGATION

The expression of any of the following meanings with regard to someone or something, or an action or state: nonexistence, rejection, cessation, denial, disappearance.

Mother: I *didn't* have any eggs. (M and C playing with tea set)

Child: *No* cookies. (C holding up empty bag)

Child: *No.* (In response to M's question)

ATTRIBUTE

An adjectival description of the size, shape, or quality of an object or person; also, noun adjuncts which modify nouns for a similar purpose (e.g., *gingerbread* man). Excluded are the semantically coded categories of RECURRENCE and QUANTIFIER.

Mother: Where's the *little* ones? (M and C playing with toy animals)

Child: *Big* animal. (Same as above)

ADVERBIAL

Included in this category are the two subcategories of ACTION/ATTRIBUTE and STATE/ATTRIBUTE.

ACTION/ATTRIBUTE: A modifier of an action indicating time, manner, duration, distance, or frequency. (Direction or place of action is coded separately as LOCATIVE; repetition is coded as RECURRENCE.)

Mother: You can dump it *the next time*. (M dumps puzzle, against C's protest)

Child: *Now* go. (C pushing truck)

STATE/ATTRIBUTE: A modifier indicating time, manner, quality, or intensity of a state.

Mother: They've got their fancy socks on *today*. (M raises dolls' feet to show socks)

Child: I'm *full*. (C puts fork down and looks at mother)

For most utterances, the relationship between major semantic roles will be easily identifiable. In utterances longer than two semantic roles in relationship, some semantic roles are considered an expansion of one of the major roles in the semantic relation. Typically, these are expansions of the AGENT or OBJECT as described by Brown (1973). When a semantic role is an expansion of one of the major roles in the semantic relation, it should be set off with parentheses to indicate this relationship. For example, the utterance "big boy jump" is coded (ATTRIBUTE) AGENT-ACTION, indicating that AGENT-ACTION is the major semantic relation and ATTRIBUTE is an expansion of the AGENT in that relation.

The occurrence of grammatical morphemes including number, tense, modal, and auxiliary aspects of the verb system; catenative verbs; articles; plural and possessive inflections; and prepositions are coded within the semantic category of the major semantic role. For example, "is jumping" is coded as ACTION, as are "jumped," "can jump," and "jumps." An utterance containing "the doll" is coded ENTITY, unless it is in relationship with an ACTION, when it becomes AGENT. In the utterance "Daddy's hat," "Daddy's" is coded POSSESSOR. The entire utterance "in the bed" is coded LOCATIVE. Thus, semantic roles may encompass more than one word and must be viewed as units of meaning not directly translated by single words. Examples of the use of this convention of using one semantic role for more than one word will be demonstrated in the practice items that follow.

A few other coding conventions need to be highlighted to assist in coding. As with aspects of the auxiliary system, separable or two-part verbs are coded ACTION. Separable verbs that should be coded in this manner include *pick up, put away, get out, put down, put on, stand up, eat up, call up, put in, pull out, put back, turn over, sit down, fall down,* and *go back.* LOCATIVE is used with separable verbs only

when the location is mentioned (e.g., "Mama sit down here"). State verbs typically coded as STATE include *want, need, like, taste, wish, hurt, matter with, have on, smell, feel, fit,* and *hope. See* or *look* are coded as STATE except when it occurs at the beginning of an imperative pointing out something (e.g., "See the doggie?" meaning, "Look at the doggie"). A small number of verbs which might be considered part of the STATE verb category are coded as ACTION because of their relation to specific intentional verbs also coded as ACTION: *forget (remember), stay (leave), know (think).* When *being* is used as a main verb, as in "You are being silly," it is also coded ACTION; otherwise forms of *be* are coded STATE (e.g., "They are funny"). The main verb *have* is coded as STATE when it implies possession, but as ACTION in contexts where an action verb synonym could be substituted (e.g., "What did you have for lunch?"). Changes in the state of an experiencer, where context makes the change clear, are coded as ACTION; the EXPERIENCER or AGENT, in these cases, is coded AGENT. For example, "I go night-night," as the child moves to the bedroom, is coded AGENT-ACTION-LOCATIVE. In this coding scheme, AGENTs and EXPERIENCERs can be either animate or inanimate. Thus, "the truck hit the wall" would be coded AGENT-ACTION-OBJECT. And "the truck feels so sad" would be coded EXPERIENCER-STATE-STATE/ATTRIBUTE. These additional coding conventions will become clear as experience is gained in coding multi-word utterances.

The examples in Table 2.3 can be helpful in determining the semantic role that individual words play in an utterance, but coding an entire utterance may be more difficult. The following examples of coded utterances with explanations are provided for practice in coding entire utterances. Cover the right side of the page and code the utterances on the left side. Check coding with those provided. The explanations should clear up any discrepancies.

(C is pointing to picture in book)

doggie jump/   AGENT-ACTION

In this example, the *doggie* is the AGENT of the ACTION of *jumping.*

(C is pointing to picture in book)
the doggie is jumping/

AGENT-ACTION

The semantic code for this utterance is the same as for the preceding utterance. Articles and auxiliary verbs are not assigned a separate semantic role; they are collapsed within the major role.

(M says, "What happened?" while pointing to picture)
the boy kicked the ball/

AGENT-ACTION-OBJECT

In this example, *the boy* is the AGENT of the ACTION of *kicking* the OBJECT, *ball*. Again, articles are not assigned a separate semantic role.

(M says, "What happened?" while pointing to picture)
that boy kick/

(DEMONSTRATIVE) AGENT-ACTION

This example introduces the convention used to reflect expansions of major semantic roles. The word *that* is considered a DEMONSTRATIVE expansion of the AGENT, *boy*, who is engaged in the ACTION of *kicking*.

(C reaches for wind-up rabbit)
more jump/

RECURRENCE-ACTION

In this example, *more* is an expansion, reflecting RECURRENCE of the ACTION of *jumping*. While this appears to be an inconsistency in the use-of-parentheses convention to indicate expansions of major semantic roles, it more adequately reflects the child's development of major semantic roles in relationship to other semantic roles.

The preceding five examples demonstrate the various semantic roles that typically combine with the semantic role ACTION. In addition, major semantic roles and expansions of major semantic roles were demonstrated. Remember that each single word is not necessarily coded by a single semantic role. Semantic roles may encompass more than one word and must be viewed as units of meaning, not directly translated by single words.

Following are a few more practice utterances. These will examine the use of another major semantic role, LOCATIVE. Code the following examples.

(C drops spoon in toy cup)
spoon in/

ENTITY-LOCATIVE

In this example, the *spoon* is a multi-term ENTITY situated *in* (LOCATIVE) something.

(M asks, "Where is that spoon?")
the spoon in the cup/

ENTITY-LOCATIVE

The semantic coding for this utterance is the same as for the preceding for two reasons. First, as has already been demonstrated, articles are considered part of the major semantic relation. Second, *in the cup* and *in* both describe the location of the spoon and thus are coded LOCATIVE.

(M says, "Tell me about this," pointing to picture)

the spoon is in the cup/

EXPERIENCER-STATE-LOCATIVE

Although the overall meaning of this example is similar to the previous two examples, one striking difference is in the use of the copula, or main verb, *is*. In this example, the semantic role, STATE, is used to reflect the use of the state verb. Consequently, the ENTITY becomes an EXPERIENCER. Ultimately this utterance translates: *the spoon* (EXPERIENCER) is in the state (STATE) of being located *in the cup* (LOCATIVE).

(C points to spoons in a coffee pot)

two spoon there/

(QUANTIFIER) ENTITY-LOCATIVE

Again, this is a multi-term ENTITY, *spoon,* that is LOCATED somewhere, *there.* But in this example there is also an expansion of the major relation, ENTITY. It indicates the number of spoons that are located there and reflects the semantic role QUANTIFIER. But the QUANTIFIER is not a major semantic role in this utterance; it is an expansion of the major semantic role, ENTITY.

These examples have demonstrated variations in the use of the semantic roles ENTITY and LOCATIVE. Examples in which more than one word was coded by using only one semantic role were provided. In addition, more practice using the convention that reflects the difference between major semantic roles and expansions of major semantic roles was provided. Now, for some practice with other semantic roles, code the following.

(C points to picture in book)

big baby/

ATTRIBUTE-ENTITY

In this example, *big* is an ATTRIBUTE of the ENTITY, *baby.*

(C points to next picture)

big baby cry/

(ATTRIBUTE) AGENT-ACTION

With the use of the ACTION verb *cry,* the *baby* becomes an AGENT of that ACTION. In addition, now that a major semantic relation is expressed by the roles AGENT and ACTION in combination, the ATTRIBUTE *big* becomes an expansion of the major role, AGENT.

(C pulls baby doll away from M)

my baby/

POSSESSOR-ENTITY

In this example, the use of the pronoun *my* reflects the POSSESSOR of the ENTITY, *baby.*

(C holds up sock)

this mine/

DEMONSTRATIVE-POSSESSIVE

In this example, *this* is a DEMONSTRATIVE, and the pronoun *mine* is the POSSESSOR.

(C rocking baby doll in arms)

my baby cry/

(POSSESSOR) AGENT-ACTION

With the use of the ACTION *cry,* the *baby* becomes an AGENT and the POSSESSOR role becomes an expansion of the AGENT.

(C pulls tiny doll out of bag)

another baby/

RECURRENCE-ENTITY

The word *another* reflects an additional instance (RECURRENCE) of the ENTITY, *baby.*

(C hears baby crying in another room) another baby cry/	**(RECURRENCE) AGENT-ACTION** Once again, the use of the ACTION, *cry*, changes the *baby* into an AGENT and the role of RECURRENCE becomes an expansion of the AGENT. RECURRENCE typically is a major role when forms of it occur in two-term utterances in conjunction with ENTITIES or ACTIONS. When the role of RECURRENCE describes an AGENT or OBJECT in a relationship with an ACTION, it is not considered a major role, but an expansion of a major role. This example demonstrates this convention.
(M says, "What should we take to the other room?") that baby/	**DEMONSTRATIVE-ENTITY** The demonstrative pronoun *that* points out a particular instance of the ENTITY, *baby*.
that baby cry/	**(DEMONSTRATIVE) AGENT-ACTION** Here the DEMONSTRATIVE role becomes an expansion of the AGENT with the addition of the ACTION, *cry*.

These examples clearly point out the different relationship between major semantic relations and expansions of major semantic roles. It is important to keep in mind the circumstances that account for a semantic role being used as a major role in one instance and not in another. Typically, if an ATTRIBUTE, POSSESSOR, RECURRENCE, or DEMONSTRATIVE is used alone with an ENTITY, then each role is considered a major role. If, however, an ACTION appears in the semantic relation, then the ATTRIBUTE, POSSESSOR, RECURRENCE, or DEMONSTRATIVE becomes an expansion of the AGENT or OBJECT. Unfortunately, there are some exceptions to these circumstances. They will be demonstrated in the following practice items.

(C looks in bag where tiny dolls had been) no baby/	**NEGATION-ENTITY** The word *no* is an example of nonexistence, which is a type of NEGATION. In this case it refers to the nonexistence of the ENTITY, *baby*.
(baby in other room stops crying) no cry/	**NEGATION-ACTION** Here the word *no* refers to the lack or cessation (type of NEGATION) of the ACTION, *cry*.
(baby in other room stops crying) baby no cry/	**AGENT-NEGATION-ACTION** Now *baby* is the AGENT of the ACTION, *cry*, but the use of the word *no* relates to the entire semantic relation. Thus, NEGATION is considered a major semantic role and not an expansion of the ACTION.
(M is changing C's sister's diaper) baby wet/	**ENTITY-STATE/ATTRIBUTE** The word *wet* describes the quality of the state that the ENTITY, *baby*, is in. The state verb does not have to be present to use the STATE/ATTRIBUTE role.

(C hands doll to M)
baby is wet/

EXPERIENCER-STATE-STATE/ATTRIBUTE
But as can be seen from this example, the STATE, *is*, can be present. And when the STATE is specified, the ENTITY becomes an EXPERIENCER.

(C runs into M's arms)
run fast/

ACTION-ACTION/ATTRIBUTE
The word *fast* describes the manner in which the ACTION is performed.

(M and C looking at book)
I can run fast/

AGENT-ACTION-ACTION/ATTRIBUTE
Now there is an AGENT, *I*, performing an ACTION, *can run*, in a particular manner (ACTION/ATTRIBUTE). The use of the modal verb *can* is coded ACTION along with the main verb *run*.

These examples demonstrate the use of semantic roles and categories that can be used in combination with ENTITIES or AGENTS and ACTIONS. In addition, the ADVERBIAL categories of ACTION/ATTRIBUTE and STATE/ATTRIBUTE were demonstrated. Perhaps more importantly, the preceding practice items demonstrate the exceptions to the rule for determining when a semantic role is a major role or an expansion of a major role. In the preceding examples, each semantic role was considered to be a major role regardless of the presence of other semantic roles.

NEGATION, STATE/ATTRIBUTE, and ACTION/ATTRIBUTE are always considered to be major semantic roles regardless of the presence of other semantic roles, as are AGENT, OBJECT, EXPERIENCER, ACTION, STATE, and LOCATIVE. Some additional coding categories also are always considered to be major roles, but they occur less frequently than the preceding. The following practice items are provided to demonstrate semantic coding using some of these less frequently occurring semantic roles and grammatical categories.

(C pats baby doll on back)
baby sleep/

EXPERIENCER-STATE
In this example, the *baby* is the EXPERIENCER of the STATE, *sleep*.

(M is holding C's baby sister who is sleeping; C pats doll on back)
my baby sleep/

(POSSESSOR) EXPERIENCER-STATE
Now a particular *baby*, *my* (POSSESSOR) *baby* (EXPERIENCER), is experiencing the STATE of *sleep*. Consequently, the role of POSSESSOR is an expansion of the major role, EXPERIENCER.

(M and C are eating cookies in therapy room)
I like cookies/

EXPERIENCER-STATE-ENTITY
The pronoun *I* is the EXPERIENCER of the STATE of *liking* an ENTITY, *cookies*.

(C addressing M while the clinician, Anna, looks on)
give Anna the cookies/

ACTION-RECIPIENT-OBJECT
The ACTION is *giving* an OBJECT, *cookies*, to a RECIPIENT, *Anna*. RECIPIENTS receive the OBJECT of an ACTION.

(M and C are making clay
cookies)
the cookies are for Anna/   EXPERIENCER-STATE-BENEFICIARY

The *cookies* (EXPERIENCER) are in the STATE of *being* for *Anna* (BENEFICIARY).

(C crumbles clay on top of
clay cookies)
make chocolate chip cookies/   ACTION-(ATTRIBUTE) CREATED OBJECT

The ACTION of *making* creates the *chocolate chip* (ATTRIBUTE) *cookies* (CREATED OBJECT).

(C turns to M, who is
rocking baby)
make cookies with me/   ACTION-CREATED OBJECT-COMITATIVE

The ACTION of *making* creates the *cookies* (CREATED OBJECT) and the AGENT (who is not specified) is to participate with the child, *me* (COMITATIVE).

These examples contain some of the infrequently occurring semantic roles and grammatical categories. Even though they may not occur in every transcript, it is important to be able to recognize them when they do occur. In addition, changes in frequency of use over time of the infrequently occurring categories may provide valuable diagnostic information. This will be discussed in more detail in the interpretation section.

Question forms also can be coded using the preceding semantic roles. Questions are treated like any other utterance; however, the semantic role that the wh-word in the question is querying is coded using the following semantic roles: ENTITY, OBJECT, or CREATED OBJECT for *what*; ACTION for *what doing*; LOCATIVE for *where*; QUANTIFIER for *how many*; ADVERBIAL (ACTION/ATTRIBUTE or STATE/ATTRIBUTE as appropriate) for *how*, *how long*, and *when*; ATTRIBUTE or DEMONSTRATIVE for *which*; AGENT, EXPERIENCER, or ENTITY for *who*; and ATTRIBUTE for *what kind of*. Keep in mind that presence of forms of the verb *to be* as a copula must be reflected in the semantic coding as STATE. Auxiliary verbs are coded with the main verb using the ACTION category. Remember to check the appropriate column on the coding sheet whenever a question is coded, because the coding of the utterances will not reflect the question form. The following practice items demonstrate coding of question forms using the semantic roles specified above.

(clock in room buzzes;
C looks up from toy)
what that?/   ENTITY-DEMONSTRATIVE

In this example, the word *what* is querying the semantic role of ENTITY. It is querying the semantic role of a particular ENTITY, *that* (DEMONSTRATIVE).

(C digs in toy box)
where's the ball?/   LOCATIVE-STATE-ENTITY

The wh-word *where* is querying the location (LOCATIVE) of an ENTITY, *the ball*.

(C and M looking at book)
what him doing?/   AGENT-ACTION

Here the semantic role being queried is ACTION. The child is using the *what doing* form to query the ACTION of the AGENT, *him*.

(C and M looking at book)
what are they doing?/

AGENT-ACTION
Again, the semantic role being queried is ACTION. The child is seeking a label for the ACTION *they* (AGENT) are engaged in. The auxiliary verb, *are*, is part of that ACTION.

(C hears talking in the hallway)
who that?/

ENTITY-DEMONSTRATIVE
In this case, it is impossible to know if *who* is an AGENT or an ENTITY, so the more neutral ENTITY is used. A particular ENTITY is being requested: *that* (DEMONSTRATIVE) ENTITY.

(C, holding bag of marbles, looks at M)
how many you got?/

EXPERIENCER-STATE-QUANTIFIER
Here the semantic role being queried is QUANTIFIER. The child is using the QUANTIFIER to ask his mother (EXPERIENCER) how many marbles she has (STATE).

(C putting pretend bandage on M's arm)
how that feels?/

DEMONSTRATIVE-STATE-STATE/ATTRIBUTE
The child is asking for a description of the quality or intensity (ADVERBIAL) of his mother's particular (DEMONSTRATIVE) STATE.

(C and M are playing with model cars on a real track)
what kinda car you driving?/

AGENT-ACTION-(ATTRIBUTE) OBJECT
The child is seeking a description (ATTRIBUTE) of the *car* (OBJECT) that the mother (AGENT) is *driving* (ACTION).

Question forms are quite simple once it becomes possible to think in terms of semantic roles and categories and not in words. Again, remember to indicate when a question form is coded by checking the appropriate column on the coding sheet. As can be seen in the preceding examples, once the question is semantically coded, it is impossible to tell that the original utterance was in the form of a question. In the final analysis of semantic roles and relations, it is important to be able to differentiate question forms from other utterances. How to differentiate question forms will be explained in the next paragraph. Differentiation is necessary because some comparison data excludes question forms from analysis.

The preceding practice items should be helpful as coding of the sample transcript is begun. Progress through the transcript and determine the appropriate combination of roles and/or categories for each utterance. The semantic code for each utterance should be recorded on the Semantic Analysis Coding Sheet. Record the utterance number and the semantic coding for each utterance. If the utterance is a question, be certain to put a check in the question column to differentiate it from non-questions. For utterances that do not appear to be codable using the 21 semantic roles and grammatical categories, record the utterance number but leave the coding column blank. These utterances will be characterized using three additional categories which will be discussed in Table 2.4. The partially completed Semantic Analysis Coding Sheets can be found on pages 56–59.

Semantic Analysis
Coding Sheet

Name of Child ___*Bridget*___

Utterance Number	Semantic Coding	Question
1		
2	ACTION	
3	NEGATION	
4		
5	STATE-(POSSESSOR) ENTITY-LOCATIVE	
6	DEMONSTRATIVE	✓
7	ENTITY-RECURRENCE	✓
8	ENTITY	
9	ENTITY	
10		
11	ACTION-ACTION/ATTRIBUTE	
12		
13	LOCATIVE	
14	LOCATIVE	
15		
16	ENTITY-RECURRENCE	✓
17	ACTION-LOCATIVE	
18	DEMONSTRATIVE-STATE-NEGATION-QUANTIFIER	
19	ENTITY-RECURRENCE	✓
20	EXPERIENCER-STATE-NEGATION-LOCATIVE	
21	EXPERIENCER-NEGATION-STATE	
22	ACTION-OBJECT	
23	LOCATIVE-EXPERIENCER-STATE	✓
24	LOCATIVE-(DEMONSTRATIVE) EXPERIENCER-STATE	✓
25	ENTITY	

© **1993 Thinking Publications** *Duplication permitted for educational use only.*

Semantic Analysis
Coding Sheet

Name of Child _*Bridget*_

Utterance Number	Semantic Coding	Question
26	ACTION	
27	ENTITY	
28	ACTION	
29		
30		
31	AGENT-ACTION-ACTION/ATTRIBUTE	
32	DEMONSTRATIVE-STATE-ENTITY	
33		
34		
35	LOCATIVE-STATE-(RECURRENCE) EXPERIENCER	✓
36	AGENT-ACTION-OBJECT	
37		
38	ACTION	
39		
40	ENTITY	
41	ENTITY	
42		
43	ATTRIBUTE-STATE/ATTRIBUTE	
44	AGENT-ACTION	
45	AGENT-ACTION-OBJECT	
46		
47		
48		
49		
50	ENTITY	

Semantic Analysis
Coding Sheet

Name of Child ___*Bridget*___

Utterance Number	Semantic Coding	Question
51		
52		
53		
54		
55		
56	AGENT-ACTION-OBJECT	
57		
58	ENTITY	
59		
60	DEMONSTRATIVE-STATE-ENTITY	✓
61	DEMONSTRATIVE-STATE-ENTITY	
62	DEMONSTRATIVE-POSSESSOR	
63		
64		
65	DEMONSTRATIVE-STATE-POSSESSOR	
66	ENTITY-RECURRENCE	✓
67	RECURRENCE	
68		
69		
70	RECURRENCE	✓
71		
72		
73		
74		
75	STATE-STATE/ATTRIBUTE	

© **1993 Thinking Publications** *Duplication permitted for educational use only.*

Semantic Analysis
Coding Sheet

Name of Child __Bridget__

Utterance Number	Semantic Coding	Question
76		
77		
78	NEGATION-ENTITY	
79	NEGATION	
80		
81	AGENT-ACTION-OBJECT	
82		
83	STATE/ATTRIBUTE-LOCATIVE	
84	ENTITY	
85		
86	ACTION-POSSESSOR	
87	ACTION-OBJECT	
88	ACTION-OBJECT	
89		
90		
91		
92		
93	ENTITY	
94	ENTITY	
95		
96	ACTION	✓
97	(DEMONSTRATIVE) LOCATIVE	
98		
99	ENTITY-LOCATIVE	
100	AGENT-ACTION	

© 1993 Thinking Publications *Duplication permitted for educational use only.*

With the majority of utterances semantically coded, return to the utterances left blank on the coding form because the use of the 21 semantic roles and residual grammatical categories did not seem to fit. Typically, there are three reasons that an utterance is not semantically codable using the 21 semantic roles and residual grammatical categories: (1) the utterance is a complex sentence, requiring syntactic categories to reflect the complexity; (2) the utterance is a conversational device that may have been acquired as a whole unit rather than as individual roles; or (3) the utterance is a communication routine that also may have been acquired as a whole unit, and semantically coding it may inflate the semantic complexity of the child's productions. The types of conversational devices and communication routines frequently occurring in child language transcripts are captured in Table 2.4.

TABLE 2.4
CATEGORIES USED TO CODE UTTERANCES NOT CODABLE
USING SEMANTIC ROLES AND RESIDUAL GRAMMATICAL CATEGORIES
(Retherford, Schwartz, and Chapman, 1981)

Conversational Devices

The following categories were used to code utterances not codable using semantic roles or residual grammatical categories. These categories were judged to reflect pragmatic conventions governing conversation rather than semantic intentions.

ATTENTION   Use of an individual's name to gain attention.

Mother: Abigail! (M calling C, who is climbing on sofa)
Child: Mama! (M dressing C while talking to another adult)

AFFIRMATION   Use of affirmative terms to assert that a previous utterance or behavior is correct or to indicate compliance with request from previous utterance.

Mother: Okay. (following C's request for assistance in putting puzzle together)
Child: Yeah. (in response to M's offer of assistance)

POSITIVE EVALUATION   Use of positive terms to evaluate an utterance or behavior of the other speaker.

Mother: Right. (C manipulating puzzle, fits piece in correctly)
Child: Very good. (M places block on top of stack and C responds)

INTERJECTION   Use of words like *um*, *oh*, etc. to hold a speaking turn and/or as a searching strategy for conversational contribution.

Mother: Oh. (following C's affirmative response to M's question of activity)
Child: Um. (C looking at M who has just queried C about doll's name)

POLITE FORM   Use of terms like *please*, *thank you*, etc. in absence of other semantic content (e.g., "Please help me." = ACTION/ATTRIBUTE-ACTION-OBJECT)

Mother: Thank you. (C pouring M an imaginary cup of coffee)
Child: Pretty please. (M offers imaginary plate of cookies to C)

REPETITION REQUEST   Use of terms like *what*, *huh*, etc. to request repetition of another speaker's utterance.

Mother: What? (C describing toy people's activities)
Child: Hum? (following M's question)

ACCOMPANI-MENT   Use of *there* (in the absence of pointing or directional/locational intent) or *there you go* to accompany an action by one speaker.

Mother: There you go. (C attempting to wrap herself in blanket, finally succeeds)
Child: There, there. (C patting doll on back)

Continued on next page

TABLE 2.4—*Continued*

Communication Routines

The following categories were used to code utterances not codable using semantic roles or residual grammatical categories. These categories were judged to reflect pragmatic conventions of frequently occurring routines rather than semantic intentions.

ANIMAL

Utterances used to engage in routines about animal sounds and behaviors. Also use of animal sounds with no referent present. When animal sounds are used to label an animal, the residual grammatical category of ENTITY is used.

Mother: The cow says, "Moo." (M and C playing with toy farm)
Child: Moo. (same as above; C previously labeled toy cow appropriately)
Child: Moo. (no referent present; C pretending to be cow)

STORY/SONG/ POEM

Utterances which consist of all or part of story text, songs, nursery rhymes, or poems.

Mother: Where is thumbkin? Where is thumbkin? (M and C singing along with finger play)
Child: Here I am. (same as above)

COUNTING/ ALPHABET

Utterances which consist of rote counting or recitation of all or part of alphabet. When context indicates counting of referents or labeling/identifying letters, the residual grammatical category of ENTITY is used.

Mother: A B C D. (M singing, no referent present)
Child: One, two, three. (no referent present)

GREETING

Use of greeting and leave-taking forms reflecting adherence to routines rather than semantic intent.

Mother: How are you? (M and C talking on toy telephone)
Child: Bye-bye. (C waving to M)

SAY X

Requests for other speaker to repeat specific information.

Mother: Say I'm sorry, Eugene. (following scolding prompted by C pulling cat's tail)
Child: Say I wake up. (C picking up doll from baby bed)

SOUNDS ACCOMPANYING

Noises and/or sounds used to replicate noises/sounds of vehicles or objects.

Mother: Whoops! (toy monkey falls off trapeze)
Child: Vroom. (C moving toy car back and forth on floor)

NAME

Routine forms requesting or specifying the name of something or someone.

Mother: What's your name? (M speaking to doll C is holding)
Child: My name is Kiki. (C talking on telephone)

Identification of conversational devices and communication routines may be easier than semantically coding the utterances. The examples in Table 2.4 make them easy to identify. With practice, each type of conversational device and communication routine should stand out.

As previously stated, the first reason an utterance cannot be coded using the 21 semantic roles and residual grammatical categories is that the utterance is a complex sentence. Identification of utterances appropriately labeled COMPLEX may be more difficult than identification of conversational devices and communication routines. The decision to identify an utterance as complex when completing the semantic analysis is based on the presence of parallel semantic roles or categories within the same utterance. That is, it is not possible to have two AGENTS or two ACTIONS or two ENTITIES within the same utterance. If an utterance contains more than one of any type of major semantic category, the utterance is coded COMPLEX. This judgment of semantic complexity may be different than the judgment made when completing the syntactic analysis. In other words, an utterance could be classified COMPLEX for the semantic analysis but the same utterance would not necessarily be assigned a stage for complex sentence development when completing the syntactic analysis. The following examples of child utterances labeled COMPLEX may be helpful.

doggie barked and barked/	COMPLEX
doggie bite and I cried/	COMPLEX
I want the one what's big/	COMPLEX
my shoes and pants are dirty/	COMPLEX

When COMPLEX utterances occur in a transcript, the word "complex" is written on the coding line of the coding sheet. This permits efficient identification of the number of complex sentences occurring in a transcript. Identification and analysis of complex sentences will be completed in the syntactic analysis of a transcript using slightly different criteria. These procedures will be described in Chapter 3.

One more convention in coding utterances needs to be discussed. This is the convention used for utterances that have semantic content and are codable using the 21 semantic roles and residual grammatical categories, but that also contain a conversational device or a conjunction. For example, in the utterance, "Mommy, big truck," the child is requesting the mother's attention and commenting on a big truck. The procedure used in this case is to indicate that a conversational device was used by recording CD in parentheses prior to the semantic code for the comment. The coding for this utterance would be: (CD) ATTRIBUTE-ENTITY. This same procedure can be used with utterance-initial conjunctions. While the use of a conjunction typically signals a complex sentence, if the utterance is not a complete sentence and only begins with a conjunction, the conjunction is noted in parentheses and the utterance is semantically coded. Communication routines rarely occur within the context of a semantically codable utterance.

Now, from the coding sheet, identify the utterances that were left blank. Determine whether each is a conversational device, a communication routine, or a complex sentence and mark them appropriately. A completed analysis has been provided on pages 63–66 to check correct identification of each of the aforementioned circumstances for not using one of the 21 semantic roles and residual grammatical categories. One more completed coding sheet, corresponding to Sara's transcript in Appendix B, can be found in Appendix C.

Summary and Interpretation of Semantically Coded One- and Multi-Word Utterances

Following the semantic coding of utterances in the sample transcript, tally the frequency of occurrence of each role or category. Using the Total Use of Individual Semantic Roles analysis sheet, progress utterance by utterance through the coding sheets and tally each semantic role in each utterance. For example, in the coded utterance AGENT-ACTION-OBJECT, mark one tally in the AGENT row, one tally in the ACTION row, and one tally in the OBJECT row. When all roles on the coding sheet have been tallied, count the number of instances of each semantic role and record this number in the number column of that row. In the sample transcript, there were 24 instances of the ACTION role, 11 one-term ENTITY roles, 10 multi-term ENTITY roles, 11 LOCATIVES, and so on.

The next step is to compute the percentage of semantic roles accounted for by each role. To do this, add all totals in the number column and put this sum in the TOTAL box at the lower right of the analysis sheet. In the sample transcript, there was a total of 126 individual roles used. Divide each individual role total by 126 to obtain the percentage of total roles accounted for by each role. For ACTION, 24 divided by 126 yields .1904. Rounding this off and multiplying by 100 (to convert to a percentage) reveals that 19 percent of all semantic roles were coded ACTION. Progress through the analysis sheet, dividing each total by the overall total and multiplying by 100 to get the percentage for each semantic role. These percentages can be added together to double-check computations. If the total is more than .3 percent above or below 100 percent, a miscalculation may have occurred. A completed analysis sheet is provided on page 67 to check computations.

Semantic Analysis
Coding Sheet

Name of Child *Bridget*

Utterance Number	Semantic Coding	Question
1	CR-sounds accompanying	
2	ACTION	
3	NEGATION	
4	CD-affirmation	
5	STATE-(POSSESSOR) ENTITY-LOCATIVE	
6	DEMONSTRATIVE	✓
7	ENTITY-RECURRENCE	✓
8	ENTITY	
9	ENTITY	
10	CD-accompaniment	
11	ACTION-ACTION/ATTRIBUTE	
12	CD-affirmation	
13	LOCATIVE	
14	LOCATIVE	
15	(CD) AGENT-ACTION	
16	ENTITY-RECURRENCE	✓
17	ACTION-LOCATIVE	
18	DEMONSTRATIVE-STATE-NEGATION-QUANTIFIER	
19	ENTITY-RECURRENCE	✓
20	EXPERIENCER-STATE-NEGATION-LOCATIVE	
21	EXPERIENCER-NEGATION-STATE	
22	ACTION-OBJECT	
23	LOCATIVE-EXPERIENCER-STATE	✓
24	LOCATIVE-(DEMONSTRATIVE) EXPERIENCER-STATE	✓
25	ENTITY	

© 1993 Thinking Publications *Duplication permitted for educational use only.*

Semantic Analysis
Coding Sheet

Name of Child ___*Bridget*___

Utterance Number	Semantic Coding	Question
26	ACTION	
27	ENTITY	
28	ACTION	
29	CD-repetition request	
30	CD-affirmation	
31	AGENT-ACTION-ACTION/ATTRIBUTE	
32	DEMONSTRATIVE-STATE-ENTITY	
33	(CD)EXPERIENCER-STATE-STATE/ATTRIBUTE	
34	CD-affirmation	
35	LOCATIVE-STATE-(RECURRENCE) EXPERIENCER	✓
36	AGENT-ACTION-OBJECT	
37	CD-affirmation	
38	ACTION	
39	CR-sounds accompanying	
40	ENTITY	
41	ENTITY	
42	CD-affirmation	
43	ATTRIBUTE-STATE/ATTRIBUTE	
44	AGENT-ACTION	
45	AGENT-ACTION-OBJECT	
46	ACTION (CD)	
47	CD-affirmation	
48	CD-affirmation	
49	CD-affirmation	
50	ENTITY	

© 1993 **Thinking Publications** *Duplication permitted for educational use only.*

**Semantic Analysis
Coding Sheet**

Name of Child ___Bridget___

Utterance Number	Semantic Coding	Question
51	CD-affirmation	
52	complex	
53	CR-sounds accompanying	
54	CR-greeting	
55	CD-affirmation	
56	AGENT-ACTION-OBJECT	
57	CD-affirmation	
58	ENTITY	
59	CD-repetition request	
60	DEMONSTRATIVE-STATE-ENTITY	✓
61	DEMONSTRATIVE-STATE-ENTITY	
62	DEMONSTRATIVE-POSSESSOR	
63	CD-polite form	
64	CD-affirmation	
65	DEMONSTRATIVE-STATE-POSSESSOR	
66	ENTITY-RECURRENCE	✓
67	RECURRENCE	
68	CD-repetition request	
69	CD-affirmation	
70	RECURRENCE	✓
71	CD-attention	
72	ACTION-OBJECT (CD)	
73	ACTION-OBJECT (CD)	
74	CD-repetition request	
75	STATE-STATE/ATTRIBUTE	

© 1993 Thinking Publications *Duplication permitted for educational use only.*

Semantic Analysis
Coding Sheet

Name of Child *Bridget*

Utterance Number	Semantic Coding	Question
76	CD-affirmation	
77	CD-affirmation	
78	NEGATION-ENTITY	
79	NEGATION	
80	CD-affirmation	
81	AGENT-ACTION-OBJECT	
82	CD-affirmation	
83	STATE/ATTRIBUTE-LOCATIVE	
84	ENTITY	
85	CD-affirmation	
86	ACTION-POSSESSOR	
87	ACTION-OBJECT	
88	ACTION-OBJECT	
89	ACTION (CD)	
90	ACTION (CD)	
91	CD-repetition request	
92	CD-affirmation	
93	ENTITY	
94	ENTITY	
95	CD-affirmation	
96	ACTION	✓
97	(DEMONSTRATIVE) LOCATIVE	
98	CR-greeting	
99	ENTITY-LOCATIVE	
100	AGENT-ACTION	

© **1993 Thinking Publications** *Duplication permitted for educational use only.*

Semantic Analysis
Total Use of Individual Semantic Roles

Name of Child ___Bridget___

ROLES	TALLY	#	%
Action	|||| |||| |||| ||||	24	19.0
Entity (one-term)		11	8.7
Entity (multi-term)		10	7.9
Locative		11	8.7
Negation		6	4.8
Agent		8	6.3
Object		9	7.1
Demonstrative		9	7.1
Recurrence		7	5.6
Attribute		1	0.8
Possessor		4	3.2

ROLES	TALLY	#	%
Adverbial Action/Attribute or State/Attribute		6	4.8
Quantifier		1	0.8
State		13	10.3
Experiencer		6	4.8
Recipient		0	—
Beneficiary		0	—
Created Object		0	—
Comitative		0	—
Instrument		0	—
Other		0	—
TOTAL		126	

© 1993 Thinking Publications *Duplication permitted for educational use only.*

Before results of the percentage of total utterances accounted for by each semantic role can be interpreted, the percentage of total utterances that were semantically codable needs to be computed. Using the Meaning Relationships in One- and Multi-Word Utterances grid analysis sheet, progress through the coding sheet and put a check on the grid indicating whether each coded utterance is one term, two terms, three terms, four terms, or longer, a complex utterance, conversational device, communication routine, or other. Under the 100th utterance row, total each column from the entire grid. For example, in the first 25 utterances there were 8 one-term utterances; in the second 25 utterances, 8 one-term utterances; in the third 25 utterances, 3 one-term utterances; in the final 25 utterances, 8 one-term utterances. This totals 27 one-term utterances. Put 27 below the 100th row in the "One-term Utterance" column. Tallies can be checked with the sample provided on pages 70–71.

Totaling the one-, two-, three-, and four-term-plus tallies in the sample transcript reveals 65 utterances that were coded semantically. Put this number in the appropriate blank of the Summary section of the Total Use of Individual Semantic Roles analysis sheet. (See page 72.) Now divide this number by 100 total utterances. The result should be .65, and after multiplying by 100 to convert to a percentage, note that 65 percent of this child's utterances in this transcript were semantically codable. Now transfer the percentage obtained for each semantic role to the Summary section. Finally, return to the Meaning Relationships grid and tally the number of utterances that were conversational devices, communication routines, and complex sentences. In the sample transcript, there were 29 utterances coded as conversational devices, indicating that 29 percent of the child's utterances were types of conversational devices. There were also 5 utterances coded as communication routines, indicating that 5 percent of this child's utterances were types of communication routines. There was one instance of a complex utterance, indicating that 1 percent of this child's utterances were coded COMPLEX. The completed Summary section of the Total Use of Individual Semantic Roles analysis sheet is provided on page 72.

With the data summarized, interpretation of the results follows. Begin by examining the percentage of total utterances that could be coded using combinations of semantic roles and grammatical categories. Brown (1973) found that 70 percent of children's utterances in Stages I–III of linguistic development could be semantically coded using a smaller set of semantic roles than those described above. Retherford, Schwartz, and Chapman (1981) found that between 64 and 85 percent of Stage I children's utterances were codable using the combination of semantic roles and grammatical categories described above. In addition, between 47 and 85 percent of utterances by children in Stages II and III were semantically codable. The sample analysis revealed 65 percent of this child's utterances to be semantically codable. This percentage indicates that this child's productions encode meaning relations with frequencies typical of children in Brown's Stages I–III of linguistic development.

Next, the frequency of occurrence of individual semantic roles and grammatical categories will be examined. Summaries of Brown's data do not include frequency of occurrence of individual roles. Summaries of the Retherford, Schwartz, and Chapman (1977) data were presented as Time 1 and Time 2 of data collection. This organizational format resulted in data obtained from children in Brown's Stages of I–II being included in the Time 1 data, and data obtained from children in Brown's Stages I–III being included in the Time 2 data. These data have been reorganized to provide a basis of comparison for results obtained from the sample transcript. Table 2.5 summarizes the frequency of occurrence of each semantic role as a percentage of total roles used by the children in the Retherford et al. (1977) study. Data are presented in Table 2.5 by stage of linguistic production.

As can be seen in Table 2.5, the most striking change during the early stages of linguistic production is the decrease in the frequency of occurrence of the one-term ENTITY category. This, however, might be predicted on the basis of an increase in utterance length alone. In addition, substantial increases in the categories of AGENT, OBJECT, DEMONSTRATIVE, RECURRENCE, POSSESSOR, and ADVERBIAL were noted as the children advanced to higher

TABLE 2.5
MEAN FREQUENCY OF OCCURRENCE OF INDIVIDUAL SEMANTIC ROLES AND GRAMMATICAL CATEGORIES OF CHILDREN IN BROWN'S STAGE I AND STAGES II AND III
(Computed from Retherford, Schwartz, and Chapman, 1977)

Role	Stage I (N = 9)	Stages II–III (N = 3)
ACTION	13.5	15.0
ENTITY (One-Term)	30.3	6.8
ENTITY (Multi-Term)	10.5	14.1
LOCATIVE	9.5	9.1
NEGATION	8.4	5.3
AGENT	3.8	6.9
OBJECT	2.0	5.7
DEMONSTRATIVE	2.9	5.6
RECURRENCE	1.8	2.8
ATTRIBUTE	3.0	4.1
POSSESSOR	1.1	3.9
ADVERBIAL	1.4	2.8
QUANTIFIER	1.9	1.7
STATE	1.6	1.8
EXPERIENCER	2.4	1.5
RECIPIENT	0.2	0.3
BENEFICIARY	0.1	0.2
CREATED OBJECT	0.1	0.0
COMITATIVE	0.7	0.1
INSTRUMENT	0.0	0.0

stages of linguistic production. Comparison of results of the sample transcript to these data indicate that this child's use of one-term ENTITY is more typical of Stage II or III than of Stage I. In addition, this child's use of the categories AGENT, OBJECT, DEMONSTRATIVE, RECURRENCE, POSSESSOR, and ADVERBIAL is more typical of children in Stages II or III. Overall, it can be said that this child's use of individual semantic roles in combination is typical of a child at least in Brown's Stage II or III. Because the sample size is so small for the Retherford et al. (1977) data (N = 3 for Stages II and III), the reader is cautioned not to overinterpret the normative data. The important change to look for in the child's use of individual semantic roles from Stage I to Stages II and III is the shift from between 12 and 50 percent use of one-term ENTITY to 5 to 10 percent use. Obviously, this decrease in use of one-term ENTITY will be accompanied by increases in use of other categories, most often in the categories of AGENT, OBJECT, POSSESSOR, and ADVERBIAL.

Identification of Brown's Prevalent Semantic Relations

To identify Brown's Prevalent Semantic Relations, analysis will utilize data and theory summarized by Brown (1973) in his classic volume, *A First Language*. Brown contended that the eight prevalent semantic relations which he found to be frequently occurring in child language laid the foundation for longer utterances. The child, according to Brown, accomplished increases in utterance length by elaborating on one of the roles in some of the basic two-term semantic relations. The role which the child was likely to expand was found to be very predictable. Brown's eight Prevalent Semantic

Semantic Analysis
Meaning Relationships in One- and Multi-Word Utterances

Name of Child __Bridget__

Utterance Number	One-Term	Two-Term	Three-Term	Four-Term Plus	Complex	Conversational Device	Communication Routine	Other
1							✓	
2	✓							
3	✓							
4						✓		
5			✓					
6	✓							
7		✓						
8	✓							
9	✓							
10						✓		
11		✓						
12						✓		
13	✓							
14	✓							
15		✓						
16		✓						
17		✓						
18				✓				
19		✓						
20				✓				
21			✓					
22		✓						
23			✓					
24			✓					
25	✓							

Utterance Number	One-Term	Two-Term	Three-Term	Four-Term Plus	Complex	Conversational Device	Communication Routine	Other
26	✓							
27	✓							
28	✓							
29						✓		
30						✓		
31			✓					
32			✓					
33			✓					
34						✓		
35			✓					
36			✓					
37						✓		
38	✓							
39							✓	
40	✓							
41	✓							
42						✓		
43		✓						
44		✓						
45			✓					
46	✓							
47						✓		
48						✓		
49						✓		
50	✓							

© 1993 Thinking Publications *Duplication permitted for educational use only.*

Name of Child __Bridget__

Utterance Number	One-Term	Two-Term	Three-Term	Four-Term Plus	Complex	Conversational Device	Communication Routine	Other
51						✓		
52					✓			
53							✓	
54							✓	
55						✓		
56			✓					
57						✓		
58	✓							
59						✓		
60			✓					
61			✓					
62		✓						
63						✓		
64						✓		
65			✓					
66		✓						
67	✓							
68						✓		
69	✓							
70						✓		
71		✓						
72		✓						
73						✓		
74		✓						
75		✓						

Utterance Number	One-Term	Two-Term	Three-Term	Four-Term Plus	Complex	Conversational Device	Communication Routine	Other
76						✓		
77						✓		
78		✓						
79	✓					✓		
80						✓		
81			✓					
82						✓		
83		✓						
84	✓							
85						✓		
86		✓						
87		✓						
88		✓						
89	✓							
90	✓							
91						✓		
92						✓		
93	✓							
94	✓							
95						✓		
96	✓							
97	✓							
98							✓	
99		✓						
100		✓						
Total	27	21	15	2	1	29	5	0

© 1993 Thinking Publications *Duplication permitted for educational use only.*

Summary   Name of Child *Bridget*

Total Number of Semantically Coded Utterances __65__ = __65.0__ % of Total Utterances

Percentage of Total Semantic Roles Accounted for by each Semantic Role:

ACTION	=	__19.0__ %
ENTITY (one-term)	=	__8.7__ %
ENTITY (multi-term)	=	__7.9__ %
LOCATIVE	=	__8.7__ %
NEGATION	=	__4.8__ %
AGENT	=	__6.3__ %
OBJECT	=	__7.1__ %
DEMONSTRATIVE	=	__7.1__ %
RECURRENCE	=	__5.6__ %
ATTRIBUTE	=	__0.8__ %
POSSESSOR	=	__3.2__ %
ADVERBIAL	=	__4.8__ %
QUANTIFIER	=	__0.8__ %
STATE	=	__10.3__ %
EXPERIENCER	=	__4.8__ %
RECIPIENT	=	__—__ %
BENEFICIARY	=	__—__ %
CREATED OBJECT	=	__—__ %
COMITATIVE	=	__—__ %
INSTRUMENT	=	__—__ %
OTHER	=	__—__ %

Total Number of Utterances Coded Conversational Device	__29__ =	__29.0__ %	of Total Utterances
Total Number of Utterances Coded Communication Routine	__5__ =	__5.0__ %	of Total Utterances
Total Number of Utterances Coded Complex	__1__ =	__1.0__ %	of Total Utterances

    © **1993 Thinking Publications** *Duplication permitted for educational use only.*

Relations are listed on the Brown's Prevalent Semantic Relations analysis sheet on page 74. The role that is underlined in five of the eight relations is the role that the child is most likely to expand. Across the top right are the three types of expansion most likely to occur in children's productions during Stages I–III. These include DEMONSTRATIVE, which Brown called *nomination*; ATTRIBUTIVE, which Brown considered also to include our RECURRENCE; and POSSESSIVE. The boxes which are crossed out represent impossible expansions. For example, under the two-term relations, move down to DEMONSTRATIVE-ENTITY. In this relation the ENTITY is underlined, indicating that ENTITY is the role likely to be expanded. But moving across the row, the DEMONSTRATIVE box is crossed out. This is because DEMONSTRATIVE-DEMONSTRATIVE-ENTITY (e.g., "that this ball") is not a likely combination. In addition to the eight prevalent semantic relations and expansions of prevalent semantic relations, Brown suggested that some three-term semantic relations did not represent expansions of two-term relations. These three-term relations are listed at the bottom of the analysis sheet.

To complete Brown's Prevalent Semantic Relations analysis form, the coding sheet used in the previous analysis will be used again. Progress through the coding sheet, identifying coded utterances which coincide with Brown's Two-Term Prevalent Semantic Relations, expansions of Two-Term Semantic Relations, and Three-Term Semantic Relations. Record the utterance number in the appropriate box for each type of semantic relation. Carefully consider each coded utterance because variations in word order are possible, although unlikely.

Progressing through the coding sheet, note that the first utterance coinciding with one of Brown's Multi-Term Combinations is utterance #7. This is an example of ATTRIBUTE-ENTITY even though it is listed as ENTITY-RECURRENCE. Recall that Brown's ATTRIBUTE category included the RECURRENCE category used here. In addition, keep in mind that word order is disregarded when identifying semantic relations. So, put a 7 in the "Utterance Number" column next to ATTRIBUTE-ENTITY. Moving on through

the coding sheet, note that the next utterance that coincides with one of Brown's combinations is utterance #15. This is an example of AGENT-ACTION, so put a 15 in the "Utterance Number" column next to AGENT-ACTION. Continue through the coding sheet, looking for examples of Brown's Prevalent Semantic Relations, expansions of Prevalent Semantic Relations, and Three-Term Prevalent Semantic Relations. Once all utterances have been examined and identified as either being or not being examples of Brown's Multi-Term Combinations, check results with the sample provided on page 74.

Summary and Interpretation of Brown's Analysis

Following identification of each example of Brown's Multi-Term Combinations, a summary of the frequency of occurrence of each type is completed. Count the number of instances of each type of two-term relation, two-term expansion, and three-term relation, and put these totals in the appropriate blanks on the Summary section of the analysis sheet. Add all instances of each type of two-term relation and put that total in the blank provided. In the sample transcript, there were 14 instances of Brown's Two-Term Prevalent Semantic Relations. Next, add the totals for two-term, three-term, and four-term-plus utterances from the Meaning Relationships grid to get the total number of multi-term utterances. In the sample transcript, there were 38 multi-term utterances. Divide the total number of instances of Brown's Prevalent Semantic Relations by the total number of multi-term utterances to get the percentage of multi-term utterances accounted for by Brown's Prevalent Semantic Relations. In the sample transcript, 14 instances of Brown's Prevalent Semantic Relations divided by 38 multi-term utterances yielded 36.8 (after multiplying by 100), indicating that 36.8 percent of this child's multi-term utterances were examples of Brown's Prevalent Semantic Relations. Next, divide 14 by 65 total semantically coded utterances to get the percentage of total semantically coded utterances accounted for by Brown's Prevalent Semantic Relations. In this transcript, 21.5 percent of the child's semantically coded utterances were examples of Brown's Prevalent Semantic Relations.

Semantic Analysis
Brown's Prevalent Semantic Relations

Name of Child _Bridget_

TWO-TERM	UTTERANCE NUMBER	DEMONSTRATIVE	ATTRIBUTIVE	POSSESSIVE
Agent-Action	15, 44, 100			
Action-Object	22, 72, 73, 87, 88			
Agent-Object		✕	✕	✕
Demonstrative-Entity			✕	✕
Entity-Locative	99			
Action-Locative	17	✕	✕	✕
Possessor-Possession		✕	✕	✕
Attribute-Entity	7, 16, 19, 66	✕	✕	✕
THREE-TERM				
Agent-Action-Object	36, 45, 56, 81			
Agent-Action-Locative				
Action-Object-Locative				

© 1993 **Thinking Publications** *Duplication permitted for educational use only.*

Name of Child *Bridget*

Summary

TWO-TERM PREVALENT SEMANTIC RELATIONS

3	Agent-Action	0 Dem	0 Att	0 Poss	=	Total of 0	Expansions
5	Action-Object	0 Dem	0 Att	0 Poss	=	Total of 0	Expansions
0	Agent-Object						
0	Demonstrative-Entity	0 Dem	0 Att	0 Poss	=	Total of 0	Expansions
1	Entity-Locative	0 Dem	0 Att	0 Poss	=	Total of 0	Expansions
1	Action-Locative						
0	Possessor-Possession	0 Dem	0 Att		=	Total of 0	Expansions
4	Attribute-Entity						
14	TOTAL Two-Term Prevalent Semantic Relations					TOTAL of 0	Expansions

= 36.8 % of Total Multi-Term Utterances

= 21.5 % of Total Semantically Coded Utterances

THREE-TERM PREVALENT SEMANTIC RELATIONS

4	Agent-Action-Object
0	Agent-Action-Locative
0	Action-Object-Locative
4	TOTAL Classic Three-Term Semantic Relations

= 10.5 % of Total Multi-Term Utterances

= 6.2 % of Total Semantically Coded Utterances

Percent of Total Semantically Coded Utterances = ___ %

© 1993 **Thinking Publications** *Duplication permitted for educational use only.*

The next step is to add all instances of each type of expansion of Brown's Prevalent Semantic Relations and put this number in the blank provided. In the sample transcript there were no instances of expansions of Brown's Prevalent Semantic Relations. If there had been, this total would be divided by 38 multi-term utterances to get the percentage of multi-term utterances accounted for by expansions of Brown's Prevalent Semantic Relations, and then divided by 65 semantically coded utterances to get the percentage of total semantically coded utterances accounted for by expansions of Brown's Prevalent Semantic Relations.

The last step is to add all instances of each type of three-term semantic relation and put this total in the blank provided. In the sample transcript there were four examples of Brown's Three-Term Prevalent Semantic Relations. Dividing this by 38 total multi-term utterances reveals that 10.5 percent of this child's multi-term utterances were examples of

Brown's Three-Term Semantic Relations. Now divide 4 by 65 total semantically coded utterances to get the percentage of total semantically coded utterances accounted for by Brown's Three-Term Prevalent Semantic Relations. The result indicates that 6.2 percent of this child's total semantically coded utterances were examples of three-term relations.

The first comparison in the interpretation of the summarized data is to Brown's reported frequency of occurrence of prevalent semantic relations for 12 children ranging in production abilities from Stage I to II. Table 2.6 displays the mean frequency of occurrence for each of the prevalent semantic relations and each three-term combination for three children at Stage I, eight children at Early Stage II, and one child at Stage II. Data represent a reorganization of individual child data presented by Brown (1973). Frequencies are reported as percentages of total multi-term utterances.

TABLE 2.6

MEAN FREQUENCY OF OCCURRENCE OF BROWN'S PREVALENT SEMANTIC RELATIONS IN STAGES I, EARLY II, AND II AS PERCENTAGE OF TOTAL MULTI-TERM UTTERANCES

(Computed from Brown, 1973)

	Stage I* (N = 3)	Early II* (N = 8)	Stage II* (N = 1)
AGENT-ACTION	24.0	9.4	7.0
ACTION-OBJECT	7.0	9.2	16.0
AGENT-OBJECT	3.7	1.5	0.0
DEMONSTRATIVE-ENTITY	1.3	7.9	1.0
ENTITY-LOCATIVE	12.7	3.9	2.0
ACTION-LOCATIVE	2.3	3.6	5.0
POSSESSOR-POSSESSION	9.7	7.1	11.0
ATTRIBUTE-ENTITY	7.0	5.4	5.0
TOTAL	67.7	48.0	47.0
AGENT-ACTION-OBJECT	3.7	2.9	6.0
AGENT-ACTION-LOCATIVE	1.0	2.1	3.0
ACTION-OBJECT-LOCATIVE	0.3	1.0	0.0
TOTAL	5.0	6.0	9.0

* Based on MLUs reported by Brown, children were grouped according to stages redefined by Miller and Chapman (1981).

Examination of Table 2.6 reveals increases across the three stages in ACTION-OBJECT and ACTION-LOCATIVE constructions. Decreases in AGENT-OBJECT, ACTION-OBJECT, ENTITY-LOCATIVE, and ATTRIBUTE-ENTITY constructions and the total use of Brown's combinations are present. In addition, increases in the total number of three-term constructions can be seen. Comparison of results obtained from analysis of the sample transcript and Brown's data suggest that the child in the sample transcript is using constructions with frequencies most similar to Stage II. However, it cannot be determined if this child's use of Brown's Prevalent Semantic Relations is at a level higher than Stage II. The most significant similarity is in the frequency of occurrence of the ACTION-OBJECT semantic relation. Once again, the data cannot be overinterpreted. Variations in situations are likely to elicit differences in the frequency of occurrence of specific combinations. The conservative interpretation is that this child is capable of producing Brown's Prevalent Semantic Relations with frequencies similar to children at least in Stage II. Whether this child's productions truly are more typical of children in Stage III or higher cannot be determined.

Examination of the distribution of multi-term utterances into Brown's combinations of semantic roles versus additional combinations may shed new light. Table 2.7 displays this distribution for Stages I–II for data reported by Brown (1973). Again, data represent a reorganization of individual child data presented by Brown.

To compare data obtained from the sample transcript to data presented in Table 2.7, one more computation is necessary. From the Meaning Relationships grid, it has been shown that 38 of this child's 100 utterances were multi-term combinations of semantic roles. In addition, from Brown's Prevalent Semantic Relations Summary sheet, it is clear that a total of 18 utterances were Brown's Prevalent Semantic Relations or Brown's Three-Term Prevalent Semantic Relations (14 + 4 = 18). That means that 47 percent (18 divided by 38) of this child's utterances were examples of Brown's combinations and 53 percent were examples of additional combinations. This child had no examples of "uninterpretable" utterances. Now, comparing these percentages to those reported by Brown, no apparent match can be seen. This may have been predicted on the basis of an extended set of coding categories. That is, when a set of coding categories containing 21 semantic roles and residual grammatical categories (Retherford, Schwartz, and Chapman, 1981) is used to code utterances, and results are compared to those obtained using a coding scheme containing far fewer categories, discrepancies are to be expected.

Let's compare this child's distribution of multi-term combinations to data reported by Retherford, Schwartz, and Chapman (1977).

TABLE 2.7

MEAN PERCENT OF TOTAL MULTI-TERM UTTERANCES ACCOUNTED FOR BY BROWN'S PREVALENT SEMANTIC RELATIONS AND ADDITIONAL COMBINATIONS OF SEMANTIC ROLES

(Computed from Brown, 1973)

	Brown's Semantic Relations*	Additional Combinations*
Stage I* (N=3)	73.3	9.3
Early II* (N=8)	59.8	30.6
Stage II* (N=1)	64.0	30.0

* Based on MLUs reported by Brown, children were grouped according to stages redefined by Miller and Chapman (1981); numbers do not total to 100 percent because Brown had a third category called "Uninterpretable" that is not reflected on this table.

TABLE 2.8
**MEAN PERCENT OF TOTAL SEMANTICALLY CODED UTTERANCES ACCOUNTED FOR
BY BROWN'S PREVALENT SEMANTIC RELATIONS AND ADDITIONAL COMBINATIONS**
(Computed from Retherford, Schwartz, and Chapman, 1977)

	Brown's Semantic Relations*	Additional Combinations*
Stage I (*N*=6)	55.4	21.9
Early II (*N*=3)	50.9	20.9
Stage II (*N*=2)	38.2	31.8
Stage III (*N*=1)	64.0	22.4

*Numbers do not total to 100 percent because Retherford et al. (1977) had a third category called "Multi-term OTHER" that is not reflected on this table.

The Retherford et al. data are summarized by percent of total semantically coded utterances rather than by percentage of total multi-term utterances. Table 2.8 displays the distribution of total semantically coded utterances into Brown's multi-term combinations versus additional combinations for children in Brown's Stages I–III. Keep in mind that the utterances in the sample transcript and the Retherford, Schwartz, and Chapman (1977) data were coded using the 21 semantic roles and residual grammatical categories previously described, and only those coinciding with Brown's categories in combination have been selected for comparison.

Comparison of results from the sample transcript to data reported by Retherford et al. (1977) again reveals inconsistencies. The child in the sample transcript used equal percentages of additional combinations and Brown's combinations (i.e., 27.7 percent for Brown's combinations [18 ÷ 65 total semantically coded utterances]). This is unlike the distribution in any of the stages in Table 2.8. It might be interpreted as an indication that this child is using combinations characteristic of a more advanced stage of linguistic production. This would assume that Brown's Prevalent Semantic Relations are more basic than combinations of additional categories. Brown's own data in Table 2.7 reveal a decrease in percentage of multi-term combinations accounted for by the eight prevalent semantic relations over the first three stages of linguistic production. In addition,

an increase in the use of less frequently occurring roles in combination suggests a greater attention on the part of the child to syntactic aspects of multi-term combinations. Again, overinterpretation of results is cautioned because of the small sample size. Taken together, these results suggest that this child's semantic production abilities are at or beyond Stage II. This finding indicates that analysis of syntactic aspects of the child's productions is warranted.

ANALYZING VOCABULARY DIVERSITY

The last procedure that will be used to analyze semantic aspects of this child's production abilities is one which analyzes the diversity of vocabulary used in language transcripts. Miller (1981) contends that this is a general analysis procedure in that the results obtained are not very specific. In addition, this procedure examines referential, rather than relational, aspects of production in that it analyzes vocabulary only with no attention to the use of words in combination.

The procedure that will be used to analyze the diversity of the vocabulary in the 100-utterance language transcript is the Type-Token Ratio described by Templin (1957). This procedure allows examination of the relationship between the total number of different words used and the total number of words used. For the 480 children that Templin studied, ratios of approximately 1:2 were obtained consistently for all age groups, gender groups, and socioeconomic groups, although the numbers comprising these ratios vary at each level. Because of this consistency, this procedure is particularly useful in analyzing the diversity of a child's vocabulary. However, Templin's data are applicable only with children between the ages of 3 and 8 years.

In obtaining her language samples, Templin used an adult-child interaction format, with picture books and toys as stimulus materials. On-line recording of spontaneous productions of the children yielded transcripts sufficiently long to permit analysis of the middle 50 utterances. It is possible to use transcripts longer than 50 utterances; however, only 50 consecutive utterances should be used to compute the Type-Token Ratio. Since the sample transcript is 100 utterances in length, the middle 50 utterances of the transcript—utterances #26–75—will be used.

To compute the Type-Token Ratio, each word used by the child (except repetitions) in the sample transcript will be counted. In some cases, two or three words are used together as a familiar expression, and these are counted as one word (e.g., *a lot, uh oh*). Keep in mind also that interjections like *um* and *oh* are counted. The word *well* is counted, when it is an interjec-

tion (e.g., "Well, let's go") and when it is an adverb (e.g., "He doesn't feel well"). Recall that in the semantic role analysis, interjections were not counted unless they were part of an expression that carried meaning (e.g., *uh oh, uh huh*). Table 2.9 delineates the rules used by Templin in counting words.

To aid in keeping track of each word used by the child, record each word on the Type-Token Ratio analysis sheet. This sheet is organized by parts of speech. Although the organizational scheme used for recording each word has no bearing on the final computation, a parts-of-speech organizational scheme has been used on this analysis sheet. Individual words could be organized alphabetically or on the basis of order of occurrence. A parts-of-speech organization was selected only for efficiency. To use this organizational format, progress through the transcript, recording each word according to part of speech. For example, *ball* is a noun; *throw* is a verb; *big* is an adjective; *slow* is an adverb; *to* is a preposition; *he* is a pronoun; *and* is a conjunction; *yeah* is a negative/ affirmative word; *the* is an article; *how* is a wh-word. If it is difficult to determine what part of speech a particular word represents, record it anywhere. Final computations are not based on correct differentiation of parts of speech. Accurate tallying of each individual word is crucial for final

---

TABLE 2.9
RULES FOR COUNTING NUMBER OF WORDS

1. Contractions of subject and predicate, like *it's* and *we're,* are counted as two words.

2. Contractions of the verb and the negative, such as *can't,* are counted as one word.

3. Each part of the verbal combination is counted as a separate word. Thus, *have been playing* is counted as three words.

4. Hyphenated words and compound nouns are one word.

5. Expressions that function as a unit in the child's understanding are counted as one word. Thus, *oh boy, all right,* etc., are counted as one word, while *Christmas tree* is counted as two words.

6. Articles (*the, a, an*) count as one word.

7. Bound morphemes and noun and verb inflections are not counted as separate words.

From "Certain Language Skills in Children: Their Development and Interrelationships," 1957, by Mildred C. Templin, *Institute of Child Welfare Monograph Series, 26.* © 1957 by the University of Minnesota Press, Minneapolis. © renewed 1985 by Mildred C. Templin. Reprinted by permission.

Semantic Analysis
Type-Token Ratio

Name of Child *Bridget*

Utterances *26–75*

Nouns		Verbs		Adjectives		Adverbs		Prepositions	
legs		stand /		another		up //		to	
elephant		do		pretty		upside			
owie /		is ᵗᵗᵗ		boom		down /			
stroller		kick /				heavy			
cow		gimme				ick			
ball /		fall /				better			
Bill //		go				here			
		sleep				else /			
		wake				more			
		take /				good			
		taste							
								welcome	
								goodnight	
								shh	
7	11	11	20	3	3	10	14	4	4

© **1993 Thinking Publications** *Duplication permitted for educational use only.*

Pronouns	Conjunctions	Negative/Affirmative	Articles	Wh-Words
you		yeah ~~HHT~~ ////	a //	huh ///
it /		no		where
there //		allright		what
one		okay		
I //				
him //				
he				
this				
yours /				
'em (them) /				
10 19		4 13	1 3	3 6

Total Number of Different:

Nouns	7
Verbs	11
Adjectives	3
Adverbs	10
Prepositions	4
Pronouns	10
Conjunctions	—
Negative/Affirmative	4
Articles	1
Wh-Words	3
TOTAL NUMBER OF DIFFERENT WORDS	53

Total Number of:

Nouns	11
Verbs	20
Adjectives	3
Adverbs	14
Prepositions	4
Pronouns	19
Conjunctions	—
Negative/Affirmative	13
Articles	3
Wh-Words	6
TOTAL NUMBER OF WORDS	93

$$\frac{\text{Total Number of Different Words}}{\text{Total Number of Words}} = \underline{.5698 = .57} = \text{Type-Token Ratio (TTR)}$$

TABLE 2.10
CALCULATING VOCABULARY DIVERSITY USING TYPE-TOKEN RATIO (*N* = 480)

Age	Different words		Total words		Type-Token Ratio Different words ÷ total words
	Mean	**SD**	**Mean**	**SD**	
3.0	92.5	26.1	204.9	61.3	0.45
3.5	104.8	20.4	232.9	50.8	0.45
4.0	120.4	27.6	268.8	72.6	0.45
4.5	127.0	23.9	270.7	65.3	0.47
5.0	132.4	27.2	286.2	75.5	0.46
6.0	147.0	27.6	328.0	65.9	0.45
7.0	157.7	27.2	363.1	51.3	0.43
8.0	166.5	29.5	378.8	80.9	0.44

From "Certain Language Skills in Children: Their Development and Interrelationships," by Mildred C. Templin, 1957, *Institute of Child Welfare Monograph Series, 26.* © 1957 by the University of Minnesota Press, Minneapolis. © renewed 1985 by Mildred C. Templin. Reprinted by permission.

computation. If a particular word occurs more than once, tally additional instances of the word next to the original recording of the word (e.g., "ball ///// /" means the word *ball* occurred seven times in the transcript). A completed tally of words occurring in the sample transcript is provided on pages 80–81.

To obtain the numbers needed for the final computation, count the number of different words in each column and put these totals in the spaces provided. In the sample transcript, there were 7 different nouns, 11 verbs, 3 adjectives, 10 adverbs, 4 prepositions, 10 pronouns, 0 conjunctions, 4 negative/affirmatives, 1 article, and 3 wh-words. Now add these totals to obtain the total number of different words used by this child. In the sample transcript, a total of 53 different words were used.

Now count each instance of each word in each column and put the total in the spaces provided. In this sample, there were 11 total instances of nouns used, 20 verbs, 3 adjectives, 14 adverbs, 4 prepositions, 19 pronouns, 0 conjunctions, 13 negative/affirmatives, 3 articles, and 6 wh-words. Add these totals to obtain the total number of words used. A total of 93 words was obtained.

To complete the final computation and obtain the Type-Token Ratio, divide the total number of different words (53) by the total number of words (93). This results in a Type-Token Ratio of .5698, which rounds off to .57.

SUMMARY AND INTERPRETATION OF TYPE-TOKEN RATIO

The interpretation of the obtained Type-Token Ratio is accomplished by comparing it to the normative data from Templin's analysis. Table 2.10 displays the mean and standard deviation of different words used, the mean and standard deviation of total words used, and the resulting Type-Token Ratio for each age group between 3 and 8 years.

Comparison of the Type-Token Ratio of .57 to the 3-year-old Type-Token Ratios obtained by Templin reveals that the Type-Token Ratio from the sample transcript is higher. This suggests that the child's vocabulary in the sample transcript is more diverse than would be expected for the total number of words used. Type-Token Ratios greater than .50 indicate more different words than typical for the total number of words. Is this an asset or a deficit? That is difficult to say. Type-Token Ratios significantly below .50 reflect a lack of diversity and may indicate language-specific deficiency (Miller, 1981). But greater diversity has not been implicated as a diagnostic indicator. In any event, results must be considered in greater detail before drawing a conclusion.

Although Type-Token Ratios were intended to be used only as normative data, valuable information can be gained by comparing total number of different words and total number of words to the means obtained by Templin. Reductions in the total number of different words and the total number of words have been implicated as potential indicators of developmental language delays or disorders (Miller, 1991). The sample transcript contained 53 different words. Compared to the mean obtained by Templin, this total is more than one standard deviation below the mean for 3-year-olds. In addition, the total of 93 words is also more than one standard deviation below the mean. In this case, the best interpretation is that the child in the sample transcript is younger than 3 years of age and that her vocabulary in this transcript was reasonably diverse. Some data is available for children younger than 3 years of age. Phillips (1973) reports that the mean Type-Token Ratio for 10 children, 8 months of age, was .31. For 10 children 18 months of age, a mean Type-Token Ratio of .34 was obtained, and for ten children, 28 months of age, a mean Type-Token Ratio of .41 was obtained. However, Phillips does not report the number of different words and total number of words used to compute Type-Token Ratios. Until sufficient data are obtained on the diversity of a child's vocabulary before 3 years, direct application of Type-Token Ratio norms is not appropriate.

IMPLICATIONS FOR REMEDIATION

After the selected semantic analysis procedures have been completed, examination of the results of each analysis is necessary to develop remediation goals. Data obtained from each of the analyses can lead to development of appropriate remediation goals if the results are considered in light of what is known about normal language acquisition. Based on the sequence of accomplishments in normal language acquisition, opportunities for the child to use new vocabulary, semantic roles, and/or roles in semantic relationships can be provided. Clinical experience has shown that the forms

likely to emerge next in the acquisition sequence are quite predictable; consequently, opportunities for emergence can be provided. The suggestions delineated here are general considerations for remediation, not hard and fast rules.

When children at the one-word utterance stage are identified by percentages of one-word utterances exceeding 50 percent of total utterances, and the use of categories within Bloom's or Nelson's One-Word Utterance Types are documented, opportunities for the development of additional vocabulary within Bloom's or Nelson's utterance types can be provided. That does not mean that a specific set of vocabulary words is taught. It does mean that the child can be provided with repeated exposure to vocabulary that falls within Bloom's or Nelson's categories. Early in the one-word period, the categories that the child is most likely to be producing include SUBSTANTIVE and NAMING words for Bloom's categories, and NOMINALS, MODIFIERS, and/or PERSONAL-SOCIAL words for Nelson's categories. Later, children add FUNCTION words for Bloom's categories and ACTION WORDS for Nelson's categories. Sufficient opportunities for children to acquire the new vocabulary types must be provided during therapy activities. The specific vocabulary representing these one-word utterance types should be determined by the interests of the child and the regularly reoccurring activities of the child.

When limited use of semantic roles has been identified for a particular child using Retherford, Schwartz, and Chapman's (1981) coding scheme, opportunities for encoding more diverse roles must be provided. Typically, goals and objectives related to semantic role use are combined with goals and objectives developed as a result of Brown's Prevalent Semantic Relations analysis. Clinical experience has shown that semantic roles encoding familiar objects and persons precede the production of verb relations such as AGENT-ACTION and ACTION-OBJECT. Appropriate objectives would include targeting object and person relations (DEMONSTRATIVE-ENTITY, ATTRIBUTE-ENTITY, ENTITY-LOCATIVE, POSSESSOR-POSSESSION) for the child early in the two-word period, and verb relations

(AGENT-ACTION, ACTION-OBJECT, ACTION-LOCATIVE) for the child late in the two-word period. Three-term relations can be targeted next, as can the semantic roles identified by Retherford et al. (1981) as infrequently occurring, since they are likely to occur in three-term and expanded forms. Again, specific vocabulary is not taught; opportunities for using targeted semantic relations within structured activities are provided.

Results obtained from analysis of vocabulary diversity can be used to develop goals and objectives for increasing vocabulary. Type-Token Ratios one standard deviation below the norms provided suggest a lack of vocabulary diversity. Remediation should focus on increasing vocabulary typically within developmentally appropriate semantic fields (e.g., noun categories such as vehicles, plants, animals; verb categories such as cooking, play, school; temporal terms; and polar adjectives). In this area, specific vocabulary can be taught, but the focus should be on developmentally appropriate semantic fields.

Overall, analysis of both referential aspects of semantic production and relational aspects of semantic production provides results that can be used to develop remediation goals and objectives. As the discussions in the following chapter will demonstrate, results obtained from semantic analyses can be combined with results obtained from syntactic and pragmatic analyses to develop comprehensive goals and objectives for remediation.

CHAPTER 3
Syntactic Analysis

Analysis of syntactic aspects of language transcripts provides information germane to the identification of children beyond the one-word period who have delays in language production. In addition, careful examination of the developmental level of a variety of syntactic structures is essential to the appropriate determination of remediation goals and objectives. The analysis procedures described here are compatible with the semantic analysis procedures described in the previous chapter, but are more appropriate for children whose language abilities have advanced beyond the one-word stage. It would be appropriate to analyze the semantic aspects of a child's language production using the multi-term procedures described in the previous chapter, and then to analyze the syntactic aspects using the procedures described here. Information obtained from each analysis procedure would be combined to diagnose language production delays and to develop remediation goals and objectives.

There are procedures other than the ones described here which are available to analyze syntactic aspects of language production. These include Lee's (1966, 1974) *Developmental Sentence Score (DSS)* and Lee's (1966) *Developmental Sentence Types (DST)*; Tyack and Gottsleben's (1974) *Language Sampling, Analysis, and Training (LSAT)*; Crystal, Fletcher, and Garman's (1976, 1991) *Language Assessment, Remediation and Screening Procedure (LARSP)*; and Miller's (1981) *Assigning Structural Stage (ASS)*, among others. Although the procedures described here do not differ demonstrably from those procedures developed by Miller (1981), the directions and interpretations are more explicit, and forms for

analysis are provided. The intent is not to duplicate procedures or to offer alternative procedures, but to provide experience in determining the syntactic level of language production and in interpreting results obtained from such analysis. The experience gained here will be beneficial in using any of the aforementioned procedures, as all procedures are based on the analysis of documented aspects of syntactic production.

The procedures described here permit identification of a variety of syntactic structures and documentation of the developmental level of each structure. Assignment of the Most Typical Stage and the Most Advanced Stage for each structure permits comparison to normative data for determination of the presence or absence of syntactic delays. In addition, once a delay has been documented, the stage assignments form the basis of decision rules for determining content of remediation goals and objectives.

ANALYZING MEAN LENGTH OF UTTERANCE IN MORPHEMES

The procedure that will be used to analyze utterance length is based on procedures described by Brown (1973) to examine the structural changes in children's productions on the basis of increases in utterance length. Brown documented changes in structural complexity concomitant to increases in utterance length as determined by meaning units or morphemes. The rules for assigning morphemes to utterances have been presented in the literature (Brown, 1973; Bloom and Lahey,

1978; Miller, 1981; Owens, 1992) and appear fairly straightforward. Some inconsistencies in assigning morphemes exist. In addition, problems periodically arise from analysis of utterances produced by children with language delays or language disorders because their utterances may not follow a normal developmental sequence. A modification of Brown's original decision rules will be used for assigning morphemes, and examples of utterances produced by children with language delays and language disorders will be provided. Table 3.1 summarizes the decision rules for assigning morphemes to utterances that have been used with the sample transcript.

TABLE 3.1
RULES FOR ASSIGNING MORPHEMES TO UTTERANCES

1. Morphemes are assigned only to utterances that are completely intelligible. Following the rules for numbering utterances in a transcript (see Chapter 1), only assign morphemes to utterances that are numbered. No partially intelligible or unintelligible utterances should be numbered or assigned morphemes.

2. Assign morphemes to 100 consecutive utterances. Selecting utterances for assigning morphemes can inflate the resulting MLU. Transcripts with a high number of responses to yes/no questions can deflate the resulting MLU. Select a portion of the transcript that appears to be representative of the range of the child's abilities.

3. Repetitions within an utterance as a result of stuttering or false starts are assigned morphemes only in the most complete form (e.g., given the utterance, "my dad dad is big," count only "my dad is big"). Occasionally, a child repeats a word for emphasis or part of a phrase for clarification. In these cases, each word is counted (e.g., given the utterance, "my dad is big big," count all words if the second *big* has more emphasis that the first).

4. Fillers such as *um, well,* or *oh* are not assigned morphemes. Words like *hi, yeah,* and *no* are assigned morphemes.

5. Compound words are treated as single words, even though they consist of two or more free morphemes. The reason for this is that children appear not to have use of each constituent morpheme within the compound word. Proper names and ritualized reduplications (e.g., *choo-choo, night-night, quack-quack*) are treated in the same fashion.

6. Diminutive forms of words (e.g., *doggie, mommy*) are assigned only one morpheme. The reason for this is that children do not appear to have productive control over the suffix and use many diminutive forms as the only form of the word produced.

7. Auxiliary verbs are assigned one morpheme. Catenative forms also are assigned one morpheme, even though they represent two to three morphemes in the expanded form (e.g., *gonna = going to*; *wanna = want to*; *hafta = have to*).

8. All inflections, including possessive *-s*, plural *-s*, third person singular *-s*, regular past *-ed*, and present progressive *-ing*, are assigned one morpheme. This is in addition to the morpheme assigned to the word onto which the form is inflected. Irregular past tense forms are assigned only one morpheme. The reason for this is that children do not appear to have derived these from the present tense form.

9. Negative contractions (e.g., *can't, don't, won't*) are assigned two morphemes only if there is evidence within the transcript that the child uses each part of the contraction separately. If the child does not use each part of the contraction separately, the negative contraction receives one morpheme. Again, the reason for this is that until the child uses each part separately, the child does not have productive control over the contraction.

10. Indefinite pronouns (i.e., *anybody, anyone, somebody, someone, everybody, everyone*) are assigned one morpheme. The reason for this is that the child appears to use these pronouns as single words not analyzable into two morphemes.

From *A First Language: The Early Stages* by Roger Brown, 1973, Cambridge, MA: Harvard University Press. © 1973 by the President and Fellows of Harvard College. Reprinted by permission of the publishers.

Try determining the number of morphemes in a few utterances for practice before turning to the sample transcript. As was done in the previous chapter, cover the right side of the page, determine the number of morphemes in the utterance, and then check values with those provided. Explanations should clear up any questions.

(C points to picture in
photo album)
there Daddy/

    morphemes = 2

    In this utterance, each word is equal to one morpheme.

(C puts baby doll in crib
and covers her)
go night-night/

    morphemes = 2

    In this utterance, the word *night-night* is assigned only one morpheme. This is because it is assumed that the utterance functions as a single concept for the child.

(C places empty juice cup
on table)
allgone juice/

    morphemes = 2

    Again, a word like *allgone* functions as a single word for most children and in most cases is written as one word.

(C points to picture
in picture book)
two doggies/

    morphemes = 3

    In this utterance, the use of the plural inflection accounts for the addition of one morpheme. Remember, the diminutive form does not receive a morpheme.

(C pulls circus
train out of box)
big choo-choo train/

    morphemes = 2

    Without any additional utterances, only two morphemes can be assigned to this utterance. If there is evidence that the child uses the word *train* separate from *choo-choo*, three morphemes could be assigned to this utterance. Two morphemes are never assigned to *choo-choo*.

(C picks up monkey
that fell off bar)
he fell down/

    morphemes = 3

    With just this utterance, the child is given credit for only three morphemes. No credit is given for past tense of irregular verbs, since children appear not to have derived these from the present tense form.

(C watches baby brother
eating raisins)
he likes raisins/

morphemes = 5

In this utterance, the use of the third person singular present tense receives a morpheme, as does the plural -s.

(C shakes his head and says)
I don't like raisins/

morphemes = 5/6

In this utterance, the negative contraction is assigned two morphemes only if there is evidence that each piece of the uncontracted form (*do*, *not*) is used separately or together elsewhere in the transcript.

(C kicks ball, then
turns to M)
I kicked the ball/

morphemes = 5

The regular past tense -*ed* receives a morpheme. Evidence of use in the uninflected form is not needed.

(M and C are racing cars
around track)
he's gonna catch me/

morphemes = 5

The catenative form of *going to* receives only one morpheme. Brown indicated that catenatives were assigned two morphemes in older children, but for consistency in these analyses, one morpheme will always be assigned to catenatives.

(M says to crying C,
"Did she hurt you?")
yeah she hit me/

morphemes = 4

With no boundary marker indicating a pause between *yeah* and the rest of this utterance, one morpheme is assigned to each word in this utterance.

(C pulls large stuffed dog
from surprise box)
oh that's a big doggie/

morphemes = 5

The filler *oh* does not receive a morpheme in the count, nor does the diminutive form of dog. The contractible copula is assigned one morpheme.

(C sets dog next to
middle-sized dog)
that is a big doggie/

morphemes = 5

In this utterance, the uncontracted form of the copula is used. This does not change the morpheme count, but the example is provided to demonstrate a pragmatic convention of uncontracting the copulas used for emphasis.

(C puts handful of popcorn in mouth)	
I am eating popcorn/	morphemes = 5
	In this utterance, the present progressive form of *eat* receives a morpheme, so that *eating* receives a total of two morphemes. The compound word *popcorn* receives only one morpheme.
(C is explaining why he was late)	
she couldn't find her pocketbook/	morphemes = 5/6
	In this utterance, *couldn't* receives two morphemes only if there is evidence of use of the uncontracted form elsewhere in the transcript. The word *pocketbook* receives only one morpheme.
(C is relating story to M)	
she didn't say hi/	morphemes = 4/5
	The negative contraction receives two morphemes only if there is evidence of use of the uncontracted form. Greeting terms, either within or preceding an utterance, are assigned a morpheme.
(C points to arm)	
he hitted me/	morphemes = 3
	Assigning a morpheme to incorrect use of the regular past tense *-ed* inflates MLU. Thus, no morpheme is assigned. Valuable information is obtained if attempts by the child to mark past tense are noted.
(C holds up picture)	
lookit Mommy/	morphemes = 2
	In most cases, the child's use of *lookit* functions as one word. Thus, only one morpheme is assigned. The use of *Mommy* as an attention-getter does receive a morpheme.
(C hands cars to M)	
Mommy do it/	morphemes = 2/3
	The use of *do it* also typically functions as one word. In addition, the attention-getter receives one morpheme. If there is evidence that the child uses *do* and *it* independently of one another, then each is counted as a separate morpheme.

(C pours milk from pitcher)
I didn't spilled it/

morphemes = 4/5

In this utterance, the child is attempting to mark the past tense but has not realized that the rule for marking the past tense is to mark it on the auxiliary verb. Therefore, the child has marked past tense on both the main verb *spill* and the auxiliary *did*. Counting double marking of past tense in auxiliary and main verb inflates MLU, so count the past tense only once. The rule for assigning morphemes to negative contractions holds here as in previous examples, resulting in four or five total morphemes.

(M asks, "And who knocked the cart over?")
the man the man the big man/

morphemes = 3

The use of false starts in an utterance is disregarded. Count only the most complete form.

(C pulls truck away from other child)
that's my big my big truck/

morphemes = 5

Again, false starts, even if they occur within an utterance, are disregarded. Count only the most complete form.

(C continues arguing with other child)
that's my new one my new truck/

morphemes = 8

This utterance is different from the previous two in that the repetition is not considered a false start but a clarification of an unclear sentence constituent. The child apparently decided that the listener might not know what *one* referred to and therefore provided additional information. This is not considered a false start, and as a result each word in the repetition receives a morpheme.

With that practice, assigning morphemes to the utterances in the sample transcript should be easier. The transcript used for semantic analysis in the previous chapter will be used for syntactic analysis in this chapter. In addition, a transcript obtained from a conversation with an older child (Sara) is in Appendix B; its completed syntactic analysis is provided in Appendix D. The completed analysis in Appendix D will provide experience in making some of the more difficult judgments. Using the transcript from Chapter 1 (i.e., Bridget) and a blank Structural Stage Analysis Grid in Appendix D, proceed utterance by utterance and record the number of morphemes in each utterance in the "Number of Morphemes" column. When the number of morphemes in each utterance has been recorded, add the morphemes for each utterance to obtain the total number of morphemes in this 100-utterance sample. Now divide this total by 100 to obtain the MLU in morphemes for this transcript. Check the morpheme assignments, the total morpheme computation, and the resulting MLU in morphemes with the sample provided on pages 91–92.

Syntactic Analysis
Structural Stage Analysis Grid

Name of Child: *Bridget*

Utterance Number	Number of Morphemes	Negation	Yes/No Questions	Wh-Questions	Noun Phrase Elaboration	Verb Phrase Elaboration	Complex
1	1						
2	2						
3	1						
4	1						
5	4						
6	1						
7	2						
8	1						
9	1						
10	1						
11	3						
12	1						
13	1						
14	1						
15	4						
16	2						
17	4						
18	4						
19	2						
20	4						
21	4						
22	2						
23	3						
24	4						
25	2						

Utterance Number	Number of Morphemes	Negation	Yes/No Questions	Wh-Questions	Noun Phrase Elaboration	Verb Phrase Elaboration	Complex
26	2						
27	2						
28	2						
29	1						
30	1						
31	5						
32	4						
33	4						
34	1						
35	4						
36	3						
37	1						
38	1						
39	1						
40	1						
41	1						
42	1						
43	2						
44	2						
45	3						
46	3						
47	1						
48	1						
49	1						
50	1						
Total	105						

© 1993 **Thinking Publications** *Duplication permitted for educational use only.*

Syntactic Analysis
Structural Stage Analysis Grid

Name of Child **Bridget**

Utterance Number	Number of Morphemes	Negation	Yes/No Questions	Wh-Questions	Noun Phrase Elaboration	Verb Phrase Elaboration	Complex
51	1						
52	3						
53	1						
54	1						
55	1						
56	4						
57	1						
58	1						
59	1						
60	4						
61	4						
62	3						
63	1						
64	1						
65	4						
66	2						
67	1						
68	1						
69	1						
70	1						
71	1						
72	3						
73	3						
74	1						
75	2						

Utterance Number	Number of Morphemes	Negation	Yes/No Questions	Wh-Questions	Noun Phrase Elaboration	Verb Phrase Elaboration	Complex
76	1						
77	1						
78	3						
79	1						
80	1						
81	5						
82	1						
83	3						
84	1						
85	1						
86	2						
87	3						
88	3						
89	3						
90	3						
91	1						
92	1						
93	1						
94	1						
95	1						
96	3						
97	3						
98	1						
99	2						
100	2						
Total	95						

$200 \div 100 = 2.00$ MLU

© 1993 **Thinking Publications** *Duplication permitted for educational use only.*

TABLE 3.2
Predicted MLU Ranges and Linguistic Stages of Children
within One Predicted Standard Deviation of Predicted Mean

Age ± 1 mo.	Predicted MLU[a]	Predicted SD[b]	Predicted MLU ± 1 SD (Middle 68%)	Brown's stages within 1 SD of predicted MLU							
				EI	*LI*	*II*	*III*	*EIV*	*LIV/EV*	*LV*	*Post V*
18	1.31	.325	.99 - 1.64	X	X						
21	1.62	.386	1.23 - 2.01	X	X	X					
24	1.92	.448	1.47 - 2.37	X	X	X					
27	2.23	.510	1.72 - 2.74		X	X	X				
30	2.54	.571	1.97 - 3.11		X	X	X	X			
33	2.85	.633	2.22 - 3.48			X	X	X			
36	3.16	.694	2.47 - 3.85			X	X	X	X		
39	3.47	.756	2.71 - 4.23				X	X	X	X	
42	3.78	.817	2.96 - 4.60				X	X	X	X	X
45	4.09	.879	3.21 - 4.97					X	X	X	X
48	4.40	.940	3.46 - 5.34					X	X	X	X
51	4.71	1.002	3.71 - 5.71						X	X	X
54	5.02	1.064	3.96 - 6.08						X	X	X
57	5.32	1.125	4.20 - 6.45							X	X
60	5.63	1.187	4.44 - 6.82							X	X

[a]MLU is predicted from the equation MLU = -.548 + .103 (AGE).

[b]SD is predicted from the equation SD MLU = -.0446 + .0205 (AGE).

From "The relation between age and mean length of utterance in morphemes" by J. Miller and R. Chapman, 1981, *Journal of Speech and Hearing Research, 24*(2), p. 158. © 1981 by the American Speech-Language-Hearing Association, Rockville, MD. Reprinted by permission of the American Speech-Language-Hearing Association.

For this transcript, an MLU of 2.00 morphemes should have been obtained. This value provides very little information without additional analyses. One mechanism for analyzing this MLU is to compare it to data provided by Miller and Chapman (1981) on the predicted MLU ranges for 123 children. Table 3.2 summarizes the predicted MLUs, MLU ranges, and standard deviations for children in the Miller and Chapman (1981) study. The following computation permits evaluation of the MLU obtained from Bridget's transcript in Chapter 1 or for any obtained MLU:

$$\frac{\text{obtained MLU - predicted MLU}}{\text{predicted SD}} = \text{SD below the mean for CA}$$

$$\frac{2.00 - 2.23}{.510} = \text{-.45 SD below the mean for 27 months}$$

Although the child in the sample transcript is 28 months of age, the values for 27 month-olds are used. The MLU for the sample transcript fell .45 standard deviations below the mean for children 27 months of age. This MLU clearly reflects utterances that would be considered within normal limits in terms of mean length of morpheme. But this is a very cursory analysis. Therefore, the next step is to examine variations in utterance length by completing a length distribution analysis. This analysis can add to the interpretation of the obtained MLU. The Structural Stage Analysis Grid will be used later to fill in the remaining columns, following the analysis of variations in utterance length and identification of grammatical morphemes.

ANALYZING VARIATIONS IN UTTERANCE LENGTH

In this analysis procedure, the utterances in the sample transcript will be tallied by length in morphemes. This permits examination of the distribution of utterances by length across the range of utterance lengths within this transcript. Using the Structural Stage Analysis Grid and a blank Length Distribution Analysis Sheet from Appendix D, progress utterance by utterance through the Structural Stage Analysis Grid and tally each utterance in the box on the Length Distribution Analysis Sheet next to the number of morphemes which the utterance contains. For example, in the sample transcript, utterance number 1 contains one morpheme, so mark a tally next to the box indicating one morpheme length. Utterance number 2 contains two morphemes, so mark a tally next to the box indicating two morpheme lengths. Proceed through the Structural Stage Analysis Grid and tally each utterance. Now count the tallies in each row and record this number in the total box for that row. Check tallies and totals with the sample provided on page 95.

Totals obtained should be 51 utterances that were one morpheme in length, 16 utterances that were two morphemes in length, 17 utterances that were three morphemes in length, 14 utterances that were four morphemes in length, and the two longest utterances were five morphemes in length. Notation of upper bound length and lower bound length are reported to provide analysis of variability in utterance length. To determine the upper bound length, check the total column for the longest utterance in morphemes. In the sample transcript, there were two utterances that were five morphemes in length. Thus, in this transcript, the upper bound length, or longest utterance, was five morphemes. Put a 5 in the blank next to "Upper Bound Length." To determine the lower bound length, check the total column for the

shortest utterance in morphemes. In this sample, there were 51 utterances that were one morpheme in length. Thus, the lower bound length, or shortest utterance, is one morpheme. Put a 1 in the blank next to "Lower Bound Length."

This analysis may not appear to provide information substantially different from the MLU in morphemes. But, in fact, it does provide additional information. A length distribution analysis is necessary for interpretation of an obtained MLU. The analysis may confirm the obtained MLU by indicating that there is appropriate variation in length of utterance around the mean length. Brown (1973) has provided expected upper bound lengths significantly higher than the target MLU for each of his five stages. His target values were data sampling points across which the children used in his study were compared. These target values are not to be interpreted as midpoints or boundaries for stages. Table 3.3 summarizes the target values and the upper bound length for each stage of Brown's five stages of linguistic development.

As can be seen in Table 3.3, the upper bound length for each stage is substantially longer than the mean might indicate. The completion of a length distribution analysis provides insight into the variation in length of utterances that a particular child is capable of producing. The obtained MLU can be confirmed by completing a length distribution analysis. The MLU of 2.00 morphemes from the sample transcript implies that this child should be able to produce utterances as long as seven morphemes in length.

TABLE 3.3

BROWN'S (1973) TARGET MLU IN MORPHEMES AND UPPER BOUND LENGTHS FOR EACH STAGE

Stage	MLU	Upper Bound Length
I	1.75	5
II	2.25	7
III	2.75	9
IV	3.50	11
V	4.00	13

From *A First Language: The Early Stages* by Roger Brown, 1973, Cambridge, MA: Harvard University Press. © 1973 by the President and Fellows of Harvard College. Reprinted by permission of the publishers.

Syntactic Analysis
Length Distribution Analysis Sheet

Name of Child *Bridget*

Length in Morphemes	Tally	Total
1	┼┼┼┼ ┼┼┼┼ ┼┼┼┼ ┼┼┼┼ ┼┼┼┼ ┼┼┼┼ ┼┼┼┼ ┼┼┼┼ ┼┼┼┼ ┼┼┼┼ /	51
2	┼┼┼┼ ┼┼┼┼ ┼┼┼┼ /	16
3	┼┼┼┼ ┼┼┼┼ ┼┼┼┼ //	17
4	┼┼┼┼ ┼┼┼┼ ////	14
5	//	2
6		0
7		0
8		0
9		0
10		0
11		0
12		0
13		0
14		0
15		0

Upper Bound Length = _____ *5* _____ morphemes

Lower Bound Length = _____ *1* _____ morphemes

© 1993 Thinking Publications *Duplication permitted for educational use only.*

This child produces utterances five morphemes in length, the upper bound length for the previous stage. Are we to conclude that this child is incapable of producing utterances as long as her MLU would predict? That would be too strong a conclusion. The conservative conclusion would be that for this sample, Bridget produced utterances that did not vary around the mean as much as would be expected for her MLU.

The length distribution analysis also can confirm sample representativeness. Had the child in the sample transcript produced a great number of responses to yes/no questions, as observed directly by a preponderance of yes/no responses in the sample, a lower MLU would have been obtained and the length distribution analysis would have revealed restricted length variation. Such a finding would suggest a need for obtaining another sample of this child's language under more natural interactional conditions. A very high MLU with little variation in length around the mean may be the result of obtaining a sample under narrative or storytelling conditions. Obtaining another sample under conversational conditions or using another part of the transcript would be indicated in this case as well.

Reductions in variation in utterance length also may be indicative of additional problems beyond sample representativeness. A child with utterances clustering closely around the mean may have a specific deficit in production abilities. For example, children with apraxic-like behaviors or speech motor control problems tend to produce utterances resulting in low MLUs and minimal variation in utterance length around the mean. Children who are learning language in a very rote manner tend to produce utterances resulting in MLUs of varying lengths but with minimal variation around the mean. Children with autistic-like behaviors present profiles such as this. Chapman (1981) provides an excellent discussion of the importance of completing a length distribution analysis and the implications of results obtained from such an analysis. The appropriate interpretation of the results of the length distribution analysis performed on the sample transcript would be that this sample appears to be reasonably representative, and that there may be a restriction in the amount of variation in utter-

ance length around the obtained mean length. There also may be concern in regard to the large number of one-word utterances (51). This may have brought the MLU down, resulting in a less-than-typical profile of variability about the mean.

ANALYZING USE OF GRAMMATICAL MORPHEMES

The next analysis procedure that will be used results in a stage assignment reflecting mastery of grammatical morphemes. The stage assignments are based on data reported by de Villiers and de Villiers (1973) and indicate the stage at which each of the 14 grammatical morphemes studied by Brown (1973) are used correctly in 90 percent of the utterances where a particular grammatical morpheme is necessary. Brown designated this 90 percent correct use in obligatory contexts as mastery level. Using this 90 percent criterion, de Villiers and de Villiers (1973) reported the stage at which each of the 14 grammatical morphemes typically is mastered. Table 3.4 (see pages 102–103) summarizes the development for a variety of linguistic structures throughout Brown's stages of linguistic production including grammatical morphemes. Column 4 indicates the stage at which each of the 14 grammatical morphemes is used in 90 percent of obligatory contexts. This stage is considered mastery level. The other structures summarized in Table 3.4 are reported at their emergence level. These will be discussed individually in the sections describing the procedures for analysis of each.

To determine mastery of the 14 grammatical morphemes in the sample transcript, both the obligatory contexts for and the use of each grammatical morpheme will be identified. Obviously, instances of correct use of each grammatical morpheme are easier to identify than instances of the obligatory contexts where a grammatical morpheme is not used. With practice, it should be possible to identify each obligatory context with ease.

Before beginning the grammatical morpheme analysis, examine the practice utterances that are provided. These will provide experience in identifying the 14 grammatical morphemes and determining obligatory contexts without the use of the grammatical morpheme. Again, the right side of the page can be covered, the use of and/or the obligatory contexts for each of the 14 grammatical morphemes can be identified, and then results can be checked with the explanations provided.

(C points to picture in book)
two puppies/

This is an example of the correct use of the regular plural *-s*. Therefore, there is an obligatory context for and the correct use of the regular plural *-s* grammatical morpheme.

(C pulls second tiny doll from bag)
two baby/

In this utterance, there is an obligatory context for a plural *-s*, but the child has not used the plural inflection.

(C points to box in corner)
puppy in box/

This is an example of the obligatory context for and correct use of the preposition *in*. Determining the obligatory context for many of the grammatical morphemes, especially prepositions, requires that the transcript include detailed description of the nonlinguistic context. This utterance also contains the obligatory context for articles preceding the nouns, but the articles are not used. In addition, this utterance contains the obligatory context for the contractible copula, and, again, that grammatical morpheme is not used.

(C hears baby crying in another room)
baby cry/

If the context notes indicate that the child is describing an ongoing activity, this utterance can be considered an obligatory context for the present progressive tense of the verb. Obviously, it was not used in this utterance. In addition, there is an obligatory context for the contractible auxiliary without use. There also is questionable obligatory context for an article without use. The reason this would be considered questionable is that many times children use the word *baby* as a proper name, and an article would not be required.

(C points to puppy still in box)
puppy there/

The context notes for this utterance indicate that the child was pointing out one of the puppies that was still in the box. Therefore, this would be an obligatory context for the preposition *in*. In addition, there is an obligatory context for an article and a contractible copula (*a* / *the* puppy *is* in there).

(C hands her mother's hat to clinician)
mommy hat/

Again, from the context notes it can be seen that the child is talking about his mother's hat. Thus, there is an obligatory context for the possessive *-s* without use of that grammatical morpheme.

(clinician asks, "Where's your owie?" and C holds out hand) on finger/	This utterance contains an obligatory context for and the correct use of the preposition *on*.
(C dances doll across toy piano keys) Mommy singing/	This is an instance of the obligatory context for and the correct use of the present progressive tense of the verb (*-ing*). This utterance also contains the obligatory context for the contractible auxiliary, but the auxiliary is not used. Note that the auxiliary does not have to be present to give the child credit for correct use of *-ing*.
(C hands book to M) Daddy's book/	This utterance contains an obligatory context for and the correct use of the possessive *-s*.
(C knocks doll off barn) she falled down/	This utterance contains an obligatory context for the irregular past tense of the verb. However, the child's use is of the regular form, and thus there is incorrect use of the irregular past. This is simply the obligatory context for the irregular past.
(puppy knocks C down) puppy jumped on me/	This utterance contains the obligatory context for and the correct use of the regular past tense of the verb. It also contains the obligatory context for and correct use of the preposition *on*. In addition, it contains the obligatory context for an article.
(C points to puppy) that a puppy/	This utterance contains an obligatory context for the contractible copula, but the copula is not used. In addition, there is an obligatory context for and correct use of the article *a*.
(C points to one of the puppies) he barks/	This is an example of an obligatory context for and correct use of the regular third person singular present tense of the verb. The regular form is quite easy to identify by looking for the use of proper names or singular pronouns. These are often followed by the regular third person singular present tense of the verb.
(C points to another puppy) that's my puppy/	This utterance contains an obligatory context for and the correct use of the contractible copula. Possessive pronouns do not require use of the possessive *-s* grammatical morpheme and therefore this utterance does not contain an obligatory context for the possessive *-s*.

(C scoops raisins into a pile) these are my ones/	This utterance contains obligatory contexts for and correct use of two grammatical morphemes: the contractible copula (plural form) and the plural *-s*.
(M says, "You need to hurry," as C puts toys in bag) I'm hurrying/	This utterance also contains obligatory contexts for and correct use of two grammatical morphemes: the contractible auxiliary and the present progressive tense of the verb, *-ing*.
(C makes doll jump up and down) him jumping/	This utterance contains the obligatory context for the contractible auxiliary without the correct use. It also contains the obligatory context for and the correct use of the present progressive tense of the verb.
(M says, "Who's ready for ice cream?") I am/	This utterance is in response to a question, and in this elliptical form, the copula is uncontractible (*I'm* cannot be said as a response). Thus, this is an obligatory context for and the correct use of the uncontractible copula.
(M says, "Who's making all that noise?") he is/	This utterance is also in response to a question, and again, as a response, *he's* isn't possible. Thus, this is an obligatory context for and correct use of the uncontractible auxiliary.
(C walks dolls away from toy piano) they were singing/	This utterance contains an obligatory context for and correct use of the present progressive tense of the verb. In addition, since using the contracted form of the auxiliary eliminates the tense information, (e.g., *They are singing* and *They were singing* both contract to *They're singing*), this is an example of an uncontractible auxiliary. De Villiers and de Villiers (1978) indicate that uncontractible forms typically are syllabic, as in this example. The previous two examples are uncontractible in the elliptical form.
(C points to puppy climbing out of box) he does that every time/	This is an example of an obligatory context for and the correct use of the irregular third person singular present tense of the verb.

Now return to the transcript and examine each utterance for the use of and/or obligatory context for each of the 14 grammatical morphemes. Remember, there may be more than one instance of the use of and/or obligatory context for grammatical morphemes in each utterance. Using the Grammatical Morpheme Analysis Sheet, record the utterance number of each instance of an obligatory context for a grammatical morpheme in the appropriate box. Record the utterance number again if the grammatical morpheme was used correctly in the obligatory context. It may be easier to consider each of the 14 grammatical morphemes individually and examine each utterance for the presence of and/or obligatory context for that particular grammatical morpheme. This means that it will be necessary to go through the transcript 14 times. It is possible to examine each utterance once for the use of and/or obligatory context for all grammatical morphemes; however, some may be missed this way.

Once all obligatory contexts for and uses of the 14 grammatical morphemes have been identified, add the number of uses of each grammatical morpheme and divide this by the number of obligatory contexts for that grammatical morpheme. Multiply this number by 100 to get the percentage of use of that grammatical morpheme. Put this number in the "% Use" box on the Grammatical Morpheme Analysis Sheet. Check results with the sample provided on page 101.

As can be seen from the Grammatical Morpheme Analysis Sheet, several of the grammatical morphemes were not present in this transcript, nor were the obligatory contexts present in the transcript. For these grammatical morphemes, no statement can be made regarding mastery. In addition, several of the grammatical morphemes occurred so infrequently that the resulting percentages are questionable. Both of these problems point out the need for obtaining samples that are relatively lengthy. As discussed in Chapter 1, a sample of 100 utterances is the absolute minimum length.

What conclusions can be drawn from the grammatical morpheme analysis? First, in spite of few instances of each, this child apparently has mastered the plural -*s*, the preposition *in*, and the possessive -*s*. In addition, the con-

tractible copula appears to have been mastered. More confidence of mastery of this grammatical morpheme is warranted because there were nine instances of correct use. It also can be concluded that five grammatical morphemes appear not to have been mastered. These include the regular past tense -*ed* (with 33 percent correct use in obligatory contexts), the irregular past tense of the verb (with 43 percent correct use in obligatory contexts), articles (with 35 percent correct use in obligatory contexts), and the contractible auxiliary and uncontractible copula (with 50 percent correct use in obligatory contexts). In addition, one obligatory context was noted for two grammatical morphemes (preposition *on* and regular third person singular present tense -*s*). This single obligatory context for each with use yielded 0 percent correct use for these grammatical morphemes. Stages will be assigned reflecting mastery of grammatical morphemes in the Summary and Interpretation section of this analysis procedure.

ANALYZING COMPLEXITY OF NEGATION

Like the grammatical morpheme analysis, this analysis also results in a stage assignment reflecting the structural complexity of negation within a transcript. The stage assignments are based on data reported by Klima and Bellugi (1966); Chapman (1978); and Chapman, Paul, and Wanska (1981). Changes in the child's ability to incorporate negative elements into an utterance typically occur with increases in utterance length. Column 5 in Table 3.4 (on pages 102–103) indicates the changes in structural complexity of negation and the stage at which those changes emerge. Keep in mind that the stage assignments reflect emergence of a new way of producing negation and not mastery of this new form. In addition, note that changes do not occur at every stage.

To determine the stage which characterizes the child's level of negation, analyze each utterance within the transcript for developmental complexity. The first step is the identification of negative elements within the transcript. The identification of negative elements is easier than identification of some syntactic structures,

Syntactic Analysis
Grammatical Morpheme Analysis Sheet

Name of Child *Bridget*

Grammatical Morpheme	Obligatory Contexts	Use	% Use
1. -ing	—	—	—
2. plural -s	27, 78, 81	27, 78, 81	100%
3. IN	17, 97	17, 97	100%
4. ON	13	—	0%
5. possessive -s	62, 65	62, 65	100%
6. regular past -ed	36, 45, 96	96	33%
7. irregular past	2, 5, 44, 46, 56, 81, 86	5, 81, 86	43%
8. regular third person singular	75	—	0%
9. articles	8, 9, 13, 17, 25, 27, 32, 40, 41, 50, 58, 60, 61, 81, 84, 93, 94	17, 25, 32, 60, 61, 81	35%
10. contractible copula	18, 20, 32, 33, 35, 60, 61, 65	18, 20, 32, 33, 35, 60, 61, 65	100%
11. contractible auxiliary	21, 24	21	50%
12. uncontractible copula	23, 62	23	50%
13. uncontractible auxiliary	—	—	—
14. irregular third person singular	—	—	—

TABLE 3.4

PRODUCTION CHARACTERISTICS OF LINGUISTIC DEVELOPMENT ORGANIZED BY BROWN'S STAGES

Stage	MLU	Age (months)	Grammatical Morphemes	Negation	Yes/No Questions	Wh-Questions	Noun Phrase Elaboration	Verb Phrase Elaboration	Complex Sentences
Early I	1.01–1.49	19–22[a] 16–26[b]	Occasional use	*No* as single word utterance	Marked with rising intonation	*What* + this/that	NP → (M) + N[d] Elaborated NPs occur only alone	Main Verb: Uninflected; occasional use of *-ing* Auxiliary: not used Copula: not used Verb + Particles: occasional use	None used
Late I/ Early II	1.50–1.99	23–26 18–31	Occasional use	*No* + noun or verb *Not* + noun or verb	Rising intonation	*What* + NP or VP *Where* + NP or VP			None used
II	2.00–2.49	27–30 21–35	1. Present progressive tense of verb *-ing*[c] 2. Regular plural *-s* 3. Preposition *In*	No change	Rising intonation	No change	NP same as Stage I Elaborated NPs occur only in object position	Main Verb: Occasionally marked auxiliary: 1. Semi-auxiliary appears 2. Use of present progressive *-ing* without auxiliary Copula: Appears without tense/number inflection	Semi-auxiliary appears: *Gonna, Gotta, Wanna, Hafta*
III	2.50–2.99	31–34 24–41	4. Preposition *On* 5. Possessive *-s*	NP + (negative) + VP	Rising intonation	Wh-word + sentence *Why, Who,* and *How* questions appear	NP → {(demonstrative) (article)} + (M) + N Subject NP elaboration appears	Main Verb: 1. Obligatory 2. Overgeneralization of regular past *-ed* Auxiliary: Present tense forms appear including *Can, Will, Be*	Object NP complement: full sentence takes the place of object of the verb
Early IV	3.00–3.49	35–38 28–45	No others mastered	NP + aux + (negative) + VP	Inversion of auxiliary verb and subject noun	Inconsistent auxiliary inversion *When* questions appear			Simple infinitive clauses appear Simple wh-clauses appear Conjoined sentences with conjunction *And*

[a]Predicted age range

[b]Age range within one SD of predicted values

[c]Based on 90% use in obligatory contexts

[d]The following are definitions of sentence notation:

→ is expanded, or elaborated, as

(x) the item within the parentheses is optional

$\begin{Bmatrix} x \\ y \\ z \end{Bmatrix}$ only one item within the brackets can occur

$\begin{Bmatrix} (x) \\ (y) \\ (z) \end{Bmatrix}$ either one of the items, or none, can occur

© **1993 Thinking Publications** *Duplication permitted for educational use only.*

Stage	MLU	Age (months)	Grammatical Morphemes	Negation	Yes/No Questions	Wh- Questions	Noun Phrase Elaboration	Verb Phrase Elaboration	Complex Sentences
Late IV/ Early V	3.50–3.99	39–42 31–50	No others mastered	No change	No change	No change	NP → (demonstrative) (article) (M) (possessive) + (adjective) + N Subject NP obligatory; noun or pronoun always appears in subject position	Main Verb: Regular past -ed (double marking of main verb and auxiliary for past in negative sentences) Auxiliary: 1. Past modals appear including *Could, Would, Should, Must, Might* 2. *Be* + present progressive -ing appears Verb Phrase: Semi-auxiliary complements now take NP	Multiple embeddings Conjoined and embedded clauses in the same sentence
Late V	4.00–4.49	43–46 37–52	6. Regular past tense of verb -ed 7. Irregular past tense of verb 8. Regular third person singular present tense 9. Definite and indefinite articles 10. Contractible copula	Past tense modals and *Be* in contracted and uncontracted form	No change	No change	NP → same as Stage IV Number agreement between subject and predicate verb phrase continues to be a problem beyond Stage V	See Grammatical Morphemes column	Relative clauses appear Infinitive clauses with subjects different from that of main sentence Conjunction *If*
V+	4.50–4.99	47–50 41–59	11. Contractible auxiliary 12. Uncontractible copula 13. Uncontractible auxiliary 14. Irregular third person singular	No data	No data	No data		Main Verb/Auxiliary 1. Past tense *Be* appears as main verb and auxiliary 2. Infrequent use of present perfect tense with auxiliary marked	Gerund clauses appear Wh-infinitive clauses appear Unmarked infinitive clauses appear Conjunction *Because* used
V++	5.00–5.99	51–67 43–67	No data	No data	No data	No data			Conjunctions *When* and *So* appear

Adapted from *Assessing Language Production in Children: Experimental Procedures* by J. Miller, 1981, Baltimore, MD: University Park Press.

© 1993 **Thinking Publications** *Duplication permitted for educational use only.*

because there are a limited number of ways in which negation can be incorporated into an utterance at these developmental levels. These include the use of *no* as a single-word utterance or added to a noun or verb and the use of *not* in contracted and uncontracted forms in various sentence positions. Following the identification of utterances with negation, the determination of the stage which best characterizes each negative element may be more difficult. To increase abilities in making these judgments, use practice utterances that again have been provided. Cover the right side of the page, compare the utterance to the descriptions of variations in form provided in Table 3.4, "Production Characteristics of Linguistic Development Organized by Brown's Stages," assign a stage, and then check results with the explanations provided.

(C pushes M's hand away as she tries to wipe his mouth)
no/

Stage EI

The use of *no* as a one-word utterance is the earliest type of negation. Assigning Stage EI to this utterance in a transcript with utterances considerably longer than one word may distort the assignment of an overall stage for negation. This means that a transcript that contains many responses to yes/no questions will erroneously report the stage for negation. A transcript such as this would be rejected on the basis of a lack of representativeness prior to beginning analysis of structural complexity.

(M and C are playing with circus set; M says, "Do you want me to put him in the wagon?")
no/

This is not an example of *no* as a negative utterance. It is a one-word response to a yes/no question, so no stage is assigned.

(C hits doll with teddy bear, then looks at M and says)
no hit/

Stages LI/EII–II

This utterance is an example of a *no* + verb sentence form. This form is characteristic of Late Stage I/Early Stage II, but it continues to be used through Stage II.

(C pulls on M's arm)
not go/

Stages LI/EII–II

This utterance is an example of a *not* + verb sentence form, also characteristic of Late Stage I/Early Stage II through Stage II.

(as M leaves room, C shakes head and looks at M)
me no go/

Stage III

This utterance is an example of a negative sentence in the form NP (noun phrase) + (negative) + VP (verb phrase), with the negative element integrated into the sentence. This form emerges in Stage III.

(C puts girl doll in car)
Daddy not go/

Stage III
This is another example with the negative element integrated into the sentence. In this case, the negative element is *not* instead of *no*. This utterance and the preceding one are characteristic of the same stage.

(C opens box of people
and animals)
there aren't any kikis here/

Stages Early IV–LIV/EV
This utterance is an example of the verb *be*, in the plural present tense negative contracted form. This form appears in Early Stage IV, at the same time as auxiliary elements in contracted and uncontracted forms.

(C picks up a toy
dog and shakes her
head)
not a kiki/

Stages LI/EII–II
This utterance is an example of *not* + noun with an article included. As discussed in the first example, assigning Stage LI/EII to the utterance appears to underestimate the child's abilities to produce negative structures. Therefore, the best stage assignment that can be made is to assign the range of stages.

(puppy jumps on
clinician and C looks
at her)
he no bite you/

Stage III
This utterance contains a negative element integrated within the sentence between the NP and the VP.

(C's baby brother is
babbling and C says to M)
he isn't silly/

Stages Early IV–LIV/EV
This negative sentence contains the present tense of the verb *be*, in the negative contracted form. It is typical of examples provided in the literature for Early Stage IV.

(C turns cup upside
down on table)
no juice/

Stages LI/EII–II
This utterance is an example of the *no* + noun form of negation. It is characteristic of Late Stage I/Early Stage II, but the range of stages is recorded.

(C pushes blue crayon away)
I don't want that one/

Stages Early IV–LIV/EV
This utterance contains an auxiliary (the dummy *do*) in the negative contracted form, which appears in Early Stage IV.

(clinician drops box of little bears and begins to pick them up)

you shouldn't do that/   Late Stage V
This utterance contains the modal auxiliary verb *should* in the negative contracted form. Modals in contracted and uncontracted form appear in negative sentences at this stage.

(C turns puzzle piece around and around)

this one doesn't fit/   Stages Early IV–LIV/EV
Again, there is an auxiliary, *does,* in the negative contracted form.

(C hugs teddy bear after pulling it out of box)

I couldn't find him/   Late Stage V
This utterance contains the past tense modal auxiliary *could* in the negative contracted form.

That practice should be helpful in identifying negative elements and assigning stages to the developmental complexity of each. Now, return to the sample transcript and examine each utterance for the presence of negative elements. If there is no negative element in the utterance, mark a dash (–) for that utterance in the "Negation" column on the Structural Stage Analysis Grid. When an utterance that contains a negative element is identified, compare that utterance to the descriptions of increases in complexity provided in column 5 of Table 3.4 to determine the stage which best characterizes the complexity of the negative elements within the utterance. Then record the stage number for that utterance in the "Negation" column on the Structural Stage Analysis Grid. Be certain to record in the correct column and row reflecting utterance number and negation analysis. When each utterance has been examined for the presence of negative elements and stage assignments have been recorded, compare results with the sample provided on pages 107–108.

This transcript contained four negative utterances ranging in complexity from Early Stage I to Stage EIV. Utterance #33 poses some problems, and this is not included in the total of four negative utterances. This utterance includes a negative response to the mother's question, "Do you want to put him up there?" The child responds, "No (I don't want to put him up there because) it's heavy." The utterance is not a negative utterance in terms of the presence of negative elements incorporated into the utterance structure. It is a negative response that is elliptical in relation to the mother's utterance and is a clarification of that negative response. Therefore, it is not appropriate to include it in the total of negative utterances.

The stage assignments for individual utterances recorded on the Structural Stage Analysis Grid will be used to complete the Syntactic Analysis Data Summary in the Summary and Interpretation section of this analysis procedure. Before tallying these instances of negation on the Data Summary sheet, the complexity of several other syntactic structures will be analyzed. The tallying of stage assignments for individual utterances will allow examination of the most frequently occurring stage for negation as well as the Most Advanced Stage. These data can only be interpreted in relation to stage assignments for other structures.

Syntactic Analysis
Structural Stage Analysis Grid

Name of Child **Bridget**

response to yes/no question

Utterance Number	Number of Morphemes	Negation	Yes/No Questions	Wh-Questions	Noun Phrase Elaboration	Verb Phrase Elaboration	Complex
1	1	—					
2	2	—					
3	1	— (circled)					
4	1	—					
5	4	—					
6	1	—					
7	2	—					
8	1	—					
9	1	—					
10	1	—					
11	3	—					
12	1	—					
13	1	—					
14	1	—					
15	4	—					
16	2	—					
17	4	—					
18	4	///					
19	2	—					
20	4	///					
21	4	EIV					
22	2	—					
23	3	—					
24	4	—					
25	2	—					

response to yes/no question plus explanation

Utterance Number	Number of Morphemes	Negation	Yes/No Questions	Wh-Questions	Noun Phrase Elaboration	Verb Phrase Elaboration	Complex
26	2	—					
27	2	—					
28	2	—					
29	1	—					
30	1	—					
31	5	—					
32	4	—					
33	4	— (circled)					
34	1	—					
35	4	—					
36	3	—					
37	1	—					
38	1	—					
39	1	—					
40	1	—					
41	1	—					
42	1	—					
43	2	—					
44	2	—					
45	3	—					
46	3	—					
47	1	—					
48	1	—					
49	1	—					
50	1	—					
Total	105						

Syntactic Analysis
Structural Stage Analysis Grid

Name of Child *Bridget*

Utterance Number	Number of Morphemes	Negation	Yes/No Questions	Wh-Questions	Noun Phrase Elaboration	Verb Phrase Elaboration	Complex
51	1	–					
52	3	–					
53	1	–					
54	1	–					
55	1	–					
56	4	–					
57	1	–					
58	1	–					
59	1	–					
60	4	–					
61	4	–					
62	3	–					
63	1	–					
64	1	–					
65	4	–					
66	2	–					
67	1	–					
68	1	–					
69	1	–					
70	1	–					
71	1	–					
72	3	–					
73	3	–					
74	1	–					
75	2	–					

Utterance Number	Number of Morphemes	Negation	Yes/No Questions	Wh-Questions	Noun Phrase Elaboration	Verb Phrase Elaboration	Complex
76	1	–					
77	1	–					
78	3	//–//					
79	1	–					
80	1	–					
81	5	–					
82	1	–					
83	3	–					
84	1	–					
85	1	–					
86	2	–					
87	3	–					
88	3	–					
89	3	–					
90	3	–					
91	1	–					
92	1	–					
93	1	–					
94	1	–					
95	1	–					
96	3	–					
97	3	–					
98	1	–					
99	2	–					
100	2	–					
Total	95						

200 ÷ 100 = 2.00 MLU

© **1993 Thinking Publications** *Duplication permitted for educational use only.*

ANALYZING COMPLEXITY OF YES/NO QUESTIONS

Analysis of the complexity of yes/no questions yields a stage assignment reflecting that complexity and is done in the same manner as the analysis of developmental complexity of grammatical morphemes and negation. The developmental sequence of changes in complexity and stage assignments is based on data reported by Klima and Bellugi (1966) and Chapman, Paul, and Wanska (1981). Column 6 in Table 3.4 summarizes the sequence of developmental changes for yes/no questions. As with negation, stage assignments reflect appearance of changes in producing yes/no questions and not mastery of the changes. And like the preceding syntactic structure, changes in complexity of yes/no questions do not occur at every stage.

To determine the stage which characterizes the child's level of yes/no question production,

each yes/no question within the sample transcript will be examined for developmental complexity. First, identify the yes/no questions and then examine the way in which the question is formed. The determination of the stage which describes each individual yes/no question is made by comparing each question to descriptions provided in Table 3.4. Before the yes/no questions in the sample transcript are identified and the developmental complexity of each is determined, some practice utterances are provided. The following utterances have been selected to demonstrate some of the problems that frequently are encountered when describing the developmental complexity of yes/no questions. The practice gained in assigning stages to these utterances will be helpful when the analysis is applied to the sample transcript. As with the practice utterances in previous sections, cover the right side of the page, compare the utterance to the descriptions of developmental changes in Table 3.4, and assign a stage. Then check results with the explanations provided.

(C picks up an apple)
ball↑/

Stages EI–III
Yes/no questions are marked only with rising intonation during these three stages. It is impossible to differentiate between these stages in the child's productions, so the best way to assign a stage is to assign all three. When this information is put together with other stage assignments, the adequacy of the child's productions can be determined.

(C shows cow to M)
see↑/

Stages EI–III
This yes/no question is of the same form as the previous one, and the three stages cannot be differentiated at this point.

(C turns empty cookie box upside down)
more↑/

Stages EI–III
Again, this is a yes/no question marked only with rising intonation, and, as in the preceding two examples, these three stages cannot be differentiated.

(C hands empty cup to M)
more juice↑/

Stages EI–III
Although this utterance is longer than the preceding three, it is of the same form. Therefore, these three stages cannot be differentiated.

(C hands puzzle piece to M) da no go↑/	**Stages EI–III** Again, this is a yes/no question marked only with rising intonation. No differentiation of stages is possible.
(C picks up doll from doll bed) baby wet↑/	**Stages EI–III** One more example of a yes/no question marked only with rising intonation.
(C turns to M as she leaves the room) am I gonna go↑/	**Stage EIV** Finally, this is an example of a yes/no question with inversion of the auxiliary and the subject noun. This form emerges in Stage EIV.
(C looks on as M dumps cookie out of box) is that the only one↑/	**Stage EIV** This also is an example of a yes/no question with the inversion necessary to form a question. But in this utterance, the main verb, *be*, is inverted. The ability to invert all or part of the verb phrase with the noun phrase appears in Stage EIV.
(C picks up last cupcake) can I eat this one↑/	**Stage EIV** This yes/no question also contains auxiliary inversion. Although assigning the same stage to each of these three utterances seems to distort the apparent differences in complexity, it appears to be the best alternative. The differences in complexity will be captured in the verb phrase analysis.
(C hands wind-up toy to M) will you fix this↑/	**Stage EIV** This yes/no question is of the same auxiliary inversion form. The obviously higher level of complexity will be credited to the child in the verb phrase analysis.

These practice utterances should have clarified the two ways in which children construct yes/no questions. Although other changes in complexity are apparent within yes/no questions, those changes in complexity reflect changes in structures other than the formation of the question. Now, return to the sample transcript and examine each utterance for the presence of rising intonation or verb phrase inversion. Progress through the transcript, recording a dash (–) for each utterance that is not a type of yes/no question in the "Yes/No Questions" column on the Structural Stage Analysis Grid. If the utterance is a type of yes/no question, compare that utterance to the descriptions of increases in complexity provided in column 6 of Table 3.4 to determine the stage which best describes the complexity of that yes/no question. Then record the stage number or range of stages for that utterance in the "Yes/No Questions" column on the Structural Stage Analysis Grid. After each yes/no question in the transcript has been analyzed, compare results with the completed section of the Structural Stage Analysis Grid on pages 111–112.

Syntactic Analysis
Structural Stage Analysis Grid

Name of Child __Bridget__

response to yes/no question

Utterance Number	Number of Morphemes	Negation	Yes/No Questions	Wh-Questions	Noun Phrase Elaboration	Verb Phrase Elaboration	Complex
1	1	–	–				
2	2	–	–				
3	1	(–)	–				
4	1	–	–				
5	4	–	–				
6	1	–	EI–III				
7	2	–	–				
8	1	–	–				
9	1	–	–				
10	1	–	–				
11	3	–	–				
12	1	–	–				
13	1	–	–				
14	1	–	–				
15	4	–	–				
16	2	–	–				
17	4	–	–				
18	4	///	–				
19	2	–	–				
20	4	///	–				
21	4	EIV	–				
22	2	–	–				
23	3	–	–				
24	4	–	–				
25	2	–	–				

response to yes/no question plus explanation

Utterance Number	Number of Morphemes	Negation	Yes/No Questions	Wh-Questions	Noun Phrase Elaboration	Verb Phrase Elaboration	Complex
26	2	–	–				
27	2	–	–				
28	2	–	–				
29	1	–	–				
30	1	–	–				
31	5	–	–				
32	4	–	–				
33	4	(–)	–				
34	1	–	–				
35	4	–	–				
36	3	–	–				
37	1	–	–				
38	1	–	–				
39	1	–	–				
40	1	–	–				
41	1	–	–				
42	1	–	–				
43	2	–	–				
44	2	–	–				
45	3	–	–				
46	3	–	–				
47	1	–	–				
48	1	–	–				
49	1	–	–				
50	1	–	–				
Total	105						

Syntactic Analysis
Structural Stage Analysis Grid

Name of Child _Bridget_

Utterance Number	Number of Morphemes	Negation	Yes/No Questions	Wh-Questions	Noun Phrase Elaboration	Verb Phrase Elaboration	Complex
51	1	—	—				
52	3	—	—				
53	1	—	—				
54	1	—	—				
55	1	—	—				
56	4	—	—				
57	1	—	—				
58	1	—	—				
59	1	—	EI–III				
60	4	—	—				
61	4	—	—				
62	3	—	—				
63	1	—	—				
64	1	—	—				
65	4	—	—				
66	2	—	—				
67	1	—	—				
68	1	—	—				
69	1	—	—				
70	1	—	EI–III				
71	1	—	—				
72	3	—	—				
73	3	—	—				
74	1	—	—				
75	2	—	—				

Utterance Number	Number of Morphemes	Negation	Yes/No Questions	Wh-Questions	Noun Phrase Elaboration	Verb Phrase Elaboration	Complex
76	1	—	—				
77	1	—	—				
78	3	LI–II	—				
79	1	—	—				
80	1	—	—				
81	5	—	—				
82	1	—	—				
83	3	—	—				
84	1	—	—				
85	1	—	—				
86	2	—	—				
87	3	—	—				
88	3	—	—				
89	3	—	—				
90	3	—	—				
91	1	—	—				
92	1	—	—				
93	1	—	—				
94	1	—	—				
95	1	—	—				
96	3	—	—				
97	3	—	—				
98	1	—	—				
99	2	—	—				
100	2	—	—				
Total	95						

$200 \div 100 = 2.00$ MLU

© 1993 Thinking Publications *Duplication permitted for educational use only.*

Three utterances should have been identified as types of yes/no questions in the sample transcript. Each of these yes/no questions was formed using rising intonation and thus were typical of Stages EI–III. Although these utterances appear to be a minimal amount of data for analysis of the developmental level of yes/no questions, it is not uncommon to find that only a small percentage of the utterances are question forms. These instances of yes/no questions will be tallied on the Syntactic Analysis Data Summary sheet after analyzing the complexity of a few other syntactic structures. Final interpretation of the level of complexity of yes/no questions can be made only after summary of the developmental level of all other syntactic structures to be analyzed.

ANALYZING COMPLEXITY OF WH-QUESTIONS

Analysis of the developmental level of wh-questions, like the preceding analyses, results in a stage assignment reflecting the complexity of the questions. Unlike the preceding analyses, the analysis of wh-questions considers two aspects of the structure to be analyzed. The first consideration in determining the developmental level of a wh-question is the type of wh-question. For example, WHAT questions appear quite early in the developmental sequence, but WHEN questions appear much later. A stage is assigned to a particular wh-question on the basis of which type of wh-question it is. The second consideration in determining the developmental level of a wh-question is the form of the question. For example, WHAT + NP question forms occur early in the developmental sequence, but questions with auxiliary inversion occur considerably later in the sequence. The form of the wh-question is to refine the judgments about stage assignment. A WHAT question with auxiliary inversion is assigned a higher stage than a WHAT question without auxiliary inversion.

Both aspects of the wh-question are considered in assigning a stage to each utterance. The changes in type and form of the wh-questions are summarized in column 7 of Table 3.4. The stage assignments are based on data reported by Klima and Bellugi (1966); Ervin-Tripp (1970); Tyack and Ingram (1977); and Chapman, Paul, and Wanska (1981). Changes in type and form reflect the appearance of these changes and not mastery of the changes.

To determine the stage which characterizes the child's level of wh-question development, analyze each wh-question within the sample transcript for type and form. To increase abilities in identifying changes in type and form, practice analyzing the utterances that are provided. As with other practice utterances, cover the right side of the page, make the stage assignment, and then check the assignments with those provided. The explanations should clear up any discrepancies.

(C points to donut and looks at M)
wazit?/

Stage EI
This probably is the most basic type of wh-question in that it functions as a generic question type. It is a WHAT question type and is in the form of a reduced WHAT + *this*.

(clock makes noise and C looks to M)
what that?/

Stage EI
This question is characteristic of the same stage as the preceding example, even though it is more complex.

(C holds up small plastic animal)
what this one?/

Stages LI/EII–II
Although this is the same type of question as the preceding two (WHAT), it is in a more complex form: WHAT + NP. Consequently, it is assigned a more advanced stage range.

(C hears voices outside door and asks M)
where Daddy?/

Stages LI/EII–II
This question is of a different type (WHERE) than the preceding questions but it is in the same form: WHERE + NP. Thus, it is assigned the same stage.

(C is drawing with marking pens)
where the green one is?/

Stage III
This question is the same type of question as the preceding one (WHERE), but it is in a more complex form: wh-word + sentence. This form emerges in Stage III.

(C is digging through toy box)
where's the big one?/

Stage EIV
Again, this is a WHERE question, but this one reflects inversion of the verb and noun phrase. This form emerges in Early Stage IV.

(clinician enters room and adjusts remote control camera)
what him doing?/

Stages LI/EII–II
This is an example of a simple WHAT-DOING question that emerges in Late Stage I/Early Stage II and does not change in form through Stage II.

(C searching through bag of small plastic animals)
where that elephant?/

Stages LI/EII–II
This is another WHERE + NP question form that emerges in Late Stage I/Early Stage II and does not change in form through Stage II.

(clinician enters room to adjust camera)
who that is?/

Stage III
The WHO question type emerges in Stage III, and the form of this particular WHO question is typical of Stage III (wh-word + sentence).

(someone shouts in hallway)
who is that?/

Stage EIV
This WHO question shows evidence of inversion of the verb and noun phrase. So even though it is a Stage III question type, it is in the Early Stage IV form.

(C pushes puppy away)

why him bite me?/   Stage III

This type of question emerges in Stage III, and it is in the Stage III form (no inversion).

(C fitting blocks together)

how this one go?/   Stage III

This is another question type to emerge in Stage III, and the uninverted form continues.

(C looks at clinician)

when is my mom coming?/   Stage EIV

WHEN questions emerge in Early Stage IV, so the assignment is quite simple on those grounds. But notice that this utterance also contains an example of auxiliary inversion, which also emerges at this stage. Consequently, it is assigned Early Stage IV on the basis of type and form.

This practice should be helpful in assigning stages on the basis of both the type and the form of the wh-question. Now, return to the sample transcript and determine the stage which best characterizes the type and form of each wh-question in the transcript. Progress through the transcript, recording a dash (−) for each utterance that is not a wh-question and the appropriate stage for each wh-question in the "Wh-Questions" column on the Structural Stage Analysis Grid. When a dash or a stage has been recorded for each utterance, compare your results with the sample provided on pages 116–117.

This transcript contained eight wh-questions ranging in complexity from Early Stage I to Late Stage V. These wh-questions will be recorded on the Syntactic Analysis Data Summary sheet, but before moving on to the analysis of other structures, one type of wh-question not included in the total needs to be examined. Five questions might have been assigned Early Stage I. All of these were a type of WHAT question and all were in the form of "huh?" Although these are WHAT questions, and the only information to go on in assigning a stage to them is the type, tallying these in Early Stage I may distort the child's level of wh-question development. These WHAT questions are quite different from other Early Stage I WHAT questions in that they are not querying a specific semantic role. Typically, Early Stage I WHAT

questions are used by children to query the label of an object. The five WHAT questions in this transcript appear to have been used to request repetition of the mother's utterance, not to obtain the label for an object. This use of *what?* or *huh?* serves a pragmatic function, not a semantic one. Analysis of the syntactic form of these questions underestimates the child's syntactic abilities. Therefore, these five questions will be eliminated from the syntactic analysis. They will be considered in the next chapter when pragmatic aspects of this child's productions are examined.

Thus, the total number of wh-questions is eight. But one more type of wh-question should be re-examined. Utterances 7, 16, 19, and 66 are all examples of a routine form for this child, "What else?" She appears to use this in various places in conversation when she wants to move on to play with and talk about other toys. If she had used the fully elaborated form, "What else is in the box?" or "What else should we do?", Stage EIV would be the more appropriate assignment. Given the abbreviated form of her utterances, Stages EI–II was judged to be the best stage assignment. Before the developmental level of wh-questions in this child's productions can be interpreted, the complexity of three more syntactic structures must be analyzed. Only after all aspects of syntactic production have been analyzed can each structure be appropriately interpreted.

Syntactic Analysis
Structural Stage Analysis Grid

Name of Child __Bridget__

response to yes/no question

repetition request

response to yes/no question plus explanation

Utterance Number	Number of Morphemes	Negation	Yes/No Questions	Wh-Questions	Noun Phrase Elaboration	Verb Phrase Elaboration	Complex
1	1	–	–	–			
2	2	–	–	–			
3	1	(–)	–	–			
4	1	–	–	–			
5	4	–	–	–			
6	1	–	EI–III	–			
7	2	–	–	EI–II			
8	1	–	–	–			
9	1	–	–	–			
10	1	–	–	–			
11	3	–	–	–			
12	1	–	–	–			
13	1	–	–	–			
14	1	–	–	–			
15	4	–	–	–			
16	2	–	–	EI–II			
17	4	–	–	–			
18	4	///	–	–			
19	2	–	–	EI–II			
20	4	///	–	–			
21	4	EIV	–	–			
22	2	–	–	–			
23	3	–	–	///			
24	4	–	–	///			
25	2	–	–	–			

Utterance Number	Number of Morphemes	Negation	Yes/No Questions	Wh-Questions	Noun Phrase Elaboration	Verb Phrase Elaboration	Complex
26	2	–	–	–			
27	2	–	–	–			
28	2	–	–	–			
29	1	–	–	(–)			
30	1	–	–	–			
31	5	–	–	–			
32	4	–	–	–			
33	4	(–)	–	–			
34	1	–	–	–			
35	4	–	–	EIV			
36	3	–	–	–			
37	1	–	–	–			
38	1	–	–	–			
39	1	–	–	–			
40	1	–	–	–			
41	1	–	–	–			
42	1	–	–	–			
43	2	–	–	–			
44	2	–	–	–			
45	3	–	–	–			
46	3	–	–	–			
47	1	–	–	–			
48	1	–	–	–			
49	1	–	–	–			
50	1	–	–	–			
Total	105						

© **1993 Thinking Publications** *Duplication permitted for educational use only.*

Syntactic Analysis
Structural Stage Analysis Grid

Name of Child _Bridget_

Utterances 51–75

Utterance Number	Number of Morphemes	Negation	Yes/No Questions	Wh- Questions	Noun Phrase Elaboration	Verb Phrase Elaboration	Complex
51	1	–	–	–			
52	3	–	–	–			
53	1	–	–	–			
54	1	–	–	–			
55	1	–	–	–			
56	4	–	–	–			
57	1	–	–	–			
58	1	–	–	–			
59	1	–	–	(–)			
60	4	–	EI–III	–			
61	4	–	–	–			
62	3	–	–	–			
63	1	–	–	–			
64	1	–	–	–			
65	4	–	–	–			
66	2	–	–	EI–IX			
67	1	–	–	–			
68	1	–	–	(–)			
69	1	–	–	–			
70	1	–	EI–III	–			
71	1	–	–	–			
72	3	–	–	–			
73	3	–	–	–			
74	1	–	–	(–)			
75	2	–	–	–			

repetition request

Utterances 76–100

Utterance Number	Number of Morphemes	Negation	Yes/No Questions	Wh- Questions	Noun Phrase Elaboration	Verb Phrase Elaboration	Complex
76	1	–	–	–			
77	1	–	–	–			
78	3	LL–II	–	–			
79	1	–	–	–			
80	1	–	–	–			
81	5	–	–	–			
82	1	–	–	–			
83	3	–	–	–			
84	1	–	–	–			
85	1	–	–	–			
86	2	–	–	–			
87	3	–	–	–			
88	3	–	–	–			
89	3	–	–	–			
90	3	–	–	–			
91	1	–	–	(–)			
92	1	–	–	–			
93	1	–	–	–			
94	1	–	–	–			
95	1	–	–	–			
96	3	–	–	–			
97	3	–	–	–			
98	1	–	–	–			
99	2	–	–	(LV)			
100	2	–	–	–			
Total	95						

based on correct use of grammatical morpheme -ed

$200 \div 100 = 2.00$ MLU

© 1993 Thinking Publications Duplication permitted for educational use only.

ANALYZING COMPLEXITY OF NOUN PHRASES

As in the analysis of each of the preceding syntactic structures, analysis of the complexity of the noun phrase results in a stage assignment. Stage assignments reflect the type and amount of elaboration of the noun phrase as well as the position of the noun phrase within the utterance. Stage assignments are based on data reported by Brown and Bellugi (1964), Cazden (1968), Ingram (1972), de Villiers and de Villiers (1973), Brown (1973), and Chapman (1978). Increases in complexity of the noun phrase occur with increases in utterance length, but the increases in complexity of the noun phrase are not simply increases in length. Column 8 of Table 3.4 summarizes the changes in the noun phrase with increases in utterance length. The summaries of changes reflect emergence of new ways to increase the complexity of the noun phrase and not mastery of the forms.

Judgments about the developmental complexity of the noun phrase are more difficult to make than with some of the preceding structures. One reason for this is that a vast majority of utterances contain a noun phrase and there is greater variability in the specificity of the noun phrase. Pragmatic requirements are such that not all utterances containing a noun phrase are in the most complex form that the child is capable of producing. In addition, many utterances contain only a noun phrase because the child is responding to a question from the other speaker or clarifying a previous utterance. Assignment of a stage to these utterances may underestimate the child's abilities. For these reasons, a greater number of practice utterances are provided to obtain experience in making these more difficult judgments. The following practice utterances have been selected to provide examples of the various types of noun phrases within transcripts and the considerations necessary for appropriately assigning stages to each. Cover the right side of the page, compare the noun phrases within the utterances to the descriptions provided in Table 3.4, and assign a stage. Then check judgments with those provided. The explanations should clarify differences.

(C reaches for box of cookies) more cookie/	Stages EI–II This utterance is an example of an elaborated noun phrase which includes an optional modifier (M) *more*. Because the noun phrase does not change in form from Early Stage I to Stage II, the range of stages is used.
(C points to picture in book) kitty/	Stages EI–II Because the modifier is optional in Stage EI and the form of the noun phrase does not change in Stage II, the stage range is the best assignment.
(C points to another picture in book) pretty kitty/	Stages EI–II This utterance includes the optional modifier that typifies the form of the elaborated noun phrase in Stages EI and II. The stage range is the best assignment.
(C watches as clinician rolls ball to M) that ball/	Stage III This utterance is an example of an elaborated noun phrase also, but it includes an optional demonstrative form, *that,* which emerges in Stage III.

(C points to picture in book)
that a baby/

Stage III
This utterance contains an elaborated noun phrase with two optional forms, a demonstrative *that* and an article *a*. It is presumed that the demonstrative represents a subject noun phrase and the article plus noun represents the object noun phrase. The verb is omitted. Utterances of this type and form emerge in Stage III. Consequently, Stage III is assigned to this utterance.

(C pulls tiny doll from bag and sets on table)
that a tiny baby/

Stage III
This utterance contains an article plus a modifier, *tiny*, plus a noun in the object noun phrase position with the demonstrative form in the subject noun phrase position. Noun phrases in this form appear in Stage III.

(C points to bus with toy kittens in it)
that alotta kikis/

Stage III
The use of *alotta* in this utterance represents an article and the optional modifier in the object position. A verb is not necessary to assign Stage III to this utterance.

(C moves to train in corner)
choo choo/

Stages EI–II
In this utterance, the noun phrase simply consists of a noun. Therefore, the stage range that should be assigned is Stage EI–II. The modifier for Stage EI through Stage II is an optional constituent.

(C holds puppy out to clinician)
kiss the puppy/

Stage III
Although this utterance contains a verb, the constituent that is the most significant is the object noun phrase, *the puppy*. This noun phrase comprises an article plus a noun. This form is characteristic of Stage III.

(C pushes puppy away)
hit that naughty puppy/

Stage III
The noun phrase in this utterance is in the object position. It contains a demonstrative, *that*, and a modifier, *naughty*, before the noun *puppy*. Noun phrases of this type are characteristic of Stage III.

(puppy jumps out of box)
that puppy jump/

Stage III

The noun phrase in this utterance is in the subject position. Subject noun phrases appear in Stage III. This is the best cue for stage assignment. But the form of this noun phrase also is consistent with Stage III in that there is a demonstrative, *that*, with the noun. No modifier is present, but the modifier is optional at this stage.

(C pushes puppy away)
that puppy licked my face/

Stage LIV/EV

There are two noun phrases in this utterance: a subject noun phrase, *that puppy,* and an object noun phrase, *my face.* The presence of a subject noun phrase suggests at least Stage III. However, the possessive pronoun *my* in the object noun phrase of a NP + VP complete utterance indicates Stage LIV/EV. The possessive is one of the optional constituents in Stage LIV/EV.

(M asks, "Where should we put the sprinkles?")
on that cookie/

Stage III

The noun phrase in this utterance contains a demonstrative, *that,* and a noun, *cookie,* in the object position. Noun phrases of this type and in this position are characteristic of Stage III.

(C points to cookie on plate)
I want that cookie/

Stage LIV/EV

There are two noun phrases in this utterance: a subject noun phrase, *I,* and an object noun phrase, *that cookie.* The object noun phrase is in Stage III form (demonstrative plus noun). The subject noun phrase is in the form of a pronoun, but stage assignment is more difficult. To assign Stage LIV, the subject noun phrase is obligatory where pragmatically appropriate, and a noun or a pronoun appears in the subject position. Because it was necessary for the child to include the subject noun phrase in his utterance due to pragmatic conventions, and he did, Stage LIV/EV is assigned.

(M points to picture in book and says, "What is that?")
a baby crying/

Stage III

The noun phrase in this utterance is in the subject position and consists of an article plus a noun. Both of these are indicative of Stage III.

(C shows finger to clinician)
hurt my little finger/

Stage LIV/EV
Although there is only one noun phrase and it is in the object position, the presence of the possessive pronoun *my* with the adjective *little* makes this noun phrase typical of Stage LIV/EV.

(C pushes puppy away)
he eatted my cookie/

Stage LIV/EV
The two noun phrases in this utterance are indicative of Stage LIV. The subject noun phrase pronoun and the object noun phrase possessive pronoun confirm Stage LIV/EV.

(C reaches for cookie on plate)
eat my big cookie/

Stage LIV/EV
This utterance contains only an object noun phrase, which could result in a lower stage assignment. But this noun phrase contains a possessive pronoun and an adjective preceding the noun. Noun phrases with these constituents are characteristic of Stage LIV/EV.

(C points to box in corner)
lotta doggies goes in there/

Stage LIV/EV
The most significant thing to note in this utterance is the lack of number agreement between the subject and the verb. Although this lack of number agreement continues to be a problem beyond Stage V, the presence of a subject noun phrase and an object noun phrase indicate at least Stage LIV. And with no further data on which to base a judgment, Stage LIV/EV is assigned. This would indicate that assigning a stage higher than Stage LIV/EV is not probable when analyzing noun phrases.

Now, with the experience gained from the practice utterances, return to the sample transcript and examine each utterance for the presence of one or more noun phrases. If there is no noun phrase in the utterance, mark a dash (–) for that utterance in the "Noun Phrase Elaboration" column on the Structural Stage Analysis Grid. When an utterance that contains a noun phrase is identified, compare that noun phrase to the descriptions of noun phrases in column 8 of Table 3.4 to determine the stage which best characterizes the complexity of the noun phrase or phrases in the utterance. Then record the stage number for that utterance in the "Noun Phrase Elaboration" column on the Structural Stage Analysis Grid. When each utterance has been examined for the presence of noun phrases and stage assignments have been recorded, compare results with the sample on pages 122–123.

Forty-six utterances containing noun phrases should have been identified. The noun phrases in this transcript ranged in complexity from Stages EI–II to Stage LIV/EV. These utterances will be tallied on the Syntactic Analysis Data Summary sheet after the complexity of two more syntactic structures have been analyzed.

Syntactic Analysis
Structural Stage Analysis Grid

Name of Child: *Bridget*

Annotations: *response to yes/no question* · *response to yes/no question plus explanation* · *repetition request*

Utterance Number	Number of Morphemes	Negation	Yes/No Questions	Wh-Questions	Noun Phrase Elaboration	Verb Phrase Elaboration	Complex
1	1	—	—	—	—		
2	2	—	—	—	—		
3	1	— (circled)	—	—	—		
4	1	—	—	—	EI–II		
5	4	—	—	—	EI–II		
6	1	—	EI–III	—	—		
7	2	—	—	EI–II	—		
8	1	—	—	—	EI–II		
9	1	—	—	—	EI–II		
10	1	—	—	—	—		
11	3	—	—	—	—		
12		—	—	—	—		
13	1	—	—	—	EI–II		
14	1	—	—	—	—		
15	4	—	—	—	LIV/EV		
16	2	—	—	EI–II	—		
17	4	—	—	—	///		
18	4	///	—	—	///		
19	2	—	—	EI–II	—		
20	4	///	—	—	LIV/EV		
21	4	EIV	—	—	LIV/EV		
22	2	—	—	—	///		
23	3	—	—	///	LIV/EV		
24	4	—	—	///	///		
25	2	—	—	—	///		

Utterance Number	Number of Morphemes	Negation	Yes/No Questions	Wh-Questions	Noun/Phrase Elaboration	Verb Phrase Elaboration	Complex
26	2	—	—	—	—		
27	2	—	—	—	EI–II		
28	2	—	—	—	—		
29	1	—	—	— (circled)	—		
30	1	—	—	—	—		
31	5	—	—	—	LIV/EV		
32	4	—	—	—	///		
33	4	— (circled)	—	—	LIV/EV		
34	1	—	—	—	—		
35	4	—	—	EIV	LIV/EV		
36	3	—	—	—	LIV/EV		
37	1	—	—	—	—		
38	1	—	—	—	—		
39	1	—	—	—	—		
40	1	—	—	—	EI–II		
41	1	—	—	—	EI–II		
42	1	—	—	—	—		
43	2	—	—	—	—		
44	2	—	—	—	LIV/EV		
45	3	—	—	—	LIV/EV		
46	3	—	—	—	—		
47	1	—	—	—	—		
48	1	—	—	—	—		
49	1	—	—	—	—		
50	1	—	—	—	EI–II		
Total	105						

© **1993 Thinking Publications** *Duplication permitted for educational use only.*

Syntactic Analysis
Structural Stage Analysis Grid

Name of Child **Bridget**

Utterance Number	Number of Morphemes	Negation	Yes/No Questions	Wh-Questions	Noun Phrase Elaboration	Verb Phrase Elaboration	Complex
51	1	—	—	—	—		
52	3	—	—	—	—		
53	1	—	—	—	—		
54	1	—	—	—	—		
55	1	—	—	—	—		
56	4	—	—	—	LIV/EV		
57	1	—	—	—	—		
58	1	—	—	—	EI–II		
59	1	—	—	— (circled)	—		
60	4	—	EI–III	—	III		
61	4	—	—	—	III		
62	3	—	—	—	III		
63	1	—	—	—	—		
64	1	—	—	—	—		
65	4	—	—	—	III		
66	2	—	—	EI–II	—		
67	1	—	—	—	—		
68	1	—	—	— (circled)	—		
69	1	—	—	—	—		
70	1	—	EI–III	—	EI–II		
71	1	—	—	—	EI–II		
72	3	—	—	—	EI–II		
73	3	—	—	—	EI–II		
74	1	—	—	— (circled)	—		
75	2	—	—	—	—		

repetition request

Utterance Number	Number of Morphemes	Negation	Yes/No Questions	Wh-Questions	Noun Phrase Elaboration	Verb Phrase Elaboration	Complex
76	1	—	—	—	—		
77	1	—	—	—	—		
78	3	LI–II	—	—	EI–II		
79	1	—	—	—	—		
80	1	—	—	—	—		
81	5	—	—	—	LIV/EV		
82	1	—	—	—	—		
83	3	—	—	—	—		
84	1	—	—	—	EI–II		
85	1	—	—	—	—		
86	2	—	—	—	EI–II		
87	3	—	—	—	EI–II		
88	3	—	—	—	EI–II		
89	3	—	—	—	EI–II		
90	3	—	—	—	EI–II		
91	1	—	—	— (circled)	—		
92	1	—	—	—	EI–II		
93	1	—	—	—	EI–II		
94	1	—	—	—	EI–II		
95	1	—	—	—	—		
96	3	—	—	LIV (circled)	—		
97	3	—	—	—	III		
98	1	—	—	—	—		
99	2	—	—	—	EI–II		
100	2	—	—	—	LIV/EV		
Total	95						

based on correct use of grammatical morpheme -ed

200 ÷ 100 = 2.00 MLU

© **1993 Thinking Publications** *Duplication permitted for educational use only.*

ANALYZING COMPLEXITY OF VERB PHRASES

The stage assignments that are made for verb phrase development are based on data reported by Klima and Bellugi (1966); Cazden (1968); Brown (1973); de Villiers and de Villiers (1973); and Chapman, Paul, and Wanska (1981). Column 9 of Table 3.4 summarizes the changes in complexity of the verb phrase and the stage at which those changes emerge. Changes in complexity of verb phrases overlap with developments in other structures more than some of the other structures analyzed. Most notably, increases in complexity of the verb phrase coincide with advances in the development of grammatical morphemes. Final interpretation of the developmental complexity of the verb phrase will be dependent upon the child's mastery of grammatical morphemes.

To determine the stage which best characterizes the child's level of verb phrase development, examine each utterance for the presence of a verb phrase. Then compare each verb phrase to the developments summarized in column 9 of Table 3.4 and assign a stage to the verb phrase in that utterance. Like the judgments made in analyzing noun phrase development, making judgments about verb phrases is more difficult than with some of the other syntactic structures. Therefore, a greater number of practice utterances will be provided for verb phrases than for some of the other structures. Cover the right side of the page, compare the utterance to the developments described in Table 3.4, and assign a stage. Check stage assignments with those provided and compare reasoning to the explanations provided.

(C falls down and looks at M)

fall down/

Stages EI–II

This utterance contains a verb plus a particle. Verb phrases of this form are used occasionally in Early Stage I but do not change in form through Stage II. The best stage assignment is the range of stages.

(puppy jumps out of box)

puppy jump/

Stages EI–II

This utterance contains a noun phrase and a verb phrase, with the verb phrase containing a main verb in an uninflected form. This form of the verb is consistent with Early Stage I through Stage II. The presence of the noun phrase has no bearing on the stage assignment.

(C curls up in doll bed, then sits up)

I is sleeping/

Stage III

The verb phrase in this utterance contains a main verb in the present progressive tense. The auxiliary is included, and even though it is in an incorrect form for first person, the inclusion of the auxiliary requires the assignment of Stage III.

(M and C looking at
picture book)

he could hit you/

Stage LIV/EV

The most significant thing to note for stage assignment is the presence of the modal auxiliary *could*. This type of auxiliary is characteristic of Stage LIV/EV.

(C points to picture in book)

baby cry/

Stages EI–II

The verb phrase in this utterance is in an uninflected form. Thus, the most appropriate stage assignment is Stage EI–II.

(another child is crying
in the hall)

baby crying/

Stages EI–II

The reason for the difficulty in assigning a stage to this utterance is that the present progressive *-ing* is used occasionally in Early Stage I and more consistently in Stage II. The best solution is to assign the range of stages.

(puppy crawls in clinician's
lap)

her gonna bite/

Stage II

The use of the semi-auxiliary *gonna* in this verb phrase indicates Stage II. The only time Stage II would be assigned as opposed to the range of Stages (EI–II) is when the semi-auxiliary or the copula is included without other information that could influence a higher stage assignment.

(C points to one of the
puppies)

she can jump/

Stage III

The presence of the present tense auxiliary *can* preceding the verb in this verb phrase indicates Stage III.

(puppy puts front paws up
on edge of box)

puppy'll jump/

Stage III

The verb phrase in this utterance also contains an auxiliary, *will*, but in this utterance it is in the contracted form.

(puppy chases heels of
clinician)
she's gonna bite you/

Stage LIV/EV

The verb phrase in this utterance contains the auxiliary *is*, the semi-auxiliary *gonna*, and the main verb *bite*. But the most important thing to take note of is that the semi-auxiliary complement *gonna bite* takes a noun phrase. Verb phrases of this type appear in Stage LIV/EV.

(clinician picks up puppy)
she bites/

Stage LV

The verb phrase in this utterance only contains a main verb. But the main verb includes correct number agreement in the use of regular third person singular present tense. This is the eighth grammatical morpheme and it is mastered in Late Stage V. The consistent use of this grammatical morpheme results in the assignment of Stage LV.

(C gestures toward puppy
in box)
she was a a naughty puppy/

Stage V+

The verb phrase in this utterance consists of the copula, or the verb *be*, as a main verb. It is in the past tense, a form that emerges in Stage V+. In addition, it is an uncontractible copula, which, as a grammatical morpheme, is mastered in Stage V+.

(C pulls toys out of toy box)
is big!/

Stage II

This utterance also contains a copula, *is,* but without tense or number inflection. The copula appears in this form in Stage II.

(as clinician leaves the
room, C turns to M)
she eatted my cookie/

Stage III

The main verb in this utterance is an irregular verb, but the child has marked the past tense of the verb by using the regular past tense *-ed* inflection. Overgeneralization of the past tense *-ed* occurs in Stage III.

(C relating story to M)
she was jumping on the couch/

Stage V+

The verb phrase in this utterance contains the past tense form of the verb *be* as an auxiliary. This form appears in Stage V+.

(C makes horse bump car
and says to M)
horsie bumped the car/

Stage LV

The main verb in this utterance includes the regular past tense
-ed inflection used correctly. Although Stage III is assigned for
incorrect or overgeneralized use, Stage LV is assigned for correct
use. This is due to the fact that the *-ed* inflection is mastered in
Late Stage V as a grammatical morpheme.

(C relating story to M)
he should go night-night/

Stage LIV/EV

This utterance contains a past tense modal auxiliary in the verb
phrase. Modals of this type appear in Stage LIV/EV.

(clinician puts cookie
toppings on table)
I have eaten those kind/

Stage V+

The verb phrase in this utterance is in the present perfect tense,
and the child has correctly marked the tense on the auxiliary
verb. This is a relatively infrequently occurring form in adult
conversation, and it is reported to be marked correctly only after
Stage V+.

(C referring to puppy)
I might get one/

Stage LIV/EV

The presence of the modal auxiliary in the verb phrase is the best
cue for stage assignment. Modals of this type appear in Stage
LIV/EV.

(clinician enters room and
C points to mat)
I was jumping on that/

Stage V+

This utterance contains the past tense form of the verb *be* as an
auxiliary verb. The verb *be* emerges in this form in Stage V+.

Now return to the sample transcript and examine each utterance for the presence of a verb phrase. As with the preceding structures, if there is no verb phrase in the utterance, mark a dash (–) for that utterance in the "Verb Phrase Elaboration" column on the Structural Stage Analysis Grid. For those utterances that do contain a verb phrase, record the stage number for the complexity of the verb phrase in that utterance in the "Verb Phrase Elaboration" column on the Structural Stage Analysis Grid. When each utterance has been examined for the presence of a verb phrase and stage assignments have been recorded, compare results with the sample on pages 128–129.

The sample transcript contained 39 utterances with verb phrases. The verb phrases in the utterances in the sample transcript ranged in complexity from Stages EI–II to Late Stage V. These verb phrases will be tallied on the Syntactic Analysis Data Summary sheet after the complexity of one more syntactic structure is analyzed.

Syntactic Analysis
Structural Stage Analysis Grid

Name of Child: Bridget

Annotations:
- *repetition request* → (Wh-Questions, Utterance 29)
- *response to yes/no question plus explanation* → (Negation, Utterance 33)

Utterance Number	Number of Morphemes	Negation	Yes/No Questions	Wh-Questions	Noun Phrase Elaboration	Verb Phrase Elaboration	Complex
26	2	–	–	–	–	EI–II	
27	2	–	–	–	EI–II	–	
28	2	–	–	–	–	EI–II	
29	1	–	–	(–)	–	–	
30	1	–	–	–	–	–	
31	5	–	–	–	LIV/EV	III	
32	4	–	–	–	–	LV	
33	4	(–)	–	–	LIV/EV	LV	
34	1	–	–	–	–	–	
35	4	–	–	EIV	LIV/EV	LV	
36	3	–	–	–	LIV/EV	III	
37	1	–	–	–	–	–	
38	1	–	–	–	–	EI–II	
39	1	–	–	–	–	–	
40	1	–	–	–	EI–II	–	
41	1	–	–	–	EI–II	–	
42	1	–	–	–	–	–	
43	2	–	–	–	–	–	
44	2	–	–	–	LIV/EV	III	
45	3	–	–	–	LIV/EV	III	
46	3	–	–	–	–	EI–II	
47	1	–	–	–	–	–	
48	1	–	–	–	–	–	
49	1	–	–	–	–	–	
50	1	–	–	–	EI–II	–	
Total	105						

Annotation:
- *response to yes/no question* → (Negation, Utterance 3)

Utterance Number	Number of Morphemes	Negation	Yes/No Questions	Wh-Questions	Noun Phrase Elaboration	Verb Phrase Elaboration	Complex
1	1	–	–	–	–	–	
2	2	–	–	–	–	EI–II	
3	1	(–)	–	–	–	–	
4	1	–	–	–	EI–II	–	
5	4	–	–	–	–	III	
6	1	–	EI–III	–	–	EI–II	
7	2	–	–	EI–II	–	–	
8	1	–	–	–	EI–II	–	
9	1	–	–	–	EI–II	–	
10	1	–	–	–	–	–	
11	3	–	–	–	–	EI–II	
12	1	–	–	–	–	–	
13	1	–	–	–	EI–II	–	
14	1	–	–	–	–	–	
15	4	–	–	–	LIV/EV	III	
16	2	–	–	EI–II	–	–	
17	4	–	–	–	III	III	
18	4	III	–	–	III	LV	
19	2	–	–	EI–II	–	–	
20	4	III	–	–	LIV/EV	LV	
21	4	EIV	–	–	LIV/EV	III	
22	2	–	–	–	III	III	
23	3	–	–	III	LIV/EV	LV	
24	4	–	–	III	III	III	
25	2	–	–	–	III	–	

128

Syntactic Analysis
Structural Stage Analysis Grid

Name of Child _Bridget_

repetition request

based on correct use of grammatical morpheme -ed

Utterance Number	Number of Morphemes	Negation	Yes/No Questions	Wh-Questions	Noun Phrase Elaboration	Verb Phrase Elaboration	Complex
51	1	–	–	–	–	–	
52	3	–	–	–	–	///	
53	1	–	–	–	–	–	
54	–	–	–	–	–	–	
55	1	–	–	–	–	–	
56	4	–	–	–	LIV/EV	///	
57	1	–	–	–	///	LV	
58	1	–	–	–	EI–II	LV	
59	1	–	EI–III	①	–	–	
60	4	–	–	–	///	LV	
61	4	–	–	–	///	LV	
62	3	–	–	–	///	–	
63	1	–	–	–	–	–	
64	1	–	–	–	///	LV	
65	4	–	EI–III	–	–	–	
66	2	–	–	EI–II	–	–	
67	1	–	–	–	–	–	
68	1	–	–	①	–	–	
69	1	–	–	–	–	–	
70	1	–	EI–III	–	–	–	
71	1	–	–	–	EI–II	EI–II	
72	3	–	–	–	EI–II	EI–II	
73	3	–	–	–	EI–II	EI–II	
74	1	–	–	①	–	–	
75	2	–	–	–	EI–II	EI–II	

Utterance Number	Number of Morphemes	Negation	Yes/No Questions	Wh-Questions	Noun Phrase Elaboration	Verb Phrase Elaboration	Complex
76	1	–	–	–	–	–	
77	1	–	–	–	–	–	
78	3	LI–II	–	–	EI–II	–	
79	1	–	–	–	–	–	
80	1	–	–	–	–	–	
81	5	–	–	–	LIV/EV	LV	
82	1	–	–	–	–	–	
83	3	–	–	–	–	–	
84	1	–	–	–	EI–II	–	
85	1	–	–	–	–	–	
86	2	–	–	–	EI–II	LV	
87	3	–	–	–	EI–II	///	
88	3	–	–	–	EI–II	///	
89	3	–	–	–	EI–II	///	
90	3	–	–	–	EI–II	///	
91	1	–	–	①	–	–	
92	1	–	–	–	EI–II	–	
93	1	–	–	–	EI–II	–	
94	1	–	–	–	EI–II	–	
95	1	–	–	–	–	–	
96	3	–	–	Ⓛ︎Ⓥ︎	–	LIV/EV	
97	3	–	–	–	///	–	
98	1	–	–	–	EI–II	–	
99	2	–	–	–	EI–II	–	
100	2	–	–	–	LIV/EV	///	
Total	95						

$200 \div 100 = 2.00$ MLU

© 1993 Thinking Publications *Duplication permitted for educational use only.*

ANALYZING COMPLEXITY OF COMPLEX SENTENCES

The last aspect of syntactic development that will be analyzed is the complex sentence. The frequency of occurrence of complex sentences in transcripts obtained from children within Brown's stages of linguistic production is very low. At the upper end of Brown's stages, typically less than 20 percent of the child's utterances are complex (Paul, 1981). And in the early stages, complex sentences are rarely used. The stage assignments that will be made for complex sentence development are based on data provided by Limber (1973) and Paul (1981). The data reported by Paul provide stage assignments on the basis of the stage at which 50 percent of the children in her sample used the structure and the stage at which 90 percent of the children in her sample used the structure. The data summarized in column 10 of Table 3.4 reflect the stage at which 50 percent of the children used the structure. The decision was made that data on complex sentence development will be at the emergence level rather than the mastery level, because this plan was followed for data on all other structures except grammatical morphemes.

To assign a stage to an utterance reflecting the developmental level of that utterance if it is a complex sentence, first identify the complex sentences in the transcript. This may be more difficult than making the stage assignments. Some practice in doing this was gained in the preceding chapter on semantic analysis. A few utterances were provided as examples of complex sentences. However, the practice provided here will be more extensive and will provide explanations for stage assignments. As described in Chapter 2, there are two main reasons that an utterance is considered complex. First, the utterance is considered complex if it contains two or more sentences within the utterance that are connected by conjunctions. These usually take the form of two or more full-sentence propositions connected by *and, but, so, or, before,* or *after*. Second, an utterance is considered complex if it contains a dependent clause (i.e., a sentence-like segment that contains a main verb) (Paul, 1981). These dependent clauses are embedded within the sentence and take a variety of forms, including infinitive clauses, wh-clauses, relative clauses, full propositional complements, and gerunds. Although the identification of these types of complex sentences becomes easier with practice, some practice utterances will be helpful before returning to the sample transcript for identification of the complex sentences. Cover the right side of the page, compare the utterance with the descriptions provided in column 10 of Table 3.4, and assign a stage. Then check assignments with the samples provided.

(C relating event to clinician)
doggie barked and barked/

Early Stage IV
This utterance contains the conjunction *and*. It is conjoining the two sentences, *the doggie barked* and *the doggie barked*.

(C continuing story)
doggie bite and I cried/

Early Stage IV
This utterance also contains the conjunction *and*. In this example, the two utterances that are conjoined are more obvious.

(C points to cookie on plate)
I want the one what's big/

Late Stage V
This utterance contains a relative clause, but the child has used a wh-word to introduce the clause. Even though the form is incorrect, Late Stage V is assigned. The relative clause modifies the noun *one*.

(C brushes flour off pants)
my shoes and pants are dirty/   Early Stage IV

This utterance is an example of another type of conjoined complex utterance. The two sentences that are conjoined are *my shoes are dirty* and *my pants are dirty*.

(C pulls on door)
I want to go/   Early Stage IV

This utterance contains a simple infinitive clause. To assign this stage, the child must use the full infinitive, not the catenative form (*wanna*) or a reduction (*go* for *to go*).

(C picks up plastic animal)
pretend he's a monster/   Stage III

This utterance contains a full propositional complement. The complement *he's a monster* is a full sentence and may or may not be introduced by the word *that*.

(C pulls plastic animal
out of bag)
I know what that is/   Early Stage IV

This example contains a simple wh-clause. The sentence *that is* is linked to the main sentence with a wh-word.

(C holds up doll dress)
this is for her to wear/   Late Stage V

This utterance contains an infinitive clause with a subject different than the subject of the main verb.

(C gestures to cupcakes
on rack)
the ones what have hats
on are mine/   Late Stage V

This utterance contains a relative clause, *what have hats on*. The relative clause modifies the noun *ones*. Again, the relative clause introducer does not have to be correct to give the child credit for use of the relative clause.

(M asks, "Why did you do
that?" after C eats handful
of cookie dough)
I felt like eating it/   Stage V+

This utterance contains a gerund clause, *eating it*. Gerund clauses include a verb plus *-ing* used within a noun clause.

(C picks up marking pen)
help me draw/   Stage V+

This utterance contains an unmarked infinitive clause. These are usually introduced by one of the following: *let, help, watch,* or *make.*

(C opens game box)
I'll show you how to do it/ Stage V+

This utterance contains a wh-infinitive clause. These are marked with both a wh-word and *to*.

(C starts to search toy box)
I think I know where it is/ Stage LIV/EV

This is an example of double embedding. It contains an embedded clause, *where it is,* that is embedded within another clause, *I know,* that is embedded within the main proposition *I think.*

These examples of types of complex sentences should be helpful in identifying complex sentences within the sample transcript. In addition, the explanations as to why each is considered complex should help in making stage assignments. Now, return to the sample transcript and examine each utterance to determine if it is an example of a complex sentence. If an utterance is not a complex sentence, mark a dash (–) in the "Complex" column on the Structural Stage Analysis Grid. If an utterance is complex, compare it to the descriptions of types of complex sentences in column 10 of Table 3.4 and assign a stage to the utterance. After each utterance has been examined to determine if it is complex and the stage assignment has been recorded, compare results to the sample provided on pages 133–134.

The sample transcript contained only one utterance that was an example of a complex sentence. With practice, the transcript can be scanned for examples of complex sentences very quickly, since very few complex sentences occur in transcripts of children within Brown's stages of linguistic production. Also, identifying complex sentences is easier to do after a verb phrase analysis has been completed. Judgments about the verb phrase typically illuminate the clause structure of the utterance, and the decision about whether the utterance is a complex sentence is made during verb phrase analysis.

Now that all the boxes on the Structural Stage Analysis Grid have been filled in, the data obtained from analyzing the preceding seven syntactic structures must be analyzed. The data obtained from analysis of these seven aspects of syntactic production will be combined with the MLU data and length distribution analysis to provide an interpretation of the structural complexity of this child's productions.

SUMMARY AND INTERPRETATION

To summarize the analysis of syntactic structures, results from the analysis of each structure must be transferred to the Syntactic Analysis Data Summary sheet. This tally sheet will display the range of performance by the child for each of the syntactic structures and the relationship between each. The visual display can be helpful in understanding the assignment of the Most Typical Stage and the Most Advanced Stage for each structure.

The first step in summarizing the analysis data is to transfer the percent use computations for each grammatical morpheme from the Grammatical Morpheme Analysis Sheet into the appropriate stage box on the Data Summary sheet. The percent use for the present progressive tense of the verb -*ing* is entered next to the number 1 in the box for Stage II—Grammatical Morphemes. But since there were no instances of the present progressive tense (i.e., present tense progressive aspect) in the sample transcript, put a dash (–) next to number 1. The percent use for the regular plural -*s* is recorded next to number 2 in the box for Stage II—Grammatical Morphemes. In the sample transcript, 100 percent correct use of the regular plural in obligatory contexts was obtained, so record 100 percent next to number 2. Now proceed through the Grammatical

Syntactic Analysis
Structural Stage Analysis Grid

Name of Child: *Bridget*

response to yes/no question

Utterance Number	Number of Morphemes	Negation	Yes/No Questions	Wh-Questions	Noun Phrase Elaboration	Verb Phrase Elaboration	Complex
1	1	–	–	–	–	–	–
2	2	–	–	–	–	EI–II	–
3	1	(–)	–	–	–	–	–
4	1	–	–	–	EI–II	–	–
5	4	–	–	–	–	III	–
6	1	–	EI–III	–	EI–II	EI–II	–
7	2	–	–	EI–II	–	–	–
8	1	–	–	–	EI–II	–	–
9	1	–	–	–	EI–II	–	–
10	1	–	–	–	–	–	–
11	3	–	–	–	–	EI–II	–
12	1	–	–	–	–	–	–
13	1	–	–	EI–II	EI–II	–	–
14	1	–	–	–	–	–	–
15	4	–	–	–	LIV/EV	III	–
16	2	–	–	EI–II	–	–	–
17	4	–	–	–	III	III	–
18	4	III	–	–	III	LV	–
19	2	–	–	EI–II	–	LV	–
20	4	III	–	–	LIV/EV	III	–
21	4	EIV	–	–	LIV/EV	III	–
22	2	–	–	–	III	III	–
23	3	–	–	III	III	LV	–
24	4	–	–	III	III	III	–
25	2	–	–	–	III	–	–

repetition request

response to yes/no question plus explanation

Utterance Number	Number of Morphemes	Negation	Yes/No Questions	Wh-Questions	Noun Phrase Elaboration	Verb Phrase Elaboration	Complex
26	2	–	–	–	–	EI–II	–
27	2	–	–	–	EI–II	–	–
28	2	–	–	–	–	EI–II	–
29	1	(–)	–	(–)	–	–	–
30	1	–	–	–	–	–	–
31	5	–	–	–	LIV/EV	III	–
32	4	–	–	–	–	LV	–
33	4	–	–	–	LIV/EV	LV	–
34	1	–	–	–	–	–	–
35	4	–	–	EIV	LIV/EV	LV	–
36	3	–	–	–	LIV/EV	III	–
37	1	–	–	–	–	–	–
38	1	–	–	–	–	EI–II	–
39	1	–	–	–	–	–	–
40	1	–	–	–	EI–II	LV	–
41	1	–	–	–	EI–II	–	–
42	1	–	–	–	–	–	–
43	2	–	–	–	–	–	–
44	2	–	–	–	LIV/EV	III	–
45	3	–	–	–	LIV/EV	III	–
46	3	–	–	–	–	EI–II	–
47	1	–	–	–	–	–	–
48	1	–	–	–	–	–	–
49	1	–	–	–	EI–II	–	–
50	1	–	–	–	EI–II	–	–
Total	105						

© 1993 Thinking Publications *Duplication permitted for educational use only.*

Syntactic Analysis
Structural Stage Analysis Grid

Name of Child: **Bridget**

Utterance Number	Number of Morphemes	Negation	Yes/No Questions	Wh-Questions	Noun Phrase Elaboration	Verb Phrase Elaboration	Complex
51	1	–	–	–	–	–	–
52	3	–	–	–	–	III	EIV
53	1	–	–	–	–	–	–
54	1	–	–	–	–	–	–
55	1	–	–	–	–	–	–
56	4	–	–	–	LIV/EV	III	–
57	1	–	–	–	–	–	–
58	1	–	–	EI-II	–	–	–
59	1	–	–	(–)	–	–	–
60	4	–	EI-III	–	III	LV	–
61	4	–	–	–	III	LV	–
62	3	–	–	–	III	–	–
63	1	–	–	–	–	–	–
64	1	–	–	–	–	–	–
65	4	–	–	–	III	LV	–
66	2	–	–	EI-II	–	–	–
67	1	–	–	(–)	–	–	–
68	1	–	–	–	EI-II	–	–
69	1	–	–	–	EI-II	EI-II	–
70	1	–	EI-III	–	EI-II	EI-II	–
71	1	–	–	–	EI-II	–	–
72	3	–	–	–	–	–	–
73	3	–	–	(–)	–	–	–
74	1	–	–	–	–	–	–
75	2	–	–	–	–	EI-II	–

(annotation: repetition request — pointing to Wh-Questions column)

Utterance Number	Number of Morphemes	Negation	Yes/No Questions	Wh-Questions	Noun Phrase Elaboration	Verb Phrase Elaboration	Complex
76	1	–	–	–	–	–	–
77	1	–	–	–	–	III	–
78	3	LI-II	–	–	EI-II	–	–
79	1	–	–	–	–	–	–
80	1	–	–	–	–	–	–
81	5	–	–	–	LIV/EV	LV	–
82	1	–	–	–	–	–	–
83	3	–	–	–	EI-II	–	–
84	1	–	–	–	EI-II	–	–
85	1	–	–	–	–	–	–
86	2	–	–	–	EI-II	LV	–
87	3	–	–	–	EI-II	III	–
88	3	–	–	–	EI-II	III	–
89	3	–	–	–	EI-II	III	–
90	3	–	–	–	EI-II	III	–
91	1	–	–	(–)	–	–	–
92	1	–	–	–	–	–	–
93	1	–	–	–	EI-II	–	–
94	1	–	–	–	EI-II	–	–
95	1	–	–	–	–	–	–
96	3	–	–	(LV)	–	LIV/EV	–
97	3	–	–	–	III	–	–
98	1	–	–	–	–	–	–
99	2	–	–	–	EI-II	–	–
100	2	–	–	–	LIV/EV	III	–
Total	95						

(annotation: based on correct use of ...tial morpheme -ed)

$$200 \div 100 = 2.00\ MLU$$

134

© 1993 **Thinking Publications** *Duplication permitted for educational use only.*

Morphemes Analysis Sheet and enter the remaining percentages for grammatical morpheme use next to the appropriate numbers on the Data Summary sheet. If there are no instances of a particular grammatical morpheme in the transcript and no obligatory contexts for that grammatical morpheme, put a dash (–) next to the number for that grammatical morpheme on the Data Summary sheet. If there were no instances of use, but some number of obligatory contexts for a particular grammatical morpheme, put a zero next to the number for that grammatical morpheme. This notation differentiates those grammatical morphemes that were not used in the obligatory contexts from those grammatical morphemes for which no data were obtained.

The next step in summarizing analysis data is to tally the occurrences of each stage for each of the syntactic structures analyzed. Using the Structural Stage Analysis Grid, record the stage number assigned to each instance of negation on the Data Summary sheet. If a particular utterance was assigned a range of stages (e.g., *no* + noun = Stages LI/EII-II), be certain to record that range on the Data Summary sheet. When all negations have been tallied, tally the stage number assigned to each yes/no question on the Data Summary sheet. Again record a range of stages if that is the notation on the Structural Stage Analysis Grid. Next, tally the stage number assigned to each wh-question on the Data Summary sheet. Then tally the stage number assigned to each noun phrase and the stage number assigned to each verb phrase. Finally, tally the stage number assigned to each complex sentence. Remember that for some structures, only a tally is entered at a particular stage. For other structures, a range of stages is tallied. This is indicated by a line drawn through as many boxes as necessary and the tally marked at the right-hand end of that line.

Once a stage has been tallied for each instance of each structure, check tallies with the sample Data Summary sheet on page 136. The Data Summary sheet provides a visual display allowing comparison of the developmental complexity of the structures analyzed for this particular child. Cursory examination of this visual display reveals a great deal of variability in the developmental complexity of the struc-

tures analyzed for this child. Although this may seem inappropriate, considerable variation in the developmental complexity of a particular structure and across structures is expected. In fact, the developmental level of a particular structure may vary as much as two stages on either side of the most frequently occurring level of that structure (Miller, 1981). This variability is the result of the ongoing nature of linguistic development. Most children do not master a single form of a particular structure (e.g., subject noun phrase elaboration) before going on to work on the production of another form of that structure (e.g., subject noun phrase pronouns). Rather, the child works on the production of a variety of forms at the same time, and a sampling of the child's production abilities at a single point in time will reveal many forms to be at a particular level of complexity, with some instances of more advanced forms and some instances of less advanced forms. Also, not all of the forms at earlier stages are incorrect (e.g., use of regular plural *-s*); rather, their continued use would be expected. This adds variability as children advance through stages of linguistic production. Ironically, minimal variability, as opposed to considerable variability, may be indicative of a problem in language production (Miller, 1981).

This expected variability does make the interpretation of the data difficult. For this reason, interpretation will be based upon two stage assignments for each syntactic structure. First, a stage number will be assigned for each syntactic structure on the basis of the most frequently occurring stage for that structure. This means that the Data Summary sheet will be examined and the number of instances of a particular stage for each structure will be counted. The stage with the greatest number of tallies is considered to be the most frequently occurring stage. This stage is considered to reflect the child's typical performance for that structure and is labeled the Most Typical Stage. Second, a stage number will be assigned for each structure on the basis of the Most Advanced Stage for that structure. The highest stage number for each structure will be identified regardless of the frequency of occurrence of that stage. This Most Advanced Stage reflects the forms the child is in the process of acquiring.

Syntactic Analysis
Data Summary

Name of Child *Bridget*

Stage	Grammatical Morphemes	Negation	Yes/No Questions	Wh-Questions	Noun Phrase	Verb Phrase	Complex Sentences
Early I							
Late I/ Early II							
II	1. — 2. *100%* 3. *100%*	/		////	HHt HHt HHt HHt //	HHt HHt	
III	4. *0%* 5. *100%*	//	///	//	HHt HHt /	HHt HHt HHt //	
Early IV		/		/			/
Late IV/ Early V					HHt HHt ///	/	
Late V	6. *33%* 7. *43%* 8. *0%* 9. *35%* 10. *100%*			/		HHt HHt /	
V+	11. *50%* 12. *50%* 13. — 14. —						
V++							

© **1993 Thinking Publications** *Duplication permitted for educational use only.*

Finally, these two stage assignments for each structure (Most Typical Stage and Most Advanced Stage) are compared to each other, to the obtained MLU, and to the child's chronological age for interpretation. Like the variability expected for an individual structure, the stage assignments are expected to vary as much as two stages on either side of the MLU stage assignment (Miller, 1981). Again, variability is expected and minimal variability may indicate a problem in syntactic aspects of language production.

Interpretation of data may be facilitated by transferring data obtained to the Syntactic Analysis Summary and Interpretation sheet (see page 139). First, record the MLU obtained from the morphemic analysis. An MLU of 2.00 morphemes was obtained for the 100-utterance sample transcript, so record this in the blank for MLU on the Summary and Interpretation sheet. Next, by comparing this to Table 3.4, it can be seen that this MLU is within the range of MLUs for Stage II (2.00–2.49 morphemes). Record Stage II in the blank indicating the stage assigned on the basis of MLU. This stage assignment is considered a pivot point to which other structures will be compared.

It is helpful also to complete the variability about the mean on the Summary and Interpretation sheet using the formula from page 93 and the values from Table 3.2. The MLU for this child was 0.45 standard deviations below the expected mean. Now record the upper and lower bound lengths obtained from the length distribution analysis. The upper bound length of 5 morphemes raises concerns about variations in utterance length for the obtained MLU.

Next, the Most Typical Stage and the Most Advanced Stage will be determined for each structure analyzed. The stage assignments for grammatical morphemes are the most difficult to make because these stage assignments are not based on the frequency of occurrence of a stage. These stage assignments are based on the percentages compiled for each grammatical morpheme. Consider the Most Typical Stage first. On the Data Summary sheet, note that of the three grammatical morphemes mastered in Stage II, this child used two at the mastery level. No data were obtained on the remaining grammatical morpheme for this stage. For

Stage III grammatical morphemes, this child used one at the mastery level. The remaining grammatical morpheme for this stage was assigned a 0 percent use, which is different from no data, as previously discussed. For Stage Late V, percentages ranging from 0 percent to 100 percent use in obligatory contexts were obtained. In Stage V+, 50 percent use for two grammatical morphemes was obtained, and no data on the remaining two grammatical morphemes were available. To assign the Most Typical Stage, the stage which reflects consistent use of the grammatical morphemes of that stage at the mastery level must be determined. Because 0 percent use was obtained for the preposition ON, grammatical morpheme #4 in Stage III, that stage cannot be assigned. Thus Stage II is assigned as the Most Typical Stage. If data on grammatical morpheme #4 had indicated greater than 90 percent correct use, Stage III would be assigned as the Most Typical Stage. Record this in the appropriate blank on the Summary and Interpretation sheet.

To assign the Most Advanced Stage for grammatical morphemes, examine the Data Summary sheet for the stage that reflects more than 0 percent use for any of the grammatical morphemes in that stage. In the sample transcript, the child used grammatical morphemes #11 and #12 in 50 percent of the obligatory contexts. Thus, Stage V+ is assigned as the Most Advanced Stage. If no data or 0 percent use had been obtained for grammatical morphemes #11 and #12, Stage Late V would be assigned as the Most Advanced Stage. But since this child is beginning to use the contractible auxiliary and the uncontractible copula (grammatical morphemes #11 and #12) in some of the obligatory contexts, Stage V+ can be considered the Most Advanced Stage for grammatical morphemes. Record this stage as the Most Advanced Stage for grammatical morphemes on the Summary and Interpretation sheet.

Determination of the Most Typical Stage and the Most Advanced Stage for the remaining structures is considerably easier than it was for grammatical morphemes. Beginning with negation, there were four negative structures in the sample transcript: one at the Stage LI/EII to Stage II level, two at the Stage III level, and one at the Early Stage IV level. The stage with the

137

greatest number of tallies is Stage III. Record this stage number as the Most Typical Stage for negation. The Most Advanced Stage for negation is Early Stage IV due to the single instance at that level. Record this stage number as the Most Advanced Stage for negation.

Turning to yes/no questions, there were three yes/no questions tallied on the Data Summary sheet and all of them were typical of Stages EI–III. Thus, Stage EI–III is assigned as the Most Typical Stage and as the Most Advanced Stage. Record this in the appropriate blanks on the Summary and Interpretation sheet.

For wh-questions, there were four questions tallied at Stages EI–II, two at Stage III, one at Stage EIV and one at Stage Late V. The Most Typical Stage is EI–II and the Most Advanced Stage is Late V. Record these in the appropriate blanks on the Summary and Interpretation sheet.

For noun phrase expansion, the Data Summary sheet reveals 22 utterances in which the noun phrase was typical of Stages EI–II, 11 utterances in which the noun phrase was typical of Stage III, and 13 utterances in which the noun phrase was typical of Stage LIV/EV. The most frequently assigned stage was Stage EI–II, so record this under the Most Typical Stage. The Most Advanced Stage was Stage LIV/EV. Record Stage LIV/EV in the blank for "Noun Phrase Expansion" under the Most Advanced Stage on the Summary and Interpretation sheet.

For verb phrase expansion, there were 10 utterances in which the verb phrase was typical of Stage EI–II, 17 utterances in which the verb phrase was typical of Stage III, 1 utterance in which the verb phrase was typical of Stage LIV/EV, and 11 utterances in which the verb phrase was typical of Stage Late V. The most frequently assigned stage was Stage III, of which there were 17 instances. Record Stage III as the Most Typical Stage for verb phrase expansion on the Summary and Interpretation Sheet. The Most Advanced Stage for Verb Phrase Expansion was Stage Late V, with 11 instances. Record Stage Late V as the Most Advanced Stage for verb phrase expansion on the Summary and Interpretation sheet.

Finally, examining complex sentences, note that only one complex sentence was in the sample transcript and it was an example of an Early Stage IV complex sentence. Thus, Stage EIV is assigned as the Most Typical Stage and the Most Advanced Stage for complex sentences. Record this on the Summary and Interpretation sheet.

Now check the recording of the stage assignments and the determination of Most Typical Stage and Most Advanced Stage for each of the syntactic structures with the sample provided on page 139. As previously mentioned, final interpretation is based upon three comparisons: (1) the Most Typical Stage to MLU stage; (2) the Most Typical Stage to the Most Advanced Stage; and (3) MLU stage to the child's chronological age.

Comparison of Most Typical Stage to MLU Stage

When comparing the Most Typical Stage for each of the syntactic structures analyzed to the stage determined by the obtained MLU, considerable variability is evident. The MLU stage is the same as the stage assigned as the Most Typical Stage for grammatical morphemes. The Most Typical Stage for negation is one stage above the MLU stage. For yes/no questions, the MLU stage is the midpoint in the range of stages assigned as the Most Typical Stage. For wh-questions, the MLU Stage is within the range of stages assigned as the Most Typical Stage.

The Most Typical Stage for noun phrase expansion is the same as the MLU stage. The Most Typical Stage for verb phrase expansion is one stage higher than the MLU stage. Finally, the Most Typical Stage for complex sentences is two stages above the MLU stage.

What is the conclusion from this first set of comparisons? For five of the structures analyzed, the variability present would be expected on the basis of the obtained MLU. But the Most Typical Stage for one of the structures appears to be higher than would be expected on the basis of MLU. The Most Typical Stage for complex sentences is two stages above the stage for MLU. One explanation could be that the sample is not representative and contains many elliptical utterances, resulting in an artificially low MLU. Another explanation could be that

Syntactic Analysis
Summary and Interpretation

Name of Child *Bridget*

1. Mean Length of Utterance
   in Morphemes (MLU): _____ 2.00 _____ morphemes

   Structural Stage by MLU: Stage _____ II _____

   Upper Bound Length: _____ 5 _____ morphemes

   Lower Bound Length: _____ 1 _____ morphemes

   CA = 28 mos.
   use 27 mos. figures
   $$\frac{2.00 - 2.23 = -.45}{.510}$$

2. Most Typical Structural Stage

   Grammatical Morphemes: Stage _____ II _____

   Negation: Stage _____ III _____

   Yes/No Questions: Stage _____ EI-III _____

   Wh-Questions: Stage _____ EI-II _____

   Noun Phrase Expansion: Stage _____ II _____

   Verb Phrase Expansion: Stage _____ III _____

   Complex Sentences: Stage _____ EIV _____

3. Most Advanced Structural Stage

   Grammatical Morphemes: Stage _____ V+ _____

   Negation: Stage _____ EIV _____

   Yes/No Questions: Stage _____ EI-III _____

   Wh-Questions: Stage _____ LV _____

   Noun Phrase Expansion: Stage _____ LIV/EV _____

   Verb Phrase Expansion: Stage _____ LV _____

   Complex Sentences: Stage _____ EIV _____

© 1993 Thinking Publications *Duplication permitted for educational use only.*

the child's MLU is lagging behind the child's abilities in formulating complex sentences, implying a length constraint. In other words, for some reason, physiological or cognitive, this child is unable to produce utterances as long as the complexity of those utterances would suggest. But this Most Typical Stage was assigned on the basis of only one utterance. Concluding a length constraint on the basis of one utterance would be inappropriate. Should a problem in terms of the length of utterance be suspected with this amount of data? Here is where the next set of comparisons enters the picture.

Comparison of Most Typical Stage to Most Advanced Stage

Results of the sample analysis revealed a difference of five stages between the Most Typical Stage and the Most Advanced Stage for grammatical morphemes. The Most Typical Stage for negation was one stage below the Most Advanced Stage. For yes/no questions, the Most Typical Stage was the same as the Most Advanced Stage. For wh-questions, the Most Advanced Stage was four stages higher than the Most Typical Stage. The Most Typical Stage for noun phrase expansion was three stages below the Most Advanced Stage. For verb phrase expansion, the Most Advanced Stage was three stages higher than the Most Typical Stage. Finally, the Most Typical Stage for complex sentences was the same as the Most Advanced Stage.

Returning to the question from the previous section, there is a reasonable gap between the Most Typical Stage and the Most Advanced Stage for five of the seven structures analyzed. This suggests that this child is exploring more sophisticated means of producing negative structures, wh-questions, noun phrases, and verb phrases as well as the consistency with which grammatical morphemes are used in obligatory contexts. For yes/no questions, her abilities appear to have plateaued. Such plateaus are common in normal language acquisition (Miller, 1981). The variability observed is typical as the child works on more sophisticated accomplishments for some structures and plateaus in her abilities in other areas. And with only one complex utterance in the sample,

it could be that no gap is present for complex sentences. The lack of a gap between the Most Typical Stage and the Most Advanced Stage for yes/no questions and complex sentences is not reason for concern for this particular child. The gap between the Most Typical Stage and the Most Advanced Stage is one of the things examined in interpreting the summary information. If no gap is observed between the Most Typical Stage and the Most Advanced Stage for most of the structures analyzed, there may be reason for concern about the child's ability to accomplish advances in form for the production of some structures. This will be discussed in greater detail with the implications for remediation.

Overall, it should be concluded that the transcript obtained from the sample child evidences a reasonable amount of variability in the developmental level of the structures analyzed. The Most Typical Stage for the seven structures analyzed are at levels appropriate for the MLU stage, and the relationship between the Most Typical Stage and the Most Advanced Stage reflects plateauing for some structures and acquisition of more sophisticated forms than typical performance for other structures. One more comparison is necessary.

Comparison of MLU Stage to Child's Age

Final interpretation of the analysis data requires comparison of the MLU stage to the child's age. Regardless of the relationship between the MLU stage and the Most Typical Stage and the relationship between the Most Typical Stage and the Most Advanced Stage, this final comparison is crucial. When the child's age is higher than the age range for the MLU Stage as reported by Miller and Chapman (1981), it might be concluded that a delay in production abilities exists. When the child's age falls within the age range for the MLU Stage, it can be assumed that the length of the child's utterances is appropriate for his age. And when the child's age is lower than the age range for the MLU Stage, the appropriate conclusion is that the child's production abilities are advanced for his age. These age ranges also can be translated into mental age expectations (Miller and Chapman, 1981). For example, a

5-year-old child with cognitive abilities of a 2-year-old would be expected to produce utterances typical in length and complexity of Stage LI/EII. Thus, the MLU stage assignment is pivotal in the interpretation of age level and structural complexity.

The age of the child in the sample transcript is 28 months. On the basis of the predicted ages for Brown's stages (Miller and Chapman, 1981), this child falls within Stage II. And the MLU stage is Stage II. Thus, this child is producing utterances that are of an appropriate length for her age. And from the previous comparisons, it was concluded that she is producing utterances that reflect an appropriate amount of variability in developmental complexity. The sample transcript reflects normal development of this child's syntax.

IMPLICATIONS FOR REMEDIATION

In review, the following are the results of comparison that are reason for concern. First, if age (or cognitive level) is higher than the age range for the MLU stage, it can be concluded that a delay in language production exists. Second, if the Most Typical Stage for some or all of the syntactic structures analyzed is lower than the MLU stage, it can be concluded that a delay in some aspect of syntax production exists. Third, if no gap is present between the Most Typical Stage and the Most Advanced Stage for most or all of the syntactic structures analyzed, it can be concluded that a delay in some aspect of syntax production exists.

As suggested by Fey (1986), factors in addition to MLU stage, Most Typical Stage, and Most Advanced Stage must be considered before concluding that the delay warrants intervention. These include no change versus dramatic change in language production during the past few months; negative versus positive reactions by parents and other caregivers to the child's communication attempts; history of middle ear problems in the child versus no such history; nonstimulating versus stimulating linguistic environments. A child with a depressed MLU in combination with recent dramatic gains in language production and a stimulating linguistic environment may not be a candidate for remediation. On the other hand, a child with a low MLU, recurrent ear infections, and parents who are reacting negatively to the delay may need remediation.

How is the information from syntactic analysis procedures used in planning remediation of the observed delays? While this could be the topic of another extensive volume, the implication is obvious. Based on the sequence of accomplishments in normal language acquisition, forms that would appear next in the sequence to increase the length and complexity of the child's utterances can be taught. This may appear to oversimplify the process, but clinical experience has shown that from the detailed analysis of syntactic aspects of language production, the forms likely to emerge next are quite predictable. Advances are likely to be seen first in structures where a gap exists between the Most Typical Stage and the Most Advanced Stage. It also has been shown that the forms occurring next in the developmental sequence can be taught even when no gap exists between the Most Typical Stage and the Most Advanced Stage.

Consideration of as many structures as have been examined in this analysis has three purposes. First, variability in performance of each structure is assumed; therefore, data on as many structures as it is possible to obtain are necessary to capture both variability and consistency. Second, stage assignments for individual structures are considered estimates of overall production abilities; therefore, data on as many structures as it is possible to obtain are necessary to be confident of the estimates. Third, each structure provides the basis for a set of remediation goals and objectives; therefore, data on as many structures as it is possible to obtain are necessary for appropriate remediation. Only with such extensive analysis is documentation of the nature of the delay possible. The goals and objectives for remediation of the identified delay are the logical outgrowth of this extensive analysis.

CHAPTER 4
Pragmatic Analysis

Analysis of language is not complete without examination of pragmatic aspects of language production. Such analysis is necessary for documenting a child's ability to use the semantic and syntactic aspects of the language system appropriately and/or for identifying a child's problems with language use. Delays in pragmatic abilities may co-occur with delays in syntax or semantics, and it appears that delays may occur in isolation. Failure to examine the pragmatic aspects of the child's linguistic production system may result in overlooking the child with normal syntax and semantics who has problems with pragmatics. In addition, for the child whose semantic and/or syntactic delays previously have been identified, failure to examine pragmatic aspects of production results in an incomplete description of the language production delay.

Procedures similar to those demonstrated here have been described in the literature as revealing developmental changes in pragmatic aspects of oral language and/or deviations from what is considered to be normal conversation (Roth and Spekman, 1984; Damico, 1985; Prutting and Kirchner, 1987; Penn, 1988; Wetherby and Prizant, 1992). Numerous studies have described differences in pragmatic aspects of oral language for individuals with language impairment. Table 4.1 summarizes potential difficulties of children with specific language impairment. The formats for identifying each of the characteristics described differ for each author. Some of the characteristics could be identified using the procedures described here.

TABLE 4.1

A PROFILE OF PRAGMATIC CHARACTERISTICS OF THE CHILD WITH SPECIFIC LANGUAGE IMPAIRMENT

CONVERSATIONAL FUNCTIONS	LINGUISTIC FORMS	INVESTIGATIONS
REQUESTING	Few requests are grammatically complete compared to normal-language children	Prinz (1982)
COMMENTING	Comments may be stereotypic in nature	Gallagher and Craig (1984) Blank, Gessner, and Esposito (1979)
REFERENCING PRESUPPOSITIONS	Their presuppositions depend more on pronominals than do those of normals	Skarakis and Greenfield (1982)
TURN TAKING	They relate to preceding discourse using more substitution devices and more inadequate forms	van Kleeck and Frankel (1981) Liles (1985a, 1985b, 1987)

Continued on next page

143

TABLE 4.1—Continued

CONVERSATIONAL FUNCTIONS	LINGUISTIC FORMS	INVESTIGATIONS
TURN TAKING (continued)	Turns involve less other-directed speech and are shorter in length	Craig and Evans (1989)
	Their utterances are less "adjacent" than age-mates so that the SLI child takes longer to follow a previous speaker with a turn of his/her own	Craig and Evans (1989)
	They do not use interruptions to gain the turn at speaking	Craig and Evans (1989)
RESPONDING	Responses to requests for clarification are structurally diffuse	Gallagher and Darnton (1978) Brinton, Fujiki, Winkler, and Loeb (1986)
	Responses to other types of speech acts are likely to be unrelated, inappropriate, and variable	Blank et al. (1979) Brinton and Fujiki (1982) Craig and Gallagher (1986) Leonard (1986) Leonard, Camarata, Rowan, and Chapman (1982)
NARRATIVES	Their narratives are less complete and include different distributions of cohesive ties	Liles (1985a, 1985b, 1987) Merritt and Liles (1987)
SPEECH ADJUSTMENTS	Their speech style modifications reflect fewer internal state questions and less adjustment of utterance length and complexity	Fey, Leonard, and Wilcox (1981)

From "Pragmatic Characteristics of the Child with Specific Language Impairment: An Interactionist Perspective" by H. Craig, 1991, (pp. 178–179) in T. Gallagher (Ed.), *Pragmatics of Language*, San Diego, CA: Singular Publishing Group. © 1991 by Singular Publishing Group. Reprinted by permission.

In spite of the attention that analysis of pragmatic aspects of conversation has received in recent years, no real normative data has emerged. According to Brinton (1990), the flurry of activity described as the pragmatic revolution has not yielded the primary goal of this activity: making "clinical research and intervention easier" (p. 8). Specific typologies of conversational moves and variations in specificity, conciseness, and style have been identified as occurring in individuals with language impairment (Fey and Leonard, 1983; Brinton and Fujiki, 1984; McTear, 1985; Brinton, Fujiki, Loeb, and Winkler, 1986; Prutting and Kirchner, 1987; Craig, 1991; McTear and Conti-Ramsden, 1991). Many of the problems identified in the studies cited above could be identified using the procedures described in this chapter. The prudent clinician would follow the use of the procedures described here with a more in-depth examination of the problems in question using experimental techniques described in the studies cited above.

Analysis of children's abilities to relate past events in storytelling frameworks has received considerable attention in recent years.

Procedures for examining the structure of narratives have been based on loose guidelines to "tell me about your favorite book, summer vacation, etc." and/or tell versus retell versions of wordless picture books (e.g., Bishop and Edmundson's [1987] use of Renfrew's [1969] "Bus Story"; Stein and Glenn's [1979] use of Mayer's "Froggie on His Own"). Work in this area is promising in that various subgroups of children with language impairments may be distinguished on the basis of narrative analysis (Liles, 1985a, 1985b, 1987; Griffith, Ripich, and Dastoli, 1986; Roth, 1986; Merritt and Liles, 1987; Carpenter, 1991). It is not within the scope of this text to present procedures for analyzing narratives. For children who demonstrate difficulties with any aspect of pragmatic analysis described here, collection and analysis of narrative samples is recommended following the examination of conversational abilities using the procedures described here.

The procedures described in this chapter are compatible with the semantic and syntactic analysis procedures described in the two preceding chapters. It would be appropriate to analyze semantic, then syntactic, and finally pragmatic aspects of an obtained language transcript. While it is not necessary to complete the analyses in this order, following this order may be the most productive. Analysis information would be combined to diagnose delays and to develop remediation goals and objectives.

Analysis procedures described in this chapter are based on information provided by Dore (1974, 1978) and Martlew (1980), and on variables identified by Keenan and Schieffelin (1976), Grice (1975), and Shatz and Gelman (1973). The procedures are designed to be used on transcripts obtained from children at the one-word stage and beyond. Not all analysis procedures described would be used for analysis of every transcript. Some procedures are appropriate for use with transcripts obtained from children at the one-word stage (Dore's Primitive Speech Acts, 1974), and other procedures are appropriate for use with transcripts obtained from children producing utterances longer than one word in length (Dore's Conversational Acts, 1978; Martlew's Conversational Moves, 1980; and Retherford Stickler's Appropriateness

Judgments, 1980). Decisions about which procedure to use with particular children can be made only after greater familiarity with each procedure.

Examination of pragmatic aspects of language production involves two major levels of distinction. The first distinction to be made is between the function of each utterance, within the range of possible purposes or intents of utterances, and the role of each utterance in the development of the overall conversation. This distinction between communicative functions and discourse relations has been recognized in the development of the procedures in this chapter. The first two procedures examine the communicative functions of utterances within children's conversation, and the last two procedures investigate the discourse relations within children's conversation.

The second distinction necessary for a thorough consideration of pragmatic aspects of language transcripts is between quantitative and qualitative analysis. For many of the analysis procedures described in previous chapters, instances of each utterance type were tallied, subjected to analysis on the basis of the frequency of occurrence of each type, and compared to frequency-of-occurrence normative data. This type of quantitative analysis ensures reasonably reliable conclusions about semantic and syntactic abilities. For some analysis procedures, particularly in the area of pragmatics, quantitative measurements are not possible. Thus, qualitative analyses are employed. Although conclusions drawn from qualitative analysis may not be as reliable as those drawn from quantitative procedures, the importance of qualitative measures cannot be denied. In the case of the role that individual utterances play in ongoing discourse, it is not possible to say that a particular number of topic initiations is "normal." Judgments are made regarding the appropriateness of conversational moves, and the overall conclusion is based on individual judgments of appropriateness. These types of judgments may be more difficult for the beginning clinician to make, but with practice, clinicians become better at drawing conclusions from qualitative analyses.

Of the three types of language production analyses presented in *Guide* (semantic, syntactic, and pragmatic), documentation of pragmatic analysis as a diagnostic tool is only beginning to emerge. Very sketchy quantitative data exist in the literature, often preventing comparison of language samples to existing norms, or making the comparison questionable because of the extreme variability of the research data reported. Perhaps at best "all a clinician can do is look at the range of normal behavior and make some educated guesses as to what normal behavior might be. Another possibility . . . is to look at the child's use of language content and form. Bottom of the range performance should be interpreted as normal if the child's language in other areas is [appropriate]." (Fey, 1987). Although pragmatic analysis is in a neophyte stage, an attempt is made in this chapter to present several pragmatic analysis procedures that can provide descriptive data and limited quantitative data, albeit extremely variable.

Some of the procedures described in this chapter will be demonstrated on the sample transcript used in the preceding chapters (i.e., Bridget's) and some will be demonstrated using a sample transcript from Appendix B (i.e., Sara's). The reasons for this will become clear as each of the analysis procedures are considered. Blank forms for each of the analysis procedures described in this chapter are provided in Appendix E.

DORE'S PRIMITIVE SPEECH ACTS

The first procedure that will be used to analyze the pragmatic content of language transcripts is based on a set of categories developed by Dore (1974).

The categories were used to code young children's utterances as they were beginning to acquire language. The categories are based on Searle's (1969) speech acts, which he contends are those that adults perform in communicating. A *speech act* is a linguistic unit of communication consisting of conceptual information, or a proposition, and an intention, or the illocutionary force. The proposition and illocutionary force are expressed following conventional grammatical and pragmatic rules. A speaker's use of Searle's speech acts requires fairly complex language by the speaker, but Dore felt that the foundations for use of speech acts were laid in the early communicative attempts of the young child. In fact, Dore contends that children can perform what he calls primitive speech acts before they have acquired sentence structures. A *primitive speech act*, according to Dore, is "an utterance, consisting formally of a single word or a single prosodic pattern which functions to convey the child's intentions before he acquires sentences" (p. 345). Table 4.2 lists and summarizes the primitive speech acts described by Dore.

TABLE 4.2
PRIMITIVE SPEECH ACTS
(Adapted from Dore, 1974)

LABELING: A word or words that function as a label produced while attending to an object. The child does not address the adult or wait for a response.

REPEATING: A word, words, or prosodic pattern that repeat part of the adult utterance and are produced while attending to the adult utterance. The child does not address the adult or wait for a response.

ANSWERING: A word or words that respond to an adult question and are produced while attending to the adult utterance which is in the form of a question. The child addresses the adult but does not necessarily wait for a response.

REQUESTING ACTION: A word, words, or prosodic pattern that function as a request for an action and are produced while attending to an object or event. The child addresses the adult and waits for a response. Often, the production is accompanied by a gesturing signal.

Continued on next page

TABLE 4.2—Continued

REQUESTING

ANSWER: A word or words that function as a request for an answer. The child addresses the adult and waits for a response. The child may gesture toward an object.

CALLING: A word or words that are used to obtain another's attention. The child addresses the adult (or other participant) and waits for a response.

GREETING: A word or words that are used to mark arrival or leave-taking and are produced while attending to the adult or an object. The child addresses the adult or object and does not necessarily wait for a response.

PROTESTING: A word, words, or prosodic pattern that express disapproval of or dislike for an object or action and are produced while attending to the adult. The child addresses the adult but does not necessarily wait for a response.

PRACTICING: A word, words, or prosodic pattern that are not contingent upon preceding utterances and are produced while attending to an object or event. The child does not address the adult and does not wait for a response. Dore suggests that this is a "catch-all category" that was used whenever an utterance could not be assigned clearly to another category.

A few utterances are provided for practice in assigning Dore's Primitive Speech Acts before attempting to categorize the utterances in the sample transcript. Similar sample utterances used for practice with Bloom's and Nelson's procedures in Chapter 2 are provided first, and then a few more examples will be considered. Cover the right side of the page and categorize each utterance using one of Dore's nine Primitive Speech Acts. Linguistic and nonlinguistic contexts are provided for each practice utterance, since this information is crucial for coding. Once coding of practice utterances is complete, check results with those provided. Explanations are provided to clarify discrepancies.

(C picks up toy horse)
horsey/

LABELING
The child produced this utterance while attending to the horse, and it is assumed that he is labeling the horse.

(C hears door open)
Dada/

GREETING, LABELING, OR CALLING
Without additional context information, it is impossible to differentiate these three categories; this underlines the necessity of noting complete contextual information.

(C reaches for cup out of reach on table)
cup/

REQUESTING ACTION
In this utterance, the child appears to desire the cup, which is out of reach. He then labels the desired cup and gesturally indicates the desire for the action of bringing it within reach.

(C reaches up to M, who has entered bedroom) up/	**REQUESTING ACTION** This utterance is also an example of a request for an action, but the child labels the action instead of the object of the action.
(family pet is barking in background) Didi/	**CALLING or LABELING** The child appears either to be calling to the dog or labeling the dog; additional context would need to be considered before coding the utterance.
(M hands cup to C, who takes a drink and says, "mmm" and then) juice/	**LABELING** The child is labeling the substance which, based on the child's previous utterance, he judged to be good.
(M is searching in closet for shoe and says to C, "where is that shoe?"; C points to chest of drawers and says) there/	**ANSWERING** The child is responding directly to the adult question.
(C points to picture of himself on table) baby/	**LABELING** The child is labeling himself in the picture. Recall that this child refers to himself as baby.
(C hands empty cup to M and says) drink/	**REQUESTING ACTION** The child is asking his mother to get him a drink.
(M attempts to wipe C's face) no/	**PROTESTING** The child is protesting his mother's attempt to wipe his face.
(C is holding box; M says, "what's in there?") /kiki/ [cookies]	**ANSWERING** The child has attended to his mother's question and is responding.
(C pulls block from bag) /bɑ/ [block]	**LABELING** The child is attending to the object retrieved from the bag and is labeling it.

(C holds up toy sheep
and looks at M)
/moo↑/

REQUESTING ANSWER

The child is asking his mother to confirm the label for the toy animal.

(C reaches arms up to M,
who is standing by door)
/ʌ/ [up]

REQUESTING ACTION

The child is requesting that his mother pick him up.

(M places C in bed and turns
to leave, saying, "Sleep
tight, Megan")
/ni ni/ [night-night]

GREETING

Remember, this category is used both for arrivals and departures.

(C is playing in crib after
nap and bats mobile
hanging in bed)
/ʌpə/

PRACTICING

The child is not addressing anyone, and therefore appears to be practicing some aspect of language.

(C is playing in crib after
nap when M walks by
the bedroom door)
/mɑ/

CALLING

The child is calling for his mother.

(M stands up and says,
"Let's have some cookies")
/kiki/ [cookies]

REPEATING

The child is repeating part of the mother's utterance without addressing her.

(M asks C, "Do you want
some cookies?")
/jɑ/

ANSWERING

In this utterance, the child is responding directly to the mother's question.

These examples should be helpful in coding the utterances in the sample transcript. Using Dore's Primitive Speech Acts analysis sheet in Appendix E, progress through the transcript of Bridget and examine each utterance to determine the type of speech act it represents. Categorize each utterance, remembering that Dore supports the notion of using the PRACTICING category as a "catch-all" category. Record the utterance number next to the appropriate speech act on Dore's Primitive Speech Acts analysis sheet. When each utterance has been coded, compare the analysis sheet with the one provided on page 150.

Pragmatic Analysis
Dore's Primitive Speech Acts

Name of Child ___Bridget___

Act	Utterance Number	Total
Labeling	1, 8, 10, 11, 13, 14, 18, 20, 26, 27, 28, 32, 40, 41, 46, 50, 53, 61, 62, 65, 83, 84, 86, 94, 99	25
Repeating		0
Answering	2, 3, 4, 5, 9, 12, 21, 25, 30, 33, 34, 36, 37, 42, 43, 44, 45, 47, 48, 49, 51, 55, 56, 57, 58, 63, 64, 69, 75, 76, 77, 78, 79, 80, 81, 82, 85, 92, 93, 95, 97	41
Requesting Action	6, 15, 17, 22, 31, 38, 52, 70, 72, 73, 87, 88, 89, 90, 100	15
Requesting Answer	7, 16, 19, 23, 24, 29, 35, 59, 60, 66, 67, 68, 74, 91, 96	15
Calling	71	1
Greeting	54, 98	2
Protesting	39	1
Practicing		0

© 1993 **Thinking Publications** *Duplication permitted for educational use only.*

TABLE 4.3
**PERCENTAGE OF TOTAL UTTERANCES ACCOUNTED FOR BY PRIMITIVE SPEECH ACT TYPES
FOR TWO CHILDREN, AGED ONE YEAR, THREE MONTHS**

(Recomputed from totals provided by Dore, 1974)

	Child "M" (based on 81 utterances)	Child "J" (based on 80 utterances)
Labeling	34.6%	17.5%
Repeating	39.5%	28.7%
Answering	14.8%	10.0%
Requesting (action and answer)	7.4%	26.2%
Calling	0	11.2%
Greeting	1.2%	6.2%
Protesting	2.5%	0
Practicing	0	0

The Primitive Speech Acts analysis sheet and the sample transcript show that 25 utterances should have been identified as examples of LABELING. In addition, 41 utterances were examples of ANSWERING; 15 utterances were examples of REQUESTING ACTION and 15 were of REQUESTING ANSWER; 2 utterances were examples of GREETING; and 1 each were examples of CALLING and PROTESTING. No instances of REPEATING or PRACTICING were identified in this transcript.

As can be seen from these totals, this child used primarily the primitive speech acts of LABELING and ANSWERING. In fact, these two acts accounted for 66 percent of the child's utterances. When the two requesting categories, REQUESTING ACTION and REQUESTING ANSWER, are added to this percentage, these four acts account for 96 percent of the child's utterances. When these results are compared to results obtained by Dore (1974), substantial differences can be found. Table 4.3 summarizes the distribution of primitive speech acts for two children, each 1 year and 3 months of age, used in Dore's (1974) study. The analysis was based on 81 and 80 utterances respectively. While there are differences between the two children on whom Dore reported, the most substantial differences are between Dore's subjects and the child in the sample transcript (i.e., Bridget). For example, the primitive speech act REPEATING accounted for 39.5 percent and

28.7 percent of utterances for Dore's subjects and 0 percent of utterances in the sample transcript. In addition, ANSWERING accounted for 14.8 percent and 10.0 percent of utterances for Dore's subjects and 41 percent of utterances in our sample transcript. These differences would not be the result of differences in total number of utterances. More likely, the observed differences are the result of the question-asking performance of the child's partner or differences in the developmental level of the children (i.e., MLU, syntactic, or semantic aspects reflecting a higher developmental level). The child in the sample transcript appears to be using a more conversational interaction style while communicating, as evidenced by the high percentage of use of REQUESTING and ANSWERING. Dore's children used primarily LABELING and REPEATING, both decidedly less conversational in style.

Other differences between Dore's subjects and the child in the sample transcript were noted but do not appear to be as substantial as these differences, primarily because of the variability between Dore's two subjects. In fact, Dore considers the differences between his two subjects to be the result of different styles of language use. The child identified as "M" in Table 4.3 apparently used language at this stage of development to "declare things about her environment." The child identified as "J" apparently used language to "manipulate other people." These differences may be similar to, or the result of differences in, semantic use at the one-word stage described in Chapter 2. For purposes of the present analysis, however, we are more concerned with the differences between our sample transcript and results of Dore's analysis. These differences are the result of age differences between the child whose sample transcript was used for analysis and the children studied by Dore. Dore's subjects were just into the one-word stage at 1 year and 3 months. The child in the sample transcript is beyond the one-word stage at the age of 2 years and 4 months. The differences in frequency of use of various speech acts are obvious for these children. As a result, analysis of primitive speech acts may not be the most revealing for children beyond the one-word stage. Such analysis, then, should be reserved for children at the one-word stage, where it can be used to identify differences in styles of language as well as differences that may be the result of a language delay or disorder.

A variation of Dore's system has been proposed by Coggins and Carpenter (1981). Their *Communicative Intention Inventory* is also based on the writings of Bates (1976), Greenfield and Smith (1976), and Halliday (1975). The *Communicative Intention Inventory* (1981) is a criterion-referenced approach (i.e., determining how well a child has established a particular behavior) rather than a norm-referenced approach (i.e., comparing the behavior of one child with that of other children). Although Coggins and Carpenter (1981) published selected percentile ranks and standard error of measurement for the frequency of eight categories of communicative intentions, the data were not intended as reference norms, but as a means "to provide the user with a perspective regarding the frequency of a set of intentional behaviors in a group of normal 16-month-old children who communicate primarily vocally and gesturally and are beginning to convey their intentions verbally" (p. 249). The inventory includes these eight intentional categories: comment on action, comment on object, request for action, request for object, request for information, answering, acknowledging, and protesting. These eight categories were selected because

they are likely communicative acts to occur in a clinical setting. Direct comparison with their frequency data is possible only if a 45-minute sample of the child and mother's interaction is video recorded in a clinical setting. Coggins and Carpenter (1981) noted, "deviations from these guidelines [i.e., conditions under which the sample is obtained] may lead to erroneous estimates of what intentions a child is capable of communicating" (p. 239). While the *Communicative Intention Inventory* (1981) has special merit for analyzing timed language samples obtained in a clinical setting, it is not appropriate to apply to these 100-utterance samples. Coggins and Carpenter's (1981) system does not analyze the communication intent of each utterance, but rather the intentional behaviors displayed (e.g., if the child repeats the word *drink* three times while drinking a glass of juice and looking toward the mother, those three utterances are tallied as one verbal comment on action, not three). Readers are urged to study Coggins and Carpenter's *Communicative Intention Inventory* (1981) and to apply it when appropriate, but its use will not be demonstrated with the language transcripts in *Guide*.

DORE'S CONVERSATIONAL ACTS

Another of Dore's (1978) analysis procedures may be more appropriate for the developmental level of the child in the sample transcript. This analysis procedure, like the preceding, examines the communicative function of utterances based on the form of those utterances and use in discourse and physical context. The procedure is based on what Dore defines as a *conversational act*. A *conversational act* consists of propositional content, a grammatical structure, and an illocutionary function. The *propositional content* refers to the conceptual information in the utterances—that is, what the utterance means. The *illocutionary function* refers to how the speaker intends his utterance to be taken. Dore contends that the grammatical structure of the utterance alters the illocutionary functions of the propositional content. Therefore, all three components must be assumed to work together in communication. Table 4.4 lists and defines the conversational acts described by Dore. Within each definition are the subcategories of conversational acts specified by Dore. He used the subcategories to identify utterances that were examples of the various types of conversational acts. Because the breakdown of subcategories within each conversational act is primarily the result of variations in form, semantic content, and/or minor shades of intention, only the major category distinctions will be used in this analysis.

TABLE 4.4
CONVERSATIONAL ACTS CATEGORIES
(Adapted from Dore, 1978)

REQUESTS: Utterances used to request information, action, or acknowledgment, including yes/no questions that seek true-false judgments; wh-questions that seek factual information; clarification questions about the content of a prior utterance; action requests that seek action from the listener; permission requests; and rhetorical questions that seek acknowledgment from the listener permitting the speaker to continue.

RESPONSES TO REQUESTS: Utterances following requests that respond directly to the request, including yes/no answers that supply true-false judgment; wh-answers that supply solicited factual information; clarifications that supply relevant repetition; compliances that verbally express acceptance, denial, or acknowledgment of a prior action or permission request; qualifications that supply unexpected information in response to the soliciting question; and repetitions of part of prior utterances.

DESCRIPTIONS: Utterances used to describe verifiable past and present facts, including identifications that label objects, events, etc.; descriptions of events, actions, propositions, etc.; descriptions of properties, traits, or conditions; expression of locations or directions; and reports of times.

STATEMENTS: Utterances used to state facts, rules, attitudes, feelings, and beliefs, including expressions of rules, procedures, definitions, etc.; evaluations that express attitudes, judgments, etc.; internal reports of emotions, sensations, and mental events, such as intents to perform future actions; attributions that report beliefs about others' internal states; and explanations that express reasons, cause, and predictions.

ACKNOWL-EDGMENTS: Utterances used to indicate recognition of responses and nonrequests, including acceptances that neutrally recognize answers and nonrequests; approvals/agreements that positively recognize answers or nonrequests; disapprovals/disagreements that negatively evaluate answers or nonrequests; and returns that acknowledge rhetorical questions and some nonrequests.

ORGANIZATIONAL DEVICES: Utterances that regulate contact and conversation, including boundary markers that indicate openings, closings, and other significant points in the conversation; calls that solicit attention; speaker selections that explicitly indicate the speaker of the next turn; politeness markers that indicate politeness; and accompaniments that maintain verbal contact.

PERFORMATIVES: Utterances that are accomplished by being said, including protests that register complaints about the listener's behavior; jokes that display nonbelief toward a proposition for humorous effect; claims that establish rights by being said; warnings that alert the listener of impending harm; and teases that taunt or playfully provoke the listener.

MISCELLANEOUS: Category used to code utterances that are uninterpretable because they are unintelligible, incomplete, or anomalous, or they contain no propositional content, such as exclamations.

Categorizing a few utterances for practice should be helpful before turning back to the sample transcript. The same utterances used for practicing Dore's Primitive Speech Acts are provided first, and then a few more are provided for additional practice.

(C picks up toy horse)
horsey/

DESCRIPTION
This utterance labels an object, the horse. Most utterances previously identified as LABELING will now be DESCRIPTION.

(C hears door opening)
Dada/

DESCRIPTION or ORGANIZATIONAL DEVICE
The problem previously encountered when differentiating primitive speech acts exists here as well. Without additional contextual information, it is impossible to differentiate these two categories.

(C reaches for cup out of reach on table)
cup/

REQUEST
In this utterance, the child is requesting his cup. Dore (1978) does not differentiate types of requests for conversational acts analysis.

(C reaches up to M, who has entered bedroom)
up/

REQUEST
Here, the child appears to be requesting to be picked up. Again, it is not necessary to differentiate types of requesting.

(family pet is barking in background)
Didi/

ORGANIZATIONAL DEVICE or DESCRIPTION
If in this utterance the child is calling the dog, then it is coded ORGANIZATIONAL DEVICE. If the child is labeling the dog, then it is coded DESCRIPTION. Analysis of additional context will determine which way to code the utterance.

(M hands cup to C, who takes a drink and says, "mmm" and then)
juice/

DESCRIPTION
This utterance identifies the delicious substance as juice, and thus is a DESCRIPTION.

(M is searching in closet for shoe and says to C, "where is that shoe?"; C points to chest of drawers and says)
there/

RESPONSE TO REQUEST
Because the mother has asked a question, the child's utterance is considered to respond to that question.

(C points to picture of
himself on table)
baby/

DESCRIPTION
Again, the child is labeling himself in the picture, and therefore this utterance is considered to be a DESCRIPTION.

(C hands empty cup to
M and says)
drink/

REQUEST
The child is requesting that his mother fill his empty cup.

(M attempts to wipe
C's face)
no/

PERFORMATIVE
This type of conversational act refers to those utterances that are accomplished simply by being said. Perhaps one of the simplest forms of performatives is the protest. This utterance is an example of a protest PERFORMATIVE.

(C is holding box; M says,
"what's in there?")
/kiki/ [cookies]

RESPONSE TO REQUEST
The child is responding directly to the mother's request.

(C pulls block from bag)
/bɑ/ [block]

DESCRIPTION
The child is labeling the block he has pulled from the bag.

(C holds up toy sheep
and looks at M)
/moo↑/

REQUEST
The child is asking his mother to confirm his label for the toy animal.

(C reaches arms up to M,
who is standing by door)
/ʌ/ [up]

REQUEST
The child is asking his mother to pick him up. All types of requests, including requests for labels and for action, are labeled REQUEST.

(M places C in bed and turns
to leave, saying, "Sleep tight,
Megan")
/ni ni/ [night-night]

ORGANIZATIONAL DEVICE
Types of greeting are labeled in this manner, primarily because of the way in which they regulate conversation.

(C is playing in crib after
nap and bats mobile
hanging in bed)
/ʌpə/

MISCELLANEOUS
This category is used for a variety of types of utterances. In this case, it is used to indicate that the propositional content of the utterance is unclear.

(C is playing in crib after nap when M walks by the bedroom door) /mɑ/	ORGANIZATIONAL DEVICE The child is soliciting his mother's attention.
(M stands up and says, "Let's have some cookies") /kiki/ [cookies]	RESPONSE TO REQUEST The child's utterance indicates recognition of the request and readiness for cookies.
(M asks C, "Do you want some cookies?") /jɑ/	RESPONSE TO REQUEST Again, the child is responding directly to the request regarding his desire for cookies.

A few more grammatically complex utterances are provided for practice. The same categories apply and, in fact, may be easier to apply, with more propositional content available to aid in coding.

(C picks up toy sheep that's in corral with cows) that's not a cow/	DESCRIPTION This utterance describes a verifiable fact regarding the sheep.
(C and M are building tower with blocks; C picks up two cylinder-shaped blocks) these are the ones what we need/	STATEMENT This utterance expresses a need statement that reports on an internal state. Because it is not verifiable, it is not a DESCRIPTION.
(C and M are playing with playground set; M puts boy doll on top of pavilion; C says) you're a silly mommy/	PERFORMATIVE In this utterance, the child is teasing his mother for her silly behavior. The utterance accomplishes the tease simply by being said. That is what makes this utterance an example of a PERFORMATIVE.
(C and M are playing with the playground set; C takes doll off swing and says) he's not feeling very good/	STATEMENT This utterance reports the child's belief about the internal state of the doll. Thus, this utterance is an example of a STATEMENT and not a DESCRIPTION of the doll.

(C pulls toy sandbox out of box and holds it up, saying) wow/	MISCELLANEOUS This category is assigned because it is an exclamation, which Dore considers to have no propositional content.
(M says to C, "I'm going to put the table in the shelter" and C says) okay/	ACKNOWLEDGMENT The child's utterance is indicating acceptance of the mother's utterance.
(M and C are playing with playground set; one of the dolls falls off swing and C picks it up) this one fell off cuz he weren't hanging on/	STATEMENT This utterance states the facts of the situation (the doll fell off the swing) but goes on to explain the reason for it (cuz he weren't hanging on). Because of the inclusion of an explanation, this utterance is an example of a STATEMENT.

These examples should be helpful in completing the analysis of the sample transcript. In many cases, conversational acts coding is easier for utterances longer than two or three words in length, because there is more language on which to base the category assignment judgments. It also should be apparent that the major developmental change in use of conversational acts occurs when the child is able to produce STATEMENTS. Now, code the sample transcript of Bridget using Dore's Conversational Acts analysis sheet from Appendix E. Progress through the transcript and determine the appropriate conversational act that characterizes each utterance. Record the utterance number next to the conversational act on the analysis sheet. When coding has been completed, check results with those provided on page 158.

Analysis of the conversational acts used by the child in the sample transcript revealed use of 32 REQUESTS, 37 RESPONSES TO REQUESTS, 18 DESCRIPTIONS, 5 STATEMENTS, 2 ACKNOWLEDGMENTS, 5 ORGANIZATIONAL DEVICES, and 1 MISCELLANEOUS. Although Dore does not provide frequency-of-occurrence data for use of conversational acts, he provides some guidelines to aid in interpretation. However, before an attempt is made to interpret the results of this analysis, another transcript obtained from an older child is provided for comparison. Using Sara's transcript in Appendix B and another Dore's Conversational Acts analysis sheet, categorize each utterance. This child's utterances are longer and may be easier to code than the utterances in Bridget's transcript, and the results obtained should be very different. When each utterance has been categorized, compare results with the sample provided on page 159.

Results of this analysis did, in fact, reveal differences: 6 of Sara's utterances were REQUESTS, 65 were RESPONSES TO REQUESTS, 17 were DESCRIPTIONS, 9 were STATEMENTS, 2 were PERFORMATIVES and 1 was MISCELLANEOUS. The most obvious difference is in the use of RESPONSES TO REQUESTS and REQUESTS. The child in the sample transcript used in all other analyses, Bridget, used 37 RESPONSES TO REQUESTS and 32 REQUESTS, but Sara, the

Pragmatic Analysis
Dore's Conversational Acts

Name of Child ___*Bridget*___

Act	Tally	Total
Requests	6, 7, 11, 15, 16, 19, 22, 23, 24, 26, 28, 29, 31, 35, 38, 52, 53, 59, 66, 67, 68, 70, 72, 73, 74, 87, 88, 89, 90, 91, 96, 100	32
Responses to Requests	2, 3, 4, 5, 9, 12, 21, 25, 30, 33, 34, 36, 37, 42, 43, 44, 45, 47, 48, 49, 51, 55, 56, 57, 58, 64, 69, 75, 76, 77, 78, 80, 81, 92, 93, 95, 97	37
Descriptions	8, 13, 14, 20, 27, 32, 40, 41, 46, 50, 60, 61, 79, 83, 84, 86, 94, 99	18
Statements	17, 18, 39, 62, 65	5
Acknowledgments	82, 85	2
Organizational Devices	10, 54, 63, 71, 98	5
Performatives		0
Miscellaneous	1	1

© 1993 Thinking Publications *Duplication permitted for educational use only.*

Pragmatic Analysis
Dore's Conversational Acts

Name of Child ___Sara___

Act	Tally	Total
Requests	*30, 37, 39, 47, 62, 98*	*6*
Responses to Requests	*1, 2, 3, 4, 5, 7, 8, 11, 12, 13, 16, 18, 19, 20, 24, 25, 28, 29, 31, 33, 34, 35, 38, 40, 41, 42, 43, 45, 46, 48, 49, 51, 52, 54, 55, 56, 57, 59, 60, 61, 63, 64, 65, 66, 69, 70, 71, 72, 75, 77, 78, 79, 81, 82, 84, 85, 87, 88, 89, 93, 94, 95, 96, 99, 100*	*65*
Descriptions	*6, 9, 10, 17, 32, 44, 53, 58, 67, 73, 74, 76, 80, 90, 91, 92, 97*	*17*
Statements	*15, 21, 22, 23, 26, 36, 50, 83, 86*	*9*
Acknowledgments		*0*
Organizational Devices		*0*
Performatives	*14, 68*	*2*
Miscellaneous	*27*	*1*

© 1993 Thinking Publications *Duplication permitted for educational use only.*

child in the second transcript, used 65 RESPONSES TO REQUESTS and only 6 REQUESTS. Dore and others have reported that the ability to initiate conversation in an appropriate manner increases as the child's developmental level increases. Using REQUESTS is one way of initiating conversation. But Sara is older than Bridget. Does this mean that Sara is pragmatically delayed? Not necessarily. There are other ways of initiating conversation besides asking questions. Dore contends that DESCRIPTIONS, STATEMENTS, and PERFORMATIVES also may function to initiate conversation. If the totals for each of these categories are added to each child's total number of REQUESTS, the difference between the two children is even greater. A total of 58 of Bridget's utterances were conversational acts that could function to initiate conversation. Only 38 of Sara's utterances could function in that capacity. This, however, still does not prove that Sara is pragmatically delayed. In fact, it may indicate a greater attention to the cohesiveness of ongoing conversation. Bloom, Rocissano, and Hood (1976) reported a decrease in spontaneous, noncontingent speech in children 21–36 months of age and an increase in topically cohesive speech. With this in mind, should both Bridget and Sara be considered developmentally normal in their patterns of initiating and responding? Before any conclusion can be drawn, two other points must be considered.

First, Sara's tendency to respond is the result of a mother who asks a considerable number of questions. In fact, if Sara had responded to all of her mother's questions, her total number of responses would be even greater. To conclude that Sara is pragmatically delayed because the majority of her utterances are RESPONSES TO REQUESTS would be inappropriate when her mother is responsible for this high number of RESPONSES TO REQUESTS. It would be important, as suggested in Chapter 1, to obtain another language sample with Sara interacting with another familiar individual. Only then could it be determined if more of Sara's utterances were used to initiate conversation and/or if she was able to maintain a topic without the assistance of questions to direct her.

The second point to consider before drawing a conclusion regarding the pragmatic abilities of these children is the setting in which the samples were obtained. While both were free play situations, Sara's mother apparently felt a greater need to direct the interaction. Before drawing a conclusion regarding the presence of a pragmatic delay, it would be important to obtain another transcript in a different setting. Only then would it be possible to determine whether Sara is unable to initiate conversation more frequently than the present sample indicates, or if she can maintain conversation without the support of a question-asking co-participant. And, as suggested earlier in this chapter, the data obtained from pragmatic analysis must be combined with data obtained from analysis of semantic and syntactic aspects of language production.

Overall, analysis of the use of Dore's Conversational Acts provides information that, when taken together with other information, can be used to describe a child's language production abilities. Identification of a pragmatic delay or disorder could not be made using this analysis procedure and one language transcript. It would be necessary to obtain samples of a particular child's language production abilities in at least one other setting and with at least one other participant. And results of analysis of conversational acts must be combined with results of semantic and syntactic analyses to be considered complete.

MARTLEW'S CONVERSATIONAL MOVES

The next analysis procedure that will be demonstrated is based on a set of discourse categories described by Martlew (1980). These categories were used to code utterances of mothers and their normally developing children at two points in time: when the children were approximately 3 years of age, and a year later when the children were approximately 4 years of age. The categories differentiate a variety of types of opening, or initiating, moves and a variety of types of responding moves. While the subcategories of INITIATING and RESPONDING MOVES are not dissimilar to Dore's

---

TABLE 4.5
CONVERSATIONAL MOVES WITH LETTER IDENTIFICATION FOR CODING
(Adapted from Martlew, 1980)

INITIATING MOVES

New Topic Introduction (N):	A new topic is introduced into the conversation.
Restarting Old Topic (R):	A previous topic is reintroduced into the conversation.
Eliciting Verbal Response (E):	The speaker invites the other participant to respond verbally, including questions.
Intruding (I):	The speaker intrudes into the conversation in an inappropriate manner or at an inappropriate time; topic may be irrelevant or a turn out of place.

RESPONDING MOVES

Acknowledging (A):	The previous speaker's utterance is acknowledged through brief remarks.
Yes/No Responses (Y):	Simple affirmation or negation of previous speaker's turn.
One-Word Answers (O):	Brief responses contingent on previous speaker's utterance; "sit" and "sit down" would both be coded O in response to "What do you want him to do?"
Repetition (R):	The previous utterance is repeated partially or wholly, with or without additional information.
Sustaining Topic (S):	The topic is maintained by reformulating content without adding new information.
Extending Topic (E):	The topic is maintained but new information is added.
False Starts (F):	An utterance is begun but is not completed; there were not really INITIATING or RESPONDING MOVES.

Conversational Acts, the focus in examining INITIATING MOVES versus conversational RESPONDING MOVES is to document discourse abilities. The unit of analysis continues to be the utterance, but in examining the role utterances play in initiating and responding to topics, the results are closer to an account of the discourse relations of the conversation. Table 4.5 lists and describes the categories of conversational moves that Martlew posited. The names for many of the categories have been changed by this author to aid in recall for coding.

Because coding of utterances is based primarily on the immediately preceding utterance of the conversational co-participant, but also at times on utterances several speaking turns prior to the utterance under consideration, it is impossible to present single utterance examples for practice. The descriptions of conversational moves should be sufficiently clear to permit successful coding of utterances from one of the sample transcripts, without the benefit of practice. In addition, final analysis of results will be based on the broad categories of INITIATING and RESPONDING MOVES; consequently, minimal variation in use of subcategories can be tolerated.

Turn to the transcript obtained from Sara and code the conversational moves using the modification of Martlew's categories. Using the first two columns of the Conversational Moves Analysis Sheet in Appendix E, record the letter code for types of INITIATING and RESPONDING MOVES under the appropriate column. For example, if Sara produces an utterance that is considered to be a New Topic Introduction, record an "N" under the "Initiating" column, next to the appropriate utterance number. Progress through the transcript and code each utterance, considering its role in relation to preceding utterances. When coding is complete, check results with the sample provided on pages 163–164.

The first two columns on the Conversational Moves Analysis Sheet and Sara's transcript show that 18 utterances should be designated as INITIATING MOVES and 82 utterances as types of RESPONDING MOVES. When these results are compared to those obtained by Martlew, there are differences. Table 4.6 summarizes the frequency of use of individual conversational moves as percentages of total utterances for eight children at approximately 3 years of age and then again at 4 years of age while conversing with their mothers.

TABLE 4.6
PERCENTAGE OF TOTAL UTTERANCES ACCOUNTED FOR BY
CONVERSATIONAL MOVE TYPES FOR EIGHT CHILDREN AT TWO POINTS IN TIME
(Adapted from Martlew, 1980)

		Time One (3 years, 3 months)	Time Two (4 years, 3 months)
INITIATING MOVES			
New Topic Introduction		5.1%	2.5%
Restarting Old Topic		7.8%	8.7%
Eliciting Verbal Response		14.4%	13.6%
Intruding		0.9%	0.7%
	TOTAL	28.3%	25.5%
RESPONDING MOVES			
Acknowledging		2.8%	3.9%
Yes/No Responses		10.3%	15.1%
One Word Answers		10.3%	8.9%
Repetition		3.8%	4.0%
Sustaining Topic		9.4%	9.2%
Extending Topic		5.0%	6.1%
	TOTAL*	66.9%[1]	68.1%[2]
FALSE STARTS		4.8%	6.4%

*This total includes a category called Comments, which Martlew does not define in his RESPONDING MOVES.

[1]This total includes 25.1% Comments.

[2]This total includes 21.0% Comments.

Pragmatic Analysis
Conversational Moves Analysis Sheet

Name of Child _Sara_

UTT#	Turn Taking — Initiating	Turn Taking — Responding	Appropriateness — Specificity	Appropriateness — Conciseness	Appropriateness — Style
1		O			
2		E			
3		R			
4		E			
5		E			
6		E			
7		E			
8		O			
9		E			
10		R			
11		E			
12		O			
13		O			
14	N				
15	N				
16		E			
17		E			
18		O			
19		E			
20		E			
21	R				
22		E			
23		E			
24		E			
25		R			

UTT#	Turn Taking — Initiating	Turn Taking — Responding	Appropriateness — Specificity	Appropriateness — Conciseness	Appropriateness — Style
26		E			
27	N				
28		O			
29		E			
30	E	O			
31		E			
32		O			
33		E			
34		O			
35		E			
36	R				
37	E	q			
38		q			
39	E	O			
40		O			
41		q			
42		q			
43		O			
44	R				
45		O			
46		E			
47	E				
48		O			
49		O			
50		E			

© 1993 **Thinking Publications** *Duplication permitted for educational use only.*

Pragmatic Analysis
Conversational Moves Analysis Sheet

Name of Child _Sara_

UTT#	Turn Taking		Appropriateness				UTT#	Turn Taking		Appropriateness			
	Initiating	Responding	Specificity	Conciseness	Style			Initiating	Responding	Specificity	Conciseness	Style	
51		O					76		E				
52		O					77		E				
53	N						78		E				
54		E					79		E				
55		O					80	R					
56		S					81		E				
57		E					82	N	E				
58		E					83	N					
59		O					84		q				
60		E					85		O				
61		q					86	R					
62	E						87		O				
63		E					88		q				
64		R					89		E				
65		q					90	N					
66		E					91	N					
67		E					92		E				
68		E					93		E				
69		E					94		O				
70		E					95		O				
71		E					96		O				
72		E					97		E				
73		S					98	E	E				
74		S					99		E				
75		E					100		E				

164

© **1993 Thinking Publications** *Duplication permitted for educational use only.*

As can be seen in Table 4.6, approximately 28 percent of the children's utterances at 3 years of age were types of INITIATING MOVES. And a year later, approximately 25 percent of their utterances were types of INITIATING MOVES. At 3 years of age, approximately 67 percent of their utterances were types of RESPONDING MOVES; at 4 years, 68 percent were types of RESPONDING MOVES. In fact, Martlew reports that for this group of mothers and children, INITIATING MOVES accounted for approximately 30 percent of utterances, and RESPONDING MOVES accounted for approximately 70 percent of utterances of the children at both points in time. Changes that occurred were primarily in the use of individual categories. Overall distribution of utterances between initiating and responding remained relatively constant over time.

The child in this sample transcript used substantially fewer INITIATING MOVES and more RESPONDING MOVES than Martlew's subjects. Should it be concluded that Sara is pragmatically delayed or disordered? These concerns are similar to those that were raised as a result of Dore's Conversational Acts analysis. In that case, as now, it is important to consider the mother's role in these results. Although the mother's use of conversational moves was not analyzed, it could be speculated that her distribution of INITIATING and RESPONDING MOVES would differ from that of the mothers in Martlew's study. So are this mother and her child, as a pair, pragmatically disordered? The same conclusion that was drawn following Dore's Conversational Acts analysis holds here as well. A minimum of two additional transcripts are needed before a conclusion can be reached: one obtained from Sara and her mother while interacting under conditions other than free play, and one obtained from Sara while interacting with another familiar adult. If the distribution of INITIATING MOVES and RESPONDING MOVES is similar in additional transcripts to the distribution obtained in the sample transcript, it would be appropriate to conclude that Sara has a limited repertoire of means available to her for initiating speaking turns. In other words, if changes in condition and/or conversational co-participant do not result in significant changes in the distribution

of INITIATING and RESPONDING MOVES, the prudent conclusion would be that Sara's ability to participate in conversation is restricted. This apparent pragmatic delay/disorder would warrant attention in remediation.

Before moving on to consider another type of discourse analysis, compare Sara's use of individual conversational moves to those of the subjects in Martlew's study. The percentages for use of individual INITIATING MOVES obtained for Sara were as follows: 7 percent (7 ÷ 100 total utterances) New Topic Introduction, 5 percent Restarting Old Topic, 6 percent Eliciting Verbal Response, and 0 percent Intruding. The totals for use of individual RESPONDING MOVES were 0 percent Acknowledging, 6 percent Yes/No Responses, 24 percent One-Word Answers, 4 percent Repetition, 3 percent Sustaining Topic, 45 percent Extending Topic, and 0 percent False Starts. The most striking differences between Sara's totals and totals for Martlew's subjects at either point in time are in the use of One-Word Answers and Extending Topic. Sara used 24 percent One-Word Answers, and Martlew's subjects used 10.3 percent at 3 years and 8.9 percent at 4 years. In addition, Sara used 45 percent Extending Topic utterances, while Martlew's subjects used 5 percent at 3 years and 6.1 percent at 4 years. These dramatic differences could be explained in one of two possible ways. First, Sara's mother asks a very high proportion of wh-questions. Since there is no conversational move specifically identified as a response to a question, the two individual conversational moves typically used in response to wh-questions are One-Word Answers and Extending Topic utterances—Sara's two most frequently occurring moves. The second explanation is a result of an ambiguity in Martlew's data. As noted in the footnote of Table 4.6, Martlew reports frequency-of-occurrence data for a conversational move that she does not define. This move, which she labels as Comments, occurred with the greatest frequency of any of her RESPONDING MOVES. If the percentages obtained for Comments and Extending Topic utterances are added together, the resulting total approaches the total Extending Topic utterances for Sara. This, combined with the tentative conclusion regarding

Sara's mother, supports the earlier contention that more transcripts must be obtained. In addition, the use of frequency-of-occurrence data on individual conversational moves may not be a valid tool in identifying differences in pragmatic abilities. Judgments are best made on overall use of the broader categories of INITIATING versus RESPONDING MOVES. Use of individual moves may support overall conclusions but should not be considered diagnostic in and of itself.

APPROPRIATENESS JUDGMENTS

This next set of analysis procedures was developed by this author and encompasses appropriateness judgments relative to three conversational variables: referent specificity, contributional conciseness, and communication style. Although little support for the reliability of appropriateness judgments exists in the literature, the three analysis procedures described in the following sections are useful for descriptive purposes. The selection of these three variables from a variety of options discussed in the literature is an attempt to capture those aspects of conversation that may be problematic for children with a language delay or language disorder. A lack of appropriateness in regard to these variables is fairly easy to identify. In addition, it appears that problems in each of these areas can be remediated. Clinical experience has shown that behaviors that will increase the level of appropriateness in each of these areas can be taught. Each of these variables will be considered individually as the sample transcript of Sara is analyzed.

Referent Specificity

In their discussion of discourse topic, Keenan and Schieffelin (1976) present a dynamic model, which includes a sequence of steps, for establishing a discourse topic in a conversation. This model is based on the assumption that speakers accomplish each step, and receive positive feedback from listeners that they have done so, before continuing the conversation. These four steps are (1) the speaker elicits the

listener's attention, (2) the speaker speaks clearly enough for the listener to hear the utterance, (3) the speaker identifies the referents in the topic, and (4) the speaker identifies the semantic relations that exist between the referents in the topic. Keenan and Schieffelin (1976) contend that all four steps may be accomplished in a single utterance or that it may take a separate utterance to accomplish each step. While all four of these steps are necessary to establish a discourse topic, each can be applied to the successful transmission of a single utterance. It is the third step that will be used in the first judgment of appropriateness. Keenan and Schieffelin (1976) report that the process of identifying the referent for the listener involves directing the listener to locate the referent in either "physical space" or "memory space." Young children rely initially on the listener's ability to locate the referent in physical space, and only later do they rely on the listener's ability to locate the referent in memory. In either case, the young child presumes the listener will do the locating with minimal assistance provided for the listener in the form of nonverbal behaviors such as looking at, pointing to, and holding up the referent. Later, children begin to use verbal means to identify referents in physical space, including the use of notice verbs (e.g., *look, see,* etc.), deictic particles (e.g., *these, this,* etc.), and interrogative forms (e.g., *what's this?*). Keenan and Schieffelin (1976) contend that children at the one-word stage can repair misunderstandings as a result of their attempts to specify referents located in physical space. Specifying the referent in memory space and/or repairing the situation when the listener fails to locate the referent in memory space is much more difficult for children. In fact, Keenan and Schieffelin report that before the age of 3 years, children experience "enormous difficulty" in specifying "non-situated" referents, or referents that are not present in the immediate situation. These researchers provide a variety of semantic, syntactic, and pragmatic reasons for this. Semantically, children do not use the previously mentioned notice verbs to assist the listener in locating the referent in memory space. Also, the notice verbs for locating referents in memory space (e.g., *remember, recall*) are not yet available to young children. Syntactically, children are not yet using tense markers consistently. Use of these and other syntactic structures (e.g., anaphoric pronouns, definite articles) would indicate to the listener that the referent is not present in the immediate context. Pragmatically, children continue to rely on nonverbal cues to locate referents for listeners, and this strategy is not useful for referents located in memory space.

This discussion should be helpful in identifying instances in which children fail to specify the referent of the topic for the listener. In adult-child conversation, the adult typically indicates to the child that the referent is not clear. The adult may do this explicitly (e.g., "I don't know what you're talking about") or indirectly, through the use of repairs. As in the previous analysis procedure, identification of instances of a lack of specificity requires examination of a sequence of utterances, and it would be impossible to provide a series of examples for practice. The example below should suffice.

In this exchange, it would be important to indicate on the Conversational Moves Analysis Sheet under the "Specificity" column that a sequence of four child utterances lacked sufficient specificity. This would be indicated by putting a dash (–) in the "Specificity" column and in the row corresponding to the utterance number. The fifth child utterance in this example would be marked with a check (✓) because the referent was specific enough to be identified. Obviously, it is impossible to consider each utterance in isolation from other utterances. The most effective method is to examine a sequence of utterances while looking for clues from the other speaker that an utterance has not been specific enough; then, backtrack and identify the child utterance that is the source of the problem. Then, the child utterance that has caused the breakdown can be marked with a dash, as would the utterances subsequent to the problem utterance. Once shared content is re-established, checks again can be used.

Turning to Sara's transcript, examine utterances for a lack of specificity. Keep in mind that an adult may choose to ignore child utterances which lack specificity; however, the typical strategy is to attempt to repair the situation. Progress through the transcript, indicating whether each utterance is sufficiently specific to allow the listener to identify the referent (✓) or whether an utterance lacks specificity (–). When the analysis is complete, compare results with the sample provided on pages 168–169.

(M and C are reading books;
C points to picture of cow and says)

C: baby cow/

M: That's not a baby cow/   (referent not identified)

C: no! a baby cow/   (repair attempted)

M: But that's not a baby calf/   (referent not identified)

C: calf/   (repair attempted)

M: Let's find a baby calf/

C: no! gramma baby/   (repair attempted)

M: Gramma baby?   (referent identified)
    Oh Gramma has a baby calf?/

C: yeah baby calf/   (referent confirmed)

167

Pragmatic Analysis
Conversational Moves Analysis Sheet

Name of Child ___Sara___

UTT#	Turn Taking Initiating	Responding	Appropriateness Specificity	Conciseness	Style
1		O	✓		
2		E	✓		
3		R	✓		
4		E	✓		
5		E	✓		
6		E	✓		
7		E	✓		
8		O	✓		
9		E	✓		
10		R	✓		
11		E	✓		
12		O	✓		
13		O	✓		
14	N		✓		
15	N		✓		
16		E	✓		
17		E	✓		
18		O	✓		
19		E	✓		
20		E	✓		
21	R		✓		
22		E	✓		
23		E	✓		
24		E	✓		
25		R	✓		

UTT#	Turn Taking Initiating	Responding	Appropriateness Specificity	Conciseness	Style
26		E	✓		
27	N		✓		
28		O	✓		
29		E	✓		
30	E		✓		
31		O	✓		
32		E	✓		
33		O	✓		
34		E	✓		
35		O	✓		
36	R		✓		
37	E		–		
38		q	✓		
39	E		✓		
40		O	✓		
41		O	✓		
42		q	✓		
43		O	✓		
44	R		✓		
45		O	✓		
46		E	✓		
47	E		✓		
48		O	✓		
49		O	✓		
50		E	✓		

© 1993 **Thinking Publications** *Duplication permitted for educational use only.*

Pragmatic Analysis
Conversational Moves Analysis Sheet

Name of Child *Sara*

UTT#	Turn Taking Initiating	Turn Taking Responding	Appropriateness Specificity	Appropriateness Conciseness	Appropriateness Style
51		O	✓		
52		O	✓		
53	N		✓		
54		E	✓		
55		O	✓		
56		S	✓		
57		E	✓		
58		E	✓		
59		O	✓		
60		E	✓		
61		q	✓		
62	E	E	✓		
63		R	—		
64		q	—		
65		E	✓		
66		E	—		
67		E	—		
68		E	—		
69		E	✓		
70		E	✓		
71		E	✓		
72		E	✓		
73		S	✓		
74		S	✓		
75		E	✓		

UTT#	Turn Taking Initiating	Turn Taking Responding	Appropriateness Specificity	Appropriateness Conciseness	Appropriateness Style
76		E	✓		
77		E	✓		
78		E	✓		
79		E	✓		
80	R		✓		
81		E	✓		
82		E	✓		
83	N		✓		
84		q	✓		
85		O	✓		
86	R		✓		
87		O	✓		
88		q	✓		
89		E	✓		
90	N		—		
91	N		✓		
92		E	✓		
93		E	✓		
94		O	✓		
95		O	✓		
96		O	✓		
97		E	✓		
98	E		✓		
99		E	✓		
100		E	✓		

© 1993 **Thinking Publications** *Duplication permitted for educational use only.*

As a result of the analysis of referent specificity, four utterance sequences should have been identified in which Sara was not specific enough in identifying the referent of her utterance so that her mother could locate it in either physical space or memory space. The first exchange in which Sara's utterance lacked specificity was at utterance #37, when Sara referred to some girl with no apparent contextual support and her mother is not quite sure to whom Sara is referring. Sara's mother's query clarifies the situation. The next exchange lacking specificity was at utterance #63, when Sara refers to "cow people." It takes three repairs from her mother to establish the referent. The next exchange lacking specificity was at utterance #66. In spite of three repairs on the part of the mother, it is not clear whether the referent eventually gets identified. The last exchange lacking specificity was at utterance #90, when Sara identifies a plate as a "cover for the pot." Again, Sara's mother attempts to repair the lack of specificity, but Sara continues with her next utterance. In three of the four instances, referents were not present and required identification in memory space. No other utterances lacking referent specificity were found in Sara's transcript.

What can be concluded from the analysis of specificity? It is obvious that Sara did not specify her referent in sufficient detail in every utterance to permit her mother to locate those referents without some follow-up clarification. But should a child of Sara's age and/or language level be expected to be specific enough in every exchange to ensure listener comprehension? Probably not. Recall that Keenan and Schieffelin (1976) report that children 3 years of age have considerable difficulty specifying referents that are not present. But before it can be concluded that Sara's lack of specificity is within normal limits, her abilities need to be analyzed under other conversational conditions. At least one other language sample in another setting and/or with another familiar adult would need to be obtained to determine whether referent specificity is a persistent problem for Sara.

Contributional Conciseness

The next variable that will be considered has to do with the amount of conversational space taken up by a single utterance and the appropriateness of the detail provided in a particular contribution. The examination of this variable is based on one of a set of conversational principles proposed by Grice (1975). He suggested four principles that contribute to an overall obligation to "be clear" in conversational endeavors. The first principle has to do with the quantity of conversational contributions, and Grice contends that speakers should make their contributions as informative as required but no more informative than required. The second principle has to do with the quality of the contribution. Grice suggests that speakers should not say what they believe to be false, nor should they say things for which they lack "adequate evidence." The third principle deals with the relations between conversational contributions and states, simply, that speakers should be relevant in their management of topics. The last principle deals with the manner of contributions and has four parts: (1) speakers should avoid obscurity, (2) speakers should avoid ambiguity, (3) speakers should be brief, and (4) speakers should be orderly. While Grice offered these as principles governing adult conversation, children demonstrate violations of these principles, thus providing evidence that they are struggling to master them. Of these four principles, the first one, the quantity principle, will be used in making the next appropriateness judgment.

Young children typically have greater difficulty providing their listeners with enough information than they do with providing too much information. However, it is the former that was considered in appropriateness judgments of referent specificity. It is the latter that will be considered in appropriateness judgments of conciseness: Does the speaker provide the listener with too much information? It is possible to think of an adult who provides the listener with so much information that the listener becomes bored or thinks, "So what?" But children violate this principle as well. In fact, children as young as 4 years of age provide the listener with too much information, as the following example indicates.

(M and C are sitting in
clinic observation area,
observing a therapy session)

C: you know the teddy what Aaron had?/   (referent identified)

M: Yes/   (identification confirmed)

C: the one what talked?/

M: Yes/

C: Aaron's teddy bear?/

M: I know which one you mean/   (identification reconfirmed)

C: well Jason gots one too/

M: Oh I see/

In appropriateness judgments regarding contributional conciseness, a judgment will be made, as Prutting and Kirchner (1983) have suggested, whether or not violation of the conciseness principle is penalizing to the child. In other words, an attempt will be made to determine if providing too much information interferes with the continuation of conversation. In the example above, the mother is on the verge of being irritated with her child for failing to see that she has enough information to know the referent of the child's sequence of utterances. But the conversation continues. Perhaps if this child had persisted in failing to be sufficiently concise, it would have had negative consequences. Without more of the conversation, we cannot be certain.

In analyzing Sara's transcript, sequences of utterances, as opposed to each utterance in isolation, will be considered in an attempt to find instances of a lack of conciseness. Progress through the transcript, examining mother and child utterances in sequence. If evidence is found of Sara providing so much information that her mother responds negatively, mark a dash (–) in the "Conciseness" column on the line corresponding to the utterance number. Keep in mind that inappropriately providing too much information often occurs over more than one utterance. When the entire transcript has been examined, compare results with the sample provided on pages 172–173.

Analysis of Sara's transcript revealed no instances where she provided so much information that it was penalizing to her as a speaker. There were two instances where she seemed to provide irrelevant information (utterances #3 and #68), but it did not appear to penalize her as a speaker; thus, these instances were judged not to be inappropriate. It could be concluded that for this listener, Sara's utterances were judged not to lack conciseness.

Again, no normative data are available to which the results can be compared. Clinical judgment regarding a child's failure to be appropriately concise must be relied upon when considering an individual child who is interacting with a variety of speakers. If the failure to be concise is penalizing to the child, intervention would be warranted. Explicit feedback would be provided to the child in order to increase awareness of listeners' reactions to providing too much information. Only then could the child be expected to make use of specific strategies for increasing the conciseness of contributions in appropriate situations.

Pragmatic Analysis
Conversational Moves Analysis Sheet

Name of Child *Sara*

UTT#	Turn Taking Initiating	Responding	Appropriateness Specificity	Conciseness	Style
1		O	✓	✓	
2		E	✓	✓	
3		R	✓	?	
4		E	✓	✓	
5		E	✓	✓	
6		E	✓	✓	
7		E	✓	✓	
8		O	✓	✓	
9		E	✓	✓	
10		R	✓	✓	
11		E	✓	✓	
12		O	✓	✓	
13		O	✓	✓	
14	N		✓	✓	
15	N		✓	✓	
16		E	✓	✓	
17		E	✓	✓	
18		O	✓	✓	
19		E	✓	✓	
20		E	✓	✓	
21	R	E	✓	✓	
22		E	✓	✓	
23		E	✓	✓	
24		E	✓	✓	
25		R	✓	✓	

UTT#	Turn Taking Initiating	Responding	Appropriateness Specificity	Conciseness	Style
26		E	✓	✓	
27	N		✓	✓	
28		O	✓	✓	
29		E	✓	✓	
30	E	O	✓	✓	
31		O	✓	✓	
32		E	✓	✓	
33		O	✓	✓	
34		E	✓	✓	
35		O	✓	✓	
36	R		✓	✓	
37	E		—	✓	
38		q	✓	✓	
39	E	q	✓	✓	
40		O	✓	✓	
41		O	✓	✓	
42		q	✓	✓	
43		O	✓	✓	
44	R	O	✓	✓	
45		O	✓	✓	
46		E	✓	✓	
47	E	O	✓	✓	
48		O	✓	✓	
49		O	✓	✓	
50		E	✓	✓	

© 1993 Thinking Publications *Duplication permitted for educational use only.*

Pragmatic Analysis
Conversational Moves Analysis Sheet

Name of Child *Sara*

UTT#	Turn Taking		Appropriateness		
	Initiating	Responding	Specificity	Conciseness	Style
51		O	✓	✓	
52		O	✓	✓	
53	N		✓	✓	
54		E	✓	✓	
55		O	✓	✓	
56		S	✓	✓	
57		E	✓	✓	
58		E	✓	✓	
59		O	✓	✓	
60		E	✓	✓	
61		q	✓	✓	
62	E		✓	✓	
63		E	—	✓	
64		R	—	✓	
65		q	✓	✓	
66		E	—	✓	
67		E	—	✓	
68		E	—	?	
69		E	✓	✓	
70		E	✓	✓	
71		E	✓	✓	
72		E	✓	✓	
73		S	✓	✓	
74		S	✓	✓	
75		E	✓	✓	

UTT#	Turn Taking		Appropriateness		
	Initiating	Responding	Specificity	Conciseness	Style
76		E	✓	✓	
77		E	✓	✓	
78		E	✓	✓	
79		E	✓	✓	
80	R		✓	✓	
81		E	✓	✓	
82		E	✓	✓	
83	N		✓	✓	
84		q	✓	✓	
85		O	✓	✓	
86	R	O	✓	✓	
87		O	✓	✓	
88		q	✓	✓	
89		E	✓	✓	
90	N		—	✓	
91	N		✓	✓	
92		E	✓	✓	
93		E	✓	✓	
94		O	✓	✓	
95		O	✓	✓	
96		O	✓	✓	
97		E	✓	✓	
98	E		✓	✓	
99		E	✓	✓	
100		E	✓	✓	

© 1993 Thinking Publications *Duplication permitted for educational use only.*

Communication Style

The final variable that will be considered in making appropriateness judgments is that of communication style, or the ability to alter the style of a contribution based on characteristics of the listener. Shatz and Gelman (1973) were the first to provide evidence indicating that young children can alter the form of their contributions on the basis of language differences of their listeners. In their study, the language of 4-year-old children was compared when the children interacted with 2-year-old children and then with adults. Results indicated that by 4 years of age, children can adjust length, complexity, and use of attention-holders in their language depending on the age and/or language abilities of conversational partners. Since this study, others have followed indicating that children as young as 3 years of age can use various styles of interacting depending on whether they are assuming a role (as of a "baby" or a "daddy"), talking with a younger child, talking with a familiar adult, or talking with an unfamiliar adult (Berko Gleason, 1973; Sachs and Devin, 1976).

The analysis of the ability to use stylistic variations in communication is based on two assumptions. The first assumption is that the child's ability to make adjustments reflects an abstract knowledge of the appropriateness of speech to the listener (Sachs and Devin, 1976). This assumption implies an integration of the cognitive system and the linguistic system. The second assumption is that a child who is unable to make adjustments will be penalized in some way as a speaker. Prutting and Kirchner (1983) suggest that a failure to adjust even loudness level can have a negative impact on the "reactions of strangers, classmates, and/or teachers" regarding the child's communication abilities. Both of these assumptions serve to justify the examination of a pragmatic variable that may occur infrequently.

In making appropriateness judgments regarding communication style, identify the child's failure to make syntactic modifications, vocal quality modifications, and vocal intensity modifications as demanded by the situation. For example, if the child is interacting with a younger child and fails to shorten the length and/or reduce the complexity of his utterances, enter a dash (—) in the "Style" column on the Conversational Moves Analysis Sheet corresponding to the utterances where those modifications would have been appropriate. If the child is role playing and fails to make vocal quality changes (e.g., lower voice for the "daddy," higher voice for the "baby") and/or syntactic changes (e.g., more imperatives for the "daddy," babbling and/or one-word utterances for the "baby") as a result of his role, again enter a dash (—) in the "Style" column corresponding to the utterances where the modifications would be appropriate. If the child failed to use politeness markers when interacting with unfamiliar adults and/or used aggressive vocal intensity when interacting with peers or adults, put a dash (—) in the "Style" column on the Conversational Moves Analysis Sheet.

Turn to Sara's transcript and consider sequences of utterances to determine whether there was a need for Sara to alter her communication style and whether she made the appropriate adjustments. If she did, put a plus (+) in the "Style" column corresponding to the utterances where the adjustments were made. If she did not make appropriate adjustments, put a dash (—) in the "Style" column corresponding to the utterances where the adjustments should have been made. All other boxes in the "Style" column should be left blank. When the entire transcript has been examined, compare results with the sample provided on pages 175–176.

Analysis of Sara's transcript revealed no instances where she should have made adjustments in her communication style and did not make them. In fact, there were no instances where she should have made adjustments and did. This clearly points out the need to have samples of communicative interaction under a variety of conditions and with a variety of partners. Only then can it be concluded that a child can or cannot make adjustments in his communication style.

And what should be done if a child is unable to make adjustments in style as situations demand? It is possible to teach the child to make the appropriate syntactic and vocal adjustments and to recognize when these adjustments are necessary. Because the ability to vary communication style is a reflection of the integration of the child's cognitive, semantic, syntactic, and pragmatic systems, this appropriateness variable is very important in determining the overall communication abilities of a child.

Pragmatic Analysis
Conversational Moves Analysis Sheet

Name of Child *Sara*

UTT#	Turn Taking — Initiating	Turn Taking — Responding	Appropriateness — Specificity	Appropriateness — Conciseness	Appropriateness — Style
1		O	✓	✓	
2		E	✓	✓	
3		R	✓	?	
4		E	✓	✓	
5		E	✓	✓	
6		E	✓	✓	
7		E	✓	✓	
8		O	✓	✓	
9		E	✓	✓	
10		R	✓	✓	
11		E	✓	✓	
12		O	✓	✓	
13		O	✓	✓	
14	N		✓	✓	
15	N		✓	✓	
16		E	✓	✓	
17		E	✓	✓	
18		O	✓	✓	
19		E	✓	✓	
20		E	✓	✓	
21	R		✓	✓	
22		E	✓	✓	
23		E	✓	✓	
24		E	✓	✓	
25		R	✓	✓	

UTT#	Turn Taking — Initiating	Turn Taking — Responding	Appropriateness — Specificity	Appropriateness — Conciseness	Appropriateness — Style
26		E	✓	✓	
27	N		✓	✓	
28		O	✓	✓	
29		E	✓	✓	
30	E	O	✓	✓	
31		E	✓	✓	
32		E	✓	✓	
33		O	✓	✓	
34		E	✓	✓	
35		O	✓	✓	
36	R		✓	✓	
37	E		—	✓	
38		Y	✓	✓	
39	E		✓	✓	
40		O	✓	✓	
41		O	✓	✓	
42		Y	✓	✓	
43		O	✓	✓	
44	R		✓	✓	
45		O	✓	✓	
46	E	E	✓	✓	
47			✓	✓	
48		O	✓	✓	
49		O	✓	✓	
50		E	✓	✓	

© 1993 **Thinking Publications** *Duplication permitted for educational use only.*

Pragmatic Analysis
Conversational Moves Analysis Sheet

Name of Child *Sara*

UTT#	Turn Taking Initiating	Turn Taking Responding	Appropriateness Specificity	Appropriateness Conciseness	Appropriateness Style
51		O	✓	✓	
52		O	✓	✓	
53	N		✓	✓	
54		E	✓	✓	
55		O	✓	✓	
56		S	✓	✓	
57		E	✓	✓	
58		E	✓	✓	
59		O	✓	✓	
60		E	✓	✓	
61		q	✓	✓	
62	E		✓	✓	
63		E	—	✓	
64		R	—	✓	
65		q	✓	✓	
66		E	—	✓	
67		E	—	✓	
68		E	—	?	
69		E	✓	✓	
70		E	✓	✓	
71		E	✓	✓	
72		E	✓	✓	
73		S	✓	✓	
74		S	✓	✓	
75		E	✓	✓	

UTT#	Turn Taking Initiating	Turn Taking Responding	Appropriateness Specificity	Appropriateness Conciseness	Appropriateness Style
76		E	✓	✓	
77		E	✓	✓	
78		E	✓	✓	
79		E	✓	✓	
80	R		✓	✓	
81		E	✓	✓	
82		E	✓	✓	
83	N		✓	✓	
84		q	✓	✓	
85		O	✓	✓	
86	R		✓	✓	
87		O	✓	✓	
88		q	✓	✓	
89		E	✓	✓	
90	N		—	✓	
91	N		✓	✓	
92		E	✓	✓	
93		E	✓	✓	
94		O	✓	✓	
95		O	✓	✓	
96		O	✓	✓	
97		E	✓	✓	
98	E		✓	✓	
99		E	✓	✓	
100		E	✓	✓	

© 1993 **Thinking Publications** *Duplication permitted for educational use only.*

IMPLICATIONS FOR REMEDIATION

Completion of each of the appropriate pragmatic analyses should be followed by a synthesis of results. The Conversational Moves Summary form can be used for this synthesis. A completed form for Sara's transcript appears on page 178.

While problems with any one of the areas analyzed may not be related to problems in another area, results of each analysis procedure completed must be reviewed to develop comprehensive goals and objectives. The sequence of normal development is not as detailed for pragmatic milestones as it is for semantic and syntactic behaviors; however, judgments about what to target in remediation for identified pragmatic problems continue to be based on what is known about normal language acquisition. Norms are not readily available, but knowledgeable judgments can be made. As in previous chapters, the suggestions provided here should be considered general guidelines for developing remediation goals and objectives, and not hard-and-fast rules.

Data obtained from frequency-of-occurrence analysis of various pragmatic categories (i.e., Dore's Primitive Speech Acts or Conversational Acts or Martlew's Conversational Moves) that indicate a limited range of categories used can provide the foundation for developing objectives that target use of a wider variety of categories. For example, if a child's language abilities overall are at a one-word level and he is using a limited number of types of primitive speech acts, it would be appropriate to provide the child with opportunities to use a broader range of types of primitive speech acts. If the child's language abilities are typical of language-normal children between 2 and 5 years of age and he is using a limited number of conversational acts, again it would be appropriate to provide opportunities for use of additional conversational acts. In either case, it would be crucial to consider the role that the conversational co-participant may play in the opportunities for expressing a variety of communicative functions such as those specified in Dore's Primitive Speech Acts and Conversational Acts. In addition, Dore (1978) concluded that variations

in setting (e.g., preschool classroom vs. supermarket) and in situation or condition (e.g., group vs. dyad; question asking vs. free play) may result in different distributions of types of conversational acts. Consequently, targeting an increase in use of particular functions or acts in a remediation goal can only be accomplished by varying the child's opportunity to engage in conversation with different partners, in different settings, and under different conditions.

Results of analysis using Martlew's Conversational Moves revealing a distribution of INITIATING and RESPONDING MOVES substantially different from results obtained by Martlew may indicate a need to teach the child additional means of initiating or responding. In other words, for a child whose INITIATING MOVES constitute substantially less than 30 percent of his speaking turns, Martlew's types of INITIATING MOVES could be taught in the context of a variety of conversational settings and situations with a variety of conversational partners. For a child whose INITIATING MOVES constitute substantially more than 30 percent of his speaking turns, it would be productive to teach the child to use various types of RESPONDING MOVES by paying attention to the contributions of his conversational co-participant and by using more diverse types of Martlew's RESPONDING MOVES. Again, attention to the setting, situation, and partner is very important when attempting to target discourse aspects of communication. Various accounts of proposed intervention formats targeting turn taking, conversational contributions, and other discourse variables are beginning to appear in the literature (Bedrosian, 1985; McTear, 1985; Fey, 1986; Beveridge and Conti-Ramsden, 1987; Brinton and Fujuki, 1989; Smedley, 1989; Norris and Damico, 1990; Gallagher, 1991; Leonard and Fey, 1991; McTear and Conti-Ramsden, 1991; Owens, 1991). Consideration of each of these will be helpful in developing intervention objectives and techniques.

Data obtained from analysis of discourse variables that result in appropriateness judgments can be used to target behaviors that would increase the appropriateness of each variable. For example, if a child lacks specificity in referent identification, he can be taught to

© 1993 Thinking Publications *Duplication permitted for educational use only.*

Pragmatic Analysis
Conversational Moves Summary

Name of Child ___Sara___

TURN TAKING

___18___ Initiating = ___18___ % of Total Utterances

___82___ Responding = ___82___ % of Total Utterances

APPROPRIATENESS JUDGMENTS

Specificity

___7___ Lacked Specificity = ___7___ % of Total Utterances

Conciseness

___0___ Lacked Conciseness = ___0___ % of Total Utterances

Style

___0___ Lacked Stylistic Variation = ___0___ % of Total Utterances

*(2 provided irrelevant information
but judged not to be inappropriate)*

© **1993 Thinking Publications** *Duplication permitted for educational use only.*

respond to explicit feedback from the conversational co-participant in order to be more specific. While the child's ability to respond to decreasing explicitness in requests for revision increases with age, children as young as 2 years of age can respond to requests for revision. In addition, the types of revisions that children are able to make change developmentally. Therefore, the expectations for adding specificity must be developmentally appropriate and based on what is known about normal language acquisition. These guidelines also hold for the child who is too informative. This child can be taught to respond to feedback from the conversational co-participant indicating that the amount of information provided is inappropriately high, resulting in the judgment of a lack of conciseness. The child can be taught various syntactic conventions for increasing conciseness (e.g., use of pronouns, anaphora, ellipsis, etc.). And he can be taught to decrease the number of speaking turns used to establish his referent. Again, behaviors targeted must be developmentally appropriate and based on normal language acquisition information. In addition, like all preceding pragmatic variables, it is crucial to consider the impact that setting, situation, and conversational co-participant will have on the child's ability to make modifications that could lead to judgments of appropriate specificity and conciseness.

Finally, the child who demonstrates an inability to vary his style of communication depending on the setting and/or conversational co-participant can be taught to recognize a need to vary his communication style, and then can be taught ways to vary his style. The ability to recognize a need to vary communication style will change developmentally, as will the conventions available to vary that style. Judgments about what behaviors to target must be based on what is known about normal language development in relation to the child's overall language production abilities.

Overall, analysis of communicative functions and discourse relations yields quantitative and qualitative data that can be used to identify children with problems in the pragmatic area of language production. These data also can be used to develop remediation goals and objectives. While the suggestions provided here can only be considered general guidelines for the development of remediation goals and objectives, use of these suggestions and information on the normal language acquisition sequence can lead to appropriate and productive goals and objectives. In addition, the variables to consider in developing goals and objectives can be used in diagnostic therapy to ensure accurate judgments of pragmatic abilities.

APPENDIX A

Blank Transcription Form

Name of Child _____ CA _____

Type of Situation _____ Date _____

Length of Tape _____ Length of Transcript _____ Time of Day _____

Materials Present _____

People Present _____

ADULT	CONTEXT	CHILD

© 1993 **Thinking Publications** Duplication permitted for educational use only.

ADULT	CONTEXT	CHILD

© 1993 **Thinking Publications** Duplication permitted for educational use only.

APPENDIX B

Unanalyzed Language Transcripts

Sara
David
Gretchen

Name of Child ___Sara___ CA ___4 years, 10 months___

Type of Situation ___free play in playroom of preschool___ Date ___10-6___

Length of Tape ___45 min___ Length of Transcript ___100 utterances___ Time of Day ___2 pm___

Materials Present ___playground set, bendable people, toy dishes___

People Present ___S = Sara; M = Mother___

ADULT	CONTEXT	CHILD	
What do you have huh?			
		toys/	1
Toys?			
What is that?	(M pointing to swingset)		
What does it look like to you?			
	(S shrugs shoulders)		
What is it?			
What does it look like?			
Where would you go to play			
with toys like this?			
		XXX/	
If we said we were going			
somewhere · to play with toys like			
this where would you play with these?			
		at the park!/	2
It looks like a park doesn't it?			
		a park/	3
What's that?			
	(S touches the slide)		
		it's a swingset/	4
	(M touches slide)		
This is?			
		no that a slide/	5

© **1993 Thinking Publications** *Duplication permitted for educational use only.*

ADULT	CONTEXT	CHILD	
	(S pointing to swingset)	there's the swingset/	*6*
What do you do with it?			
	(S climbs slide with fingers)		
	(S using finger to slide down)	climb up and wee/	*7*
Why don't you take one of the people			
and show me what you do?			
	(S picks up doll)		
Who's that?			
		Mamma/	*8*
Show me how she does it/			
	(S slides doll down slide)		
		she can't go/	*9*
		she can't go down/	*10*
How come?			
		cuz she's stuck there/	*11*
	(M points to sandbox)		
What's that?			
		sandbox/	*12*
What do you do with a sandbox?			
	(S picks up cup and puts it up		
	to her mouth)		
What are you doing?			
		drinking/	*13*
	(S picks up sand spilled on floor)		
		uh oh/	*14*
	(S puts cup in sandbox)		
		I make coffee/	*15*
Okay we'll make coffee/			
	(M pulls picnic table toward herself)		

© 1993 **Thinking Publications** *Duplication permitted for educational use only.*

ADULT	CONTEXT	CHILD	
What's this?			
		that's a picnic table/	*16*
		and that's a swingset/	*17*
What do you do on a swingset?			
		swing/	*18*
	(S pours sand into cup)		
Let's hold it over here/			
	(S stirs sand in cup with spoon)		
Now what are you doing?			
		um I mix it up/	*19*
Then what?			
	(S covers top of cup with hand)		
		then you · shake it/	*20*
	(S shakes cup)		
Who should we pretend that we are?			
		not done yet/	*21*
Oh not done yet/			
		now it's done/	*22*
	(S pours into another cup)		
Okay/			
	(S picking up spoon, stirring in cup)	I use a spoon/	*23*
What are you doing?			
		I mixing/	*24*
Mixing it up?			
		mixing it up/	*25*
		now put it in the cup/	*26*
What's that?	(M pointing to picnic table)		
		XXX/	
	(S drops cup in sandbox, spills		

© 1993 **Thinking Publications** *Duplication permitted for educational use only.*

ADULT	CONTEXT	CHILD	
	sand)		
Oops/			
		oops/	*27*
What is that over there?			
		table/	*28*
Okay/			
That looks like a picnic table/			
What do you do at a picnic table?			
		sit on it/	*29*
	(S picks up girl doll)		
Put them over there?			
Can you put them over there?			
	(S tries to bend doll's legs)		
		how do you do this?/	*30*
What do you want her to do?			
		sit down/	*31*
Okay/			
	(S looks at M)		
		also she lays down/	*32*
She can/			
	(S sits dolls at picnic table)		
What are they doing?			
		sitting/	*33*
What are they gonna do now?			
		they are um gonna eat/	*34*
They are?			
What are they gonna eat?			
		pancakes/	*35*
	(S takes another doll off		

© **1993 Thinking Publications** *Duplication permitted for educational use only.*

ADULT	CONTEXT	CHILD	
	swingset and puts it at table)		
		it's time to go/	*36*
Oh?			
	(S looking at camera)	where's that um girl?/	*37*
Beret?			
		yeah Beret/	*38*
She's in the other room/			
		cuz she isn't playing?/	*39*
Umhm/			
Now what are the people eating?			
		pancakes/	*40*
And what else?			
	(S straightens doll)		
		milk/	*41*
That's all they need?			
		yeah/	*42*
Who made the meal · who made the pancakes?			
		Mamma/	*43*
	(S picks up man doll)		
		and this is the daddy/	*44*
Okay/			
Who are these two?	(M pointing to dolls at table)		
		children/	*45*
Do you want to give them names?			
		Mark · Kristen · Pete/	*46*
	(S picks up woman doll)		
		who's this?/	*47*
That's the mommy/			

ADULT	CONTEXT	CHILD	
	(M points to swingset)		
What's this thing?			
		swingset/	*48*
And what do you do on a swingset?			
		swing/	*49*
	(S puts woman doll down and		
	picks up man doll)		
		now he's gonna go on/	*50*
What's this?	(M pointing to teeter-totter)		
	(S shrugs shoulders)		
What is this one?			
		teetotter/	*51*
What do you do on it?			
	(S puts doll on one end and		
	goes up and down)		
		teetot · teetot/	*52*
	(S sifts "sand" in sandbox)		
		this is birdseed/	*53*
It is?			
		yeah but it also's sand/	*54*
Umhm · we're pretending it's			
sand though/			
Now how does a teeter-totter work?			
	(M and S each hold doll on the		
	ends of teeter-totter)		
		teetot · teetot/	*55*
Tell me how it works/			
		teetot · teetot/	*56*
Tell me/			

 © **1993 Thinking Publications** *Duplication permitted for educational use only.*

ADULT	CONTEXT	CHILD	
		I don't know/	*57*
Well can it put ₛ/c can one person do the teeter-totter?			
	(S slides doll down teeter-totter)		
		put it down here/	*58*
How many does it take?			
		two/two/two/	*59*
	(M points to shelter)		
What's this for?			
		that's a house/	*60*
Do you know what this is called?			
		no/	*61*
		what?/	*62*
This is called a shelter/			
What do you think they would use that for?			
		for cow people/	*63*
Cow people?			
		for cow people/	*64*
What does that mean?			
	(S shrugs shoulders)		
		that means _____ /	
Cowboys?			
		yeah/	*65*
What if you saw one of these at the park?			
What do you think it's for?			
	(S picks up doll)		
		for he-mans/	*66*

© **1993 Thinking Publications** *Duplication permitted for educational use only.*

ADULT	CONTEXT	CHILD	
He-mans?			
	(S dances doll on roof of shelter)		
		this goes like this/	*67*
		he-mans · he-mans · he-mans/	*68*
Where did you learn about that?			
		at Kristi's house/	*69*
At Kristi's house?			
What would happen if it			
started to rain?			
	(S shrugging shoulders)	go in the house/	*70*
What's this called?	(M pointing to shelter)		
		shelter house/	*71*
Shelter house/			
Let's pretend it's raining/			
What would you do?			
		play with kids inside the shelter/	*72*
	(S singing and dancing dolls	inside we go go go go/	*73*
	into house)		
	(S picks up another doll)		
		inside we go/	*74*
What if they want to eat lunch now?			
		they can/	*75*
		it stopped raining/	*76*
Okay what should they do now?			
	(S taking doll out of the house)	go outside/	*77*
What do you think they would			
like to play on?			
	(S pointing to trapeze)	that/	*78*
Okay what is that?			

   © **1993 Thinking Publications** *Duplication permitted for educational use only.*

ADULT	CONTEXT	CHILD	
	(S shrugs shoulders)		
It looks like a trapeze doesn't it?			
	(S puts doll's feet through		
	trapeze rings)		
Now what are they gonna play with?			
		in the sandbox/	*79*
	(S makes doll fly to sandbox)		
	(S getting dishes out of box)	I fixed supper already/	*80*
Can you put the dishes on the table?			
	(S spoons sand into cups)		
What are you doing?			
		making popcorn/	*81*
Okay/			
What are you fixing for supper			
tonight?			
		I said popcorn/	*82*
Oh okay/			
What else?			
	(S picking up scoop)	hey this looks like a bunny ear/	*83*
A bunny ear?			
		yeah/	*84*
Let me see/	(M reaching for scoop)		
Oh it does look like a bunny's ear/			
How many ears does a bunny have?			
		two/	*85*
	(S turns scoop over)		
		and it almost like a ear/	*86*
Umhmm/			
	(M picks up another scoop		

© **1993 Thinking Publications** *Duplication permitted for educational use only.*

ADULT	CONTEXT	CHILD	
	and turns it over)		
What does this one look like?			
	(S leaning over)	a shell/	*87*
A shell?			
	(S takes scoop)		
		mhm/	*88*
	(cup of sand falls off picnic table)		
Oop · I'll clean it up · you set the			
rest of the table okay?			
	(M brushes sand into hand;		
	S puts plates on table)		
What are you doing?			
		putting the plates on/	*89*
	(S turns plate over in hand)		
		this is the cover for the pot/	*90*
The cover for the pot?			
	(S puts spoons in cups)		
		in the cups/	*91*
		that goes on there/	*92*
	(S puts knife on table)		
What are those?			
		knife and spoon/	*93*
		knife and spoon/	
How many plates are there?			
	(S pointing to each plate)	one↗/	*94*
		two↗/	*95*
		three↗/	*96*
		there's not enough/	*97*
	(S looks in box)		

© **1993 Thinking Publications** *Duplication permitted for educational use only.*

ADULT	CONTEXT	CHILD	
		how 'bout for the children?/	*98*
How 'bout for the children? Oh I			
think there's s/c how many			
do we need?			
	(S pointing to each plate)	one two three/	*99*
How many people are there?			
	(S points to each doll)		
		four/	*100*
Okay so how many plates do			
we need?			
	(S digs in box)		

© 1993 **Thinking Publications** *Duplication permitted for educational use only.*

Name of Child __*David*__   CA __*3 years, 1 month*__

Type of Situation __*free play in playroom of preschool*__   Date __*10-4*__

Length of Tape __*40 min*__   Length of Transcript __*101 utterances*__   Time of Day __*10 am*__

Materials Present __*playground set, bendable people, toy dishes*__

People Present __*M = mother; D = David*__

ADULT	CONTEXT	CHILD
	(D puts dishes on picnic table)	
Can you think of something		
you'd like for supper?		
		yeah/
What?		
What should I make for supper?		
		hot dogs/
Hot dogs?		
What else?		
What does Daddy like for supper?		
		hot dogs/
He likes hot dogs too?		
What else does Daddy like?		
		XXX/
Mhum/		
What does Daddy like for supper?		
Can you think of what Daddy		
likes for supper?		
		sandwiches/
He likes sandwiches?		
		yeah/
What kind of sandwiches?		
		big ones/
Big ones/		

© **1993 Thinking Publications** *Duplication permitted for educational use only.*

ADULT	CONTEXT	CHILD
What does he like to put inside		
of his sandwiches?		
		cheese/
Cheese and what?		
	(D looks at camera)	
		they're gonna take $_{s/c}$ that
		camera's gonna take a picture of us/
It is!/		
And what else does Dad like in		
his sandwiches?		
		things/
Things?		
What kind of things?		
		just don't worry/
Just don't worry/		
Well you have to tell me what to		
put in Daddy's sandwich so I		
can make him some supper/		
Are you going to make him		
some coffee?		
	(D scooping up sand with a dish)	yes/
		you won't find a bug in there/
You won't find a bug in there/		
What else are you going to fix		
for supper?		
		I don't know/
Don't you remember?		
		no/
	(D makes doll go down slide)	

 © **1993 Thinking Publications** *Duplication permitted for educational use only.*

ADULT	CONTEXT	CHILD
		does this little boy have to
		go go down to the slide↑/
He's gonna go down to the slide?		
	(D making doll jump on teeter-totter)	look at him/
		can he please go on this↑/
Sure/		
That looks like a fun play time		
doesn't it?		
It has swings ₛ/c who has	(M pushing swing)	
swings like this?		
		not me/
Not you?		
		Lisa/
Lisa does yeah and and where		
do we have a trapeze like that?		
	(M pushes trapeze)	
		at Lisa's/
At the cabin?		
		yeah/
Do we have a swing at the cabin?		
		yeah/
Uhum and what do you do at		
the cabin?		
		play/
Play/		
Who do you feed at the cabin?		
		Chippy/
Chippy/		
What do you feed Chippy?		

© **1993 Thinking Publications** *Duplication permitted for educational use only.*

ADULT	CONTEXT	CHILD
		nuts/
Oh does he like that?		
	(D takes dishes out of sandbox)	
		those are nuts/
Those are nuts?		
		oh these are seeds/
Seeds okay · that sounds pretty good/		
What are you doing?		
	(D spoons sand into pitcher)	
		just making/
Just making/		
Are you scooping carefully?		
		yeah/
Who are you making that for?		
		Bridge/
For Bridget?		
		yeah/
Does Bridget like that when you cook?		
		ahuh/
When is Bridget coming to see you?		
		oh nine o'clock/
At nine o'clock!/		
Oh/		
Tomorrow or today?		
		today/
Well good/		
	(D pours sand out of pitcher)	
		you know what I'm making↑/
What?		

© **1993 Thinking Publications** *Duplication permitted for educational use only.*

ADULT	CONTEXT	CHILD
		soap/
You're making soap/		
		no · I'm Papa Smurf/
Papa Smurf/		
And what are you doing Papa Smurf?		
And what are you doing Papa Smurf?		
		making something for Gargamel/
For Gargamel?		
		yeah like I'm blowing him down/
Blow him down?		
		yeah/
Poor Gargamel · I'd think		
that might hurt/		
		oh he's bad/
		he's catching all the smurfs/
Oh dear/		
		I should do something/
You should do something yes/		
	(D stirring sand in dish)	yeah Papa Smurf did this/
What does Papa Smurf do?		
		make something and Gargamel/
		he doesn't make anything for smurfs/
No for smurfs ~s/c~ what does he		
make for Gargamel?		
		things/
humm · things/		
Does he make a magic potion?		
		yeah/
And Gargamel drinks it and		

© **1993 Thinking Publications** *Duplication permitted for educational use only.*

ADULT	CONTEXT	CHILD
what happens?		
		go home/
What does say · when Gargamel		
drinks the magic potion?		
You remember what it says		
in your book?		
		yeah/
What does Gargamel s/c what		
happens when Gargamel drinks		
the magic potion?		
		thanks for this/
Does he say wamo?		
		wamo/
Yeah/		
And what else?		
		I don't know/
Do you remember in your book		
about the fake smurf?		
Who's the fake smurf?		
		that's Bob/
Oh/		
		XXX/
I see/		
		I get a new cup of coffee/
Oh good I'd like a cup of coffee/		
	(D spooning sand into cups)	I just get it right now/
All right/		
	(D gives cup to adult)	
Oh thank you very much/		

© **1993 Thinking Publications** *Duplication permitted for educational use only.*

ADULT	CONTEXT	CHILD
What do you say?		
		thank you Mom/
No I said thank you/		
What do you say?		
	(D stares at M)	
You have to say you're welcome/		
		you're welcome/
Oh you make some good coffee/		
		ahuh/
	(D spooning sand into cup)	I gonna make some for myself/
Okay/		
		you drink it up/
	(M pretends to drink)	
		gone/
mm not quite/		
		XXX/
And I'm not gonna spill/		
Are you gonna spill?		
		no/
Okay/		
	(D pours sand from cup back into sandbox)	
		alldone/
All done/		
Mine's all done too/		
	(M pours sand into sandbox)	
There mine's all done now/		
	(D scoops sand into cup)	
And now what are you doing?		

© 1993 **Thinking Publications** *Duplication permitted for educational use only.*

ADULT	CONTEXT	CHILD
		making more/
		seed/
Oh/		
Where do we put that kind of		
seed at our house?		
		XXX/
In the bird feeder?		
		yeah/
Who built us a bird feeder?		
		Dad/
		when I was taking a nap/
When you were taking a nap		
Dad built a bird feeder?		
		no/
And what else did you help Dad?		
Didn't you help Dad dig the post s/c		
dig the hole?		
		no/
No?		
What did you help Daddy with?		
		oh I did s/c I went night-night
		one day/
	(D gesturing with hands)	and then the bird feeder/
Oh I see/		
Didn't you help Dad?		
		no/
Did you help Dad with the rocks?		
		yeah/
What did you do?		

 © **1993 Thinking Publications** *Duplication permitted for educational use only.*

ADULT	CONTEXT	CHILD
		shovel them/
You shoveled them!/		
Where did you put them?		
Where did you and Dad put the rocks?		
Hmm?		
		I don't know/
You don't remember?		
When Dad shoveled them where		
did he put them?		
Did he put them in the wheelbarrow?		
		yeah/
	(D puts dishes in sandbox)	
		I'm gonna put these in the
		dishwasher/
Oh the dishwasher/		
Okay/		
	(D points to shelter house)	
		that one's for when it's raining/
Oh then we play under there?		
		yeah/
Why?		
		because/
		what if it starts to rain?/
Do you think people go under		
there when it rains?		
		yeah/
Oh look at this/	(M picking up knife)	
		it's startin' to rain/
	(D putting doll and sandbox	I'll put this under here/

© 1993 Thinking Publications *Duplication permitted for educational use only.*

ADULT	CONTEXT	CHILD
	in shelter house)	
Okay/		
		I gotta keep them in there/
Oh of course we don't want them		
to get wet when it rains/		
The picnic table can stay outside		
when it rains just like this/		
Who else has to go underneath		
there when it rains?		
		Daddy/
The dad?		
Is that like dad and mom?		
	(D pointing to mom doll)	that's the mom/
		look it they have to get inside/
They better hurry/		
	(D puts two dolls in shelter)	
		they got a raincoat/
They have a raincoat?		
Oh well maybe then they won't		
get very wet/		
		there they got in there/
Oh should we unhook her from		
the swing?		
	(M and D trying to get doll	yeah/
	off swing)	
	(D puts doll in shelter)	
		I'll turn the table this way/
	(D turns table)	
Is Dad building us a picnic table?		

 © **1993 Thinking Publications** *Duplication permitted for educational use only.*

ADULT	CONTEXT	CHILD
In the garage?		
		yeah/
What do you use when you		
help Dad build/		
		things/
		hey it stopped raining/
Oh it stopped raining?		
		they can come outside/
Oh good/		
	(D puts doll on picnic table)	
		they gonna eat something/
They're gonna eat some supper?		
	(D drops doll under table)	
		what was this boy did?/
He slipped right under the table/		
		how did he do that?/
Well you have to make him sit down/		

© **1993 Thinking Publications** *Duplication permitted for educational use only.*

Name of Child ___Gretchen___   CA ___29 months___

Type of Situation ___clinic kitchen playroom___   Date ___4-13___

Length of Tape ___50 min___   Length of Transcript ___100 utterances___   Time of Day ___1:45 pm___

Materials Present ___kitchen items___

People Present ___G = Gretchen; M = Mother; C = clinician___

ADULT	CONTEXT	CHILD
You wanna play kitchen?	(M and G moving toward play kitchen)	
		yeah/
Oh what a nice kitchen/		
They have many nice things/		
	(G picks up yellow chair)	
		/gɛtən jəo/ [Gretchen's yellow]
Gretchen's yellow chair/		
		uh huh/
	(G points to self)	
		/ʌ gɛtən/ [I'm Gretchen]
	(G points to M)	
		/ʌ/ Mama/ [you're Mama]
And I'm Mama/		
And we're in the play kitchen/		
	(G picks up pink cup)	
		/ʌ pi/ [that's pink]
Yes that's a pink one/		
Are there more in the cupboard?		
	(G opens cupboard)	
		/kiki/ [cookie]
Are there cookies in there?		
		uh huh/
	(G opens refrigerator)	
		/wʌzæ?/ [what's that?]

© **1993 Thinking Publications** *Duplication permitted for educational use only.*

ADULT	CONTEXT	CHILD
	(G pulls out egg carton with	
	Ping-Pong ball eggs)	
What are those?		
		/aɪ/ [eggs]
You're right/		
You could make scrambled eggs/		
	(G carrying eggs to stove)	yeah/
	(G starts to put eggs down	
	and turns to M)	
		/ʌ hɑt/ [that's hot]
Oh the stove is hot/		
		uh huh/
	(G looks at her finger)	
		/ʌ aʊwi/ [a owie]
Yes you have an owie/		
How did you get that owie?		
		/ʌ hɑt/ [from the hot stove]
Yes on the hot stove/		
	(G opens the oven and finds comb)	
		/ʌ hɑr/ [for hair]
A comb!/		
That's a silly thing to be in the oven/		
		/ʌ hɑr/ [your hair]
My hair?		
	(G reaches for M's hair)	
You wanna comb my hair?		
		yeah/
	(G combs M's hair and turns	
	back to cupboard)	

 © 1993 Thinking Publications *Duplication permitted for educational use only.*

ADULT	CONTEXT	CHILD
What color is that comb?		
	(G pulls on cupboard door)	
		/win/ [green]
Pull hard/		
Can you get it?		
		uh huh/
	(G gets door open)	
What's in there?		
		/kiki/ [cookies]
	(G picks up cup and turns to M)	
		/mɔr dus/ [more juice]
You want more juice?		
Well let's see/		
Here's the juice/		
	(M pours "juice" from carton)	
		/ʌ dʌ/ [thank you]
	(G opens cookie box)	
		Mama!/
What!/		
		/pupi/ [poopies]
		/aɪ pupi/ [I have poopies]
	(G and M exit)	
	(G and M return)	
What should we do now?		
	(G points to telephone)	
Oh should we play telephone?		
		uh huh/
		/ʌ hom/ [at home]
Yes we have one like that at home/		

ADULT	CONTEXT	CHILD
	(G moves to cupboard and	
	points to wooden milk bottles)	
		/ʌ mok/ [that's milk]
um hum/		
	(G putting dishes on table)	/taɪ i/ [time to eat]
Is it time to eat?		
		yeah/
What are we having?		
		/kik/ [cake]
We're having cake?		
		/æn kʊki/ [and cookies]
That's my favorite meal/		
	(G picks up box of cookies)	
		/mʌ kikiↆ/ [more cookies?]
Oh yes/		
I like cookies/		
		/no kiki/ [no cookies]
	(G sets box down)	
		/au dʌn/ [all gone or all done]
Are we all done eating?		
	(G turns to stove)	
		/ʌ hot/ [it's hot]
Yes/		
What's in the oven?		
	(G opens oven)	
		/no mor/ [nothing]
Nothing?		
Is that oven empty?		
		/ʌ no mor/ [the oven's empty]

 © **1993 Thinking Publications** *Duplication permitted for educational use only.*

ADULT	CONTEXT	CHILD
	(G turns back to table and	
	pours tea in her cup)	
		/ʌ gɛtən/ [this is Gretchen's]
Um hum/		
Do you like milk in your tea?		
		uh huh/
	(G picks up milk and hands it to M)	
		/hir/ Mom/ [here Mom]
Should I pour?		
		yeah/
Which one's yours?		
		/gɛtən ti/ [Gretchen's tea]
	(G gets up and goes to refrigerator)	
		/i · i/ [eat, eat]
Are you gonna come and eat too?		
		uh huh/
		/mor ʤus/ [more juice]
	(G gets pitcher out of refrigerator)	
		/hir/ Mom/ [here Mom]
	(G hands pitcher to M and picks	
	up cup)	
Oh thank you/		
		/aʊ doti/ [all dirty]
Is that cup dirty?		
You could wash it/		
		uh huh/
	(G carries cup to sink then turns	
	as camera moves)	
		/wʌ zæ?/ [what's that?]

ADULT	CONTEXT	CHILD
That's the camera/		
It's taking a picture of you/		
	(C enters room and talks with M, then M leaves)	
Are you playing house?		
		uh huh/
	(G brings pan from oven to table)	
		/ʌ hot/ [that's hot]
Is that cake hot?		
		uh huh/
Gretchen what's this?	(C showing teacup)	
		/ʌ hom/ [at home]
You have one at home?		
But what is this?		
		/ʌp/ [cup]
		/gɛtən/ [Gretchen's]
That's Gretchen's cup/		
You're right/		
	(C picks up bag of cars)	
What are these?		
		/ʌ hom/ [at home]
You have these at home?		
What are they?		
You tell me/		
		/arz/ [cars]
You're right/		
they're cars/		
Can you come sit down?	(C pulling out chair)	
Come sit down/		

  © **1993 Thinking Publications** *Duplication permitted for educational use only.*

ADULT	CONTEXT	CHILD
	(G walks toward table)	
		/oke/ [okay]
	(G points to chair)	
		/jɛo/ [yellow]
Yellow/		
The chair is yellow/		
Do you have a yellow chair like		
that at home?		
		yeah/
		/ʌ hom/ [at home]
You have a yellow chair at home?		
		uh huh/
Can you sit down?		
	(G turns back to refrigerator)	
		/ʌ kek/ [a cake]
	(G brings cake to table)	
Oh you need the cake/		
	(G points to table)	
		Mama /ðə/ [Momma there]
Is that Mama's place?		
		/m hm/
Do you help your mom at home?		
		/hom kek/ [home cake]
	(G picks up container of	
	raisins and looks at C)	
Those are raisins/		
		/it/ [eat]
Sure you can eat them/		
	(G opens container and takes	

© 1993 **Thinking Publications** *Duplication permitted for educational use only.*

ADULT	CONTEXT	CHILD
	out raisin)	
		/it/ [eat]
You can eat it/		
	(G puts raisin in mouth)	
		/mmm/
Is that good?		
	(G turns back to cupboard)	
Now what are you making?		
		/kiki æn dʒus/ [cookie and juice]
Cookies and juice?		
Oh boy/		
	(G walks back to table)	
		Ma /bʌ aɪ bæk/ [Mom be right back]
Yup/		
Your mom will be right back/		
		/bʌ kiki/ [bake cookies]
Oh you're going to make cookies?		
		/no Mɑ/ [no Mom]
Oh/		
Your mom is going to bake cookies?		
When she comes back in?		
		/no hom/ [no at home]
Oh I see/		
Gretchen what's this?	(C holding up blue cup)	
		/bu/ [blue]
That's what color it is/		
	(G points to pink cup)	
		/æ pi/ [that's pink]
You're right!/		

 © **1993 Thinking Publications** *Duplication permitted for educational use only.*

ADULT	CONTEXT	CHILD
That one is pink/		
Do you know what color this is?	(C holding up white fork)	
		/i ʌ aɪt/ [that is white]
Very good!/		
	(G turns to stove and picks up teapot)	
Careful you don't burn yourself/		
		/ʌ aʊwi/ [a owie]
Yes you'd get an owie/		
	(G shows C empty cookie box)	
		/no mor kiki/ [no more cookies]
Oh are the cookies all gone?		
		uh huh/
No more cookies/		
	(G turns on "water" in sink)	
		/ʌ duti/ [all dirty]
Are your hands all dirty?		
	(G nods head)	
You washed your hands/		
	(G comes back to table)	
Can I eat your mom's food?		
		/ʌ/ Mama/ [that's Mama's]
Oh that's your mother's food?		
		/ʌ Mɑmɑ it/ [Mama eat]
Okay/		
I'll leave it so Mama can eat it/		
	(C starts putting cars back in bag)	
		no/
		/maɪn/ [mine]

© **1993 Thinking Publications** *Duplication permitted for educational use only.*

ADULT	CONTEXT	CHILD
Oh don't put those away/		
Oh they're yours/		
But we need to put them in the bag/		
	(G reaches for bag)	
		/ʌ aut/ [take them out]
Do you want them out?		
Okay/		
Let's put 'em on the table/		
	(G and C take cars out of bag	
	and line them up on the table)	
There!/		
	(C picks up box of buttons)	
What are these?		
		/bʌən/ [buttons]
Buttons good/		
That's right/		
		/ʌ hom/ [at home]
Oh you have those at home too?		
	(G looking at door)	Mama/
Gretchen/		
Where is your mom?		
		/bi aɪ bæk/ [be right back]
You're right/		
She'll be right back/		
Gretchen?		
Where's the sink?		
	(G turns to sink)	
		/ʌvəðə/ [over there]
	(G walking to sink)	

 © **1993 Thinking Publications** *Duplication permitted for educational use only.*

ADULT	CONTEXT	CHILD
You're right/		
It's over there/		
	(G turns on "water")	
What's Gretchen doing?		
		/ʌ duti/ [all dirty]
I see/		
Your hands are all dirty?		
	(G starts stirring in pan on stove)	
		/ʌ/ Mama/ [for Mama]
Mama?		
Are you being a mama?		
		/ʌ/ Mama/ [for Mama]
You making something for Mama?		
	(G carries pan over to table)	
		Mama /dɪ/ [Mama sit]
Oh your mama _____ /		
	(G walks around chair, falls down)	
		oop/
		/ɔ daun/ [fall down]
	(C reaches for G)	
Woops/		
Are you okay?		
	(G gets up)	
You fell down/		
	(G looks toward door)	
		/Mama/bi aɪt bæk/ [Mama be right back]
	(camera moves)	
You're right/		
		/wʌz æt?/ [what's that?]

© **1993 Thinking Publications** *Duplication permitted for educational use only.*

APPENDIX C

Semantic Analysis
Blank Forms and
Example of Completed Analysis
Forms for Sara

Bloom's (1973) One-Word Utterance Types

Substantive	Naming	Function

Bloom's One-Word Utterance Types

_____ Substantive = _____ % of Total One-Word Utterances

_____ Naming = _____ % of Total One-Word Utterances

_____ Function = _____ % of Total One-Word Utterances

TOTAL NUMBER OF ONE-WORD UTTERANCES _____

TOTAL NUMBER OF UTTERANCES _____

_____ % OF TOTAL UTTERANCES

© 1993 **Thinking Publications** *Duplication permitted for educational use only.*

Semantic Analysis
One-Word Utterances

Name of Child _____

Nelson's (1973) One-Word Utterance Types

General Nominals	Specific Nominals	Action Words	Modifiers	Personal-Social	Function Words

Nelson's One-Word Utterance Types

_____ General Nominals = _____% of Total One-Word Utterances

_____ Specific Nominals = _____% of Total One-Word Utterances

_____ Action Words = _____% of Total One-Word Utterances

_____ Modifiers = _____% of Total One-Word Utterances

_____ Personal-Social = _____% of Total One-Word Utterances

_____ Function Words = _____% of Total One-Word Utterances

TOTAL NUMBER OF ONE-WORD UTTERANCES _____

TOTAL NUMBER OF UTTERANCES _____

_____ % OF TOTAL UTTERANCES

© **1993 Thinking Publications** *Duplication permitted for educational use only.*

Semantic Analysis
Coding Sheet

Name of Child _____

Utterance Number	Semantic Coding	Question

© 1993 Thinking Publications *Duplication permitted for educational use only.*

Semantic Analysis
Total Use of Individual Semantic Roles

Name of Child _____

ROLES	TALLY	#	%
Action			
Entity (one-term)			
Entity (multi-term)			
Locative			
Negation			
Agent			
Object			
Demonstrative			
Recurrence			
Attribute			
Possessor			

ROLES	TALLY	#	%
Adverbial Action/Attribute or State/Attribute			
Quantifier			
State			
Experiencer			
Recipient			
Beneficiary			
Created Object			
Comitative			
Instrument			
Other			
TOTAL			

© 1993 Thinking Publications Duplication permitted for educational use only.

Summary   Name of Child _____

Total Number of Semantically Coded Utterances _____ = _____% of Total Utterances

Percentage of Total Semantic Roles Accounted for by each Semantic Role:

ACTION = _____ %

ENTITY (one-term) = _____ %

ENTITY (multi-term) = _____ %

LOCATIVE = _____ %

NEGATION = _____ %

AGENT = _____ %

OBJECT = _____ %

DEMONSTRATIVE = _____ %

RECURRENCE = _____ %

ATTRIBUTE = _____ %

POSSESSOR = _____ %

ADVERBIAL = _____ %

QUANTIFIER = _____ %

STATE = _____ %

EXPERIENCER = _____ %

RECIPIENT = _____ %

BENEFICIARY = _____ %

CREATED OBJECT = _____ %

COMITATIVE = _____ %

INSTRUMENT = _____ %

OTHER = _____ %

Total Number of Utterances
Coded Conversational Device _____ = _____ % of Total Utterances

Total Number of Utterances
Coded Communication Routine _____ = _____ % of Total Utterances

Total Number of Utterances
Coded Complex _____ = _____ % of Total Utterances

© 1993 Thinking Publications *Duplication permitted for educational use only.*   **229**

Semantic Analysis
Meaning Relationships in One- and Multi-Word Utterances

Name of Child _____

Utterance Number	One-Term	Two-Term	Three-Term	Four-Term Plus	Complex	Conver-sational Device	Communi-cation Routine	Other
1								
2								
3								
4								
5								
6								
7								
8								
9								
10								
11								
12								
13								
14								
15								
16								
17								
18								
19								
20								
21								
22								
23								
24								
25								

Utterance Number	One-Term	Two-Term	Three-Term	Four-Term Plus	Complex	Conver-sational Device	Communi-cation Routine	Other
26								
27								
28								
29								
30								
31								
32								
33								
34								
35								
36								
37								
38								
39								
40								
41								
42								
43								
44								
45								
46								
47								
48								
49								
50								

© 1993 Thinking Publications *Duplication permitted for educational use only.*

Other	Communi-cation Routine	Conver-sational Device	Complex	Four-Term Plus	Three-Term	Two-Term	One-Term	Utterance Number
								76
								77
								78
								79
								80
								81
								82
								83
								84
								85
								86
								87
								88
								89
								90
								91
								92
								93
								94
								95
								96
								97
								98
								99
								100
								Total

Other	Communi-cation Routine	Conver-sational Device	Complex	Four-Term Plus	Three-Term	Two-Term	One-Term	Utterance Number
								51
								52
								53
								54
								55
								56
								57
								58
								59
								60
								61
								62
								63
								64
								65
								66
								67
								68
								69
								70
								71
								72
								73
								74
								75

© 1993 **Thinking Publications** *Duplication permitted for educational use only.*

Semantic Analysis
Brown's Prevalent Semantic Relations

Name of Child _____

TWO-TERM	UTTERANCE NUMBER	DEMONSTRATIVE	ATTRIBUTIVE	POSSESSIVE
Agent-Action				
Action-Object				
Agent-Object				
Demonstrative-Entity				
Entity-Locative				
Action-Locative				
Possessor-Possession				
Attribute-Entity				
THREE-TERM				
Agent-Action-Object				
Agent-Action-Locative				
Action-Object-Locative				

© 1993 Thinking Publications *Duplication permitted for educational use only.*

Summary

TWO-TERM PREVALENT SEMANTIC RELATIONS

_____ Agent-Action	_____ Dem	_____ Att	_____ Poss	=	Total of _____	_____ Expansions
_____ Action-Object	_____ Dem	_____ Att	_____ Poss	=	Total of _____	_____ Expansions
_____ Agent-Object						
_____ Demonstrative-Entity		_____ Att	_____ Poss	=	Total of _____	_____ Expansions
_____ Entity-Locative	_____ Dem	_____ Att	_____ Poss	=	Total of _____	_____ Expansions
_____ Action-Locative						
_____ Possessor-Possession	_____ Dem	_____ Att		=	Total of _____	_____ Expansions
_____ Attribute-Entity						

_____ TOTAL Two-Term Prevalent Semantic Relations   TOTAL of _____ = _____ Expansions

= _____ _____ % of Total Multi-Term Utterances

= _____ _____ % of Total Semantically Coded Utterances   Percent of Total Semantically Coded Utterances _____ = _____ %

THREE-TERM PREVALENT SEMANTIC RELATIONS

_____ Agent-Action-Object

_____ Agent-Action-Locative

_____ Action-Object-Locative

_____ TOTAL Classic Three-Term Semantic Relations

= _____ _____ % of Total Multi-Term Utterances

= _____ _____ % of Total Semantically Coded Utterances

© 1993 Thinking Publications *Duplication permitted for educational use only.*

Semantic Analysis
Type-Token Ratio

Name of Child _____

Utterances _____

Nouns	Verbs	Adjectives	Adverbs	Prepositions

© 1993 Thinking Publications *Duplication permitted for educational use only.*

Pronouns	Conjunctions	Negative/Affirmative	Articles	Wh-Words

Total Number of Different:

Nouns _____

Verbs _____

Adjectives _____

Adverbs _____

Prepositions _____

Pronouns _____

Conjunctions _____

Negative/Affirmative _____

Articles _____

Wh-Words _____

TOTAL NUMBER OF DIFFERENT WORDS _____

Total Number of:

Nouns _____

Verbs _____

Adjectives _____

Adverbs _____

Prepositions _____

Pronouns _____

Conjunctions _____

Negative/Affirmative _____

Articles _____

Wh-Words _____

TOTAL NUMBER OF WORDS _____

$$\frac{\text{Total Number of Different Words}}{\text{Total Number of Words}} = \underline{\hspace{1.5cm}} = \text{Type-Token Ratio (TTR)}$$

© 1993 **Thinking Publications** *Duplication permitted for educational use only.*

Semantic Analysis
Coding Sheet

Name of Child ___Sara___

Utterance Number	Semantic Coding	Question
1	ENTITY	
2	LOCATIVE	
3	ENTITY	
4	EXPERIENCER-STATE-ENTITY	
5	(CD)DEMONSTRATIVE-ENTITY	
6	DEMONSTRATIVE-STATE-ENTITY	
7	complex	
8	ENTITY	
9	AGENT-NEGATION-ACTION	
10	AGENT-NEGATION-ACTION-LOCATIVE	
11	complex	
12	ENTITY	
13	ACTION	
14	CR-sounds accompanying	
15	AGENT-ACTION-CREATED OBJECT	
16	DEMONSTRATIVE-STATE-(ATTRIBUTE)ENTITY	
17	complex	
18	ACTION	
19	AGENT-ACTION-OBJECT	
20	complex	
21	NEGATION-STATE-STATE/ATTRIBUTE	
22	STATE/ATTRIBUTE-EXPERIENCER-STATE	
23	AGENT-ACTION-INSTRUMENT	
24	AGENT-ACTION	
25	ACTION-OBJECT	

"NO" (circled, pointing to utterance 5)

© **1993 Thinking Publications** *Duplication permitted for educational use only.*

Semantic Analysis
Coding Sheet

Name of Child *Sara*

Utterance Number	Semantic Coding	Question
26	ACTION/ATTRIBUTE-ACTION-OBJECT-LOCATIVE	
27	CR-sounds accompanying	
28	ENTITY	
29	ACTION-OBJECT	
30	AGENT-ACTION-OBJECT-ACTION/ATTRIBUTE	✓
31	ACTION	
32	complex	
33	ACTION	
34	AGENT-ACTION	
35	OBJECT	
36	complex	
37	LOCATIVE-DEMONSTRATIVE-EXPERIENCER-STATE	✓
38	(CD) ENTITY	
39	complex	✓
40	OBJECT	
41	OBJECT	
42	CD-affirmation	
43	AGENT	
44	complex	
45	ENTITY	
46	other	
47	DEMONSTRATIVE-STATE-ENTITY	✓
48	ENTITY	
49	ACTION	
50	AGENT-ACTION-ACTION/ATTRIBUTE	

© 1993 **Thinking Publications** *Duplication permitted for educational use only.*

Semantic Analysis
Coding Sheet

Name of Child ___Sara___

Utterance Number	Semantic Coding	Question
51	ENTITY	
52	CR-sounds accompanying	
53	DEMONSTRATIVE-STATE-ENTITY	
54	complex	
55	CR-sounds accompanying	
56	CR-sounds accompanying	
57	EXPERIENCER-STATE-NEGATION	
58	ACTION-OBJECT-LOCATIVE	
59	QUANTIFIER	
60	DEMONSTRATIVE-STATE-ENTITY	
61	NEGATION	
62	ENTITY	✓
63	BENEFICIARY	
64	BENEFICIARY	
65	CD-affirmation	
66	BENEFICIARY	
67	AGENT-ACTION-ACTION/ATTRIBUTE	
68	CR-sounds accompanying	
69	LOCATIVE	
70	ACTION-LOCATIVE	
71	ATTRIBUTE-ENTITY	
72	ACTION-COMITATIVE-LOCATIVE	
73	AGENT-ACTION-LOCATIVE	
74	AGENT-ACTION-LOCATIVE	
75	AGENT-ACTION	

© **1993 Thinking Publications** *Duplication permitted for educational use only.*

Semantic Analysis
Coding Sheet

Name of Child ___Sara___

Utterance Number	Semantic Coding	Question
76	complex	
77	ACTION-LOCATIVE	
78	DEMONSTRATIVE	
79	LOCATIVE	
80	AGENT-ACTION-OBJECT-ACTION/ATTRIBUTE	
81	ACTION-OBJECT	
82	AGENT-ACTION-OBJECT	
83	DEMONSTRATIVE-STATE-ENTITY	
84	CD-affirmation	
85	QUANTIFIER	
86	complex	
87	ENTITY	
88	CD-affirmation	
89	ACTION-OBJECT-LOCATIVE	
90	DEMONSTRATIVE-STATE-ENTITY-POSSESSOR	
91	LOCATIVE	
92	DEMONSTRATIVE-STATE-LOCATIVE	
93	complex	
94	CR-counting/alphabet	
95	CR-counting/alphabet	
96	CR-counting/alphabet	
97	DEMONSTRATIVE-STATE-NEGATION-QUANTIFIER	
98	STATE/ATTRIBUTE-BENEFICIARY	✓
99	CR-counting/alphabet	
100	CR-counting/alphabet	

© 1993 Thinking Publications *Duplication permitted for educational use only.*

Semantic Analysis
Meaning Relationships in One- and Multi-Word Utterances

Name of Child __Sara__

Utterance Number	One-Term	Two-Term	Three-Term	Four-Term Plus	Complex	Conversational Device	Communication Routine	Other
1	✓							
2	✓							
3	✓							
4			✓					
5		✓						
6			✓					
7					✓			
8	✓							
9			✓					
10				✓				
11					✓			
12	✓							
13	✓							
14							✓	
15			✓					
16			✓					
17					✓			
18	✓							
19			✓					
20					✓			
21			✓					
22			✓					
23			✓					
24		✓						
25		✓						

Utterance Number	One-Term	Two-Term	Three-Term	Four-Term Plus	Complex	Conversational Device	Communication Routine	Other
26				✓				
27							✓	
28	✓							
29		✓						
30				✓				
31	✓							
32					✓			
33	✓							
34		✓						
35	✓							
36					✓			
37				✓				
38	✓							
39					✓			
40	✓							
41	✓							
42						✓		
43	✓							
44					✓			
45	✓							
46								✓
47			✓					
48	✓							
49	✓							
50			✓					

© **1993 Thinking Publications** *Duplication permitted for educational use only.*

Utterance Number	One-Term	Two-Term	Three-Term	Four-Term Plus	Complex	Conversational Device	Communication Routine	Other
76					✓			
77		✓						
78	✓							
79	✓							
80				✓				
81		✓						
82			✓					
83			✓					
84						✓		
85	✓							
86					✓			
87	✓							
88			✓					
89						✓		
90				✓				
91	✓							
92			✓					
93					✓			
94							✓	
95							✓	
96							✓	
97				✓				
98		✓						
99							✓	
100							✓	
Total	37	11	23	7	12	4	11	1

Utterance Number	One-Term	Two-Term	Three-Term	Four-Term Plus	Complex	Conversational Device	Communication Routine	Other
51	✓							
52							✓	
53			✓					
54					✓			
55	✓						✓	
56			✓				✓	
57			✓					
58								
59	✓		✓					
60								
61	✓							
62	✓							
63	✓							
64	✓							
65						✓		
66	✓							
67			✓				✓	
68	✓							
69			✓					
70		✓						
71		✓	✓					
72			✓					
73		✓						
74								
75								

© 1993 Thinking Publications *Duplication permitted for educational use only.*

241

Semantic Analysis
Total Use of Individual Semantic Roles

Name of Child *Sara*

ROLES	TALLY	#	%
Action	ⅢⅢ ⅢⅢ ⅢⅢ ⅢⅢ ⅢⅢ ЙЙ	29	19.2
Entity (one-term)	ⅢⅢ ⅢⅢ I	11	7.3
Entity (multi-term)	ⅢⅢ ⅢⅢ	10	6.6
Locative	ⅢⅢ ⅢⅢ ⅢⅢ	15	9.9
Negation	ⅢⅢ I	6	4.0
Agent	ⅢⅢ ⅢⅢ ⅢⅢ I	16	10.6
Object	ⅢⅢ ⅢⅢ III	13	8.6
Demonstrative	ⅢⅢ ⅢⅢ II	12	7.9
Recurrence		0	—
Attribute	II	2	1.3
Possessor	I	1	0.7

ROLES	TALLY	#	%
Adverbial Action/Attribute or State/Attribute	ⅢⅢ III	8	5.3
Quantifier	III	3	2.0
State	ⅢⅢ ⅢⅢ IIII	14	9.3
Experiencer	IIII	4	2.6
Recipient		0	—
Beneficiary	IIII	4	2.6
Created Object	I	1	0.7
Comitative	I	1	0.7
Instrument	I	1	0.7
Other	I *(Do not count in semantic roles)*	0	—
TOTAL		151	

© 1993 **Thinking Publications** *Duplication permitted for educational use only.*

Summary

Name of Child __*Sara*__

Total Number of Semantically Coded Utterances __*72*__ = __*72.0*__% of Total Utterances

Percentage of Total Semantic Roles Accounted for by each Semantic Role:

ACTION	=	*19.2* %
ENTITY (one-term)	=	*7.3* %
ENTITY (multi-term)	=	*6.6* %
LOCATIVE	=	*9.9* %
NEGATION	=	*4.0* %
AGENT	=	*10.6* %
OBJECT	=	*8.6* %
DEMONSTRATIVE	=	*7.9* %
RECURRENCE	=	— %
ATTRIBUTE	=	*1.3* %
POSSESSOR	=	*0.7* %
ADVERBIAL	=	*5.3* %
QUANTIFIER	=	*2.0* %
STATE	=	*9.3* %
EXPERIENCER	=	*2.6* %
RECIPIENT	=	— %
BENEFICIARY	=	*2.6* %
CREATED OBJECT	=	*0.7* %
COMITATIVE	=	*0.7* %
INSTRUMENT	=	*0.7* %
OTHER	=	— %

Total Number of Utterances
Coded Conversational Device __*4*__ = __*4.0*__ % of Total Utterances

Total Number of Utterances
Coded Communication Routine __*11*__ = __*11.0*__ % of Total Utterances

Total Number of Utterances
Coded Complex __*12*__ = __*12.0*__ % of Total Utterances

© **1993 Thinking Publications** *Duplication permitted for educational use only.*

Semantic Analysis
Brown's Prevalent Semantic Relations

Name of Child _Sara_

TWO-TERM	UTTERANCE NUMBER	DEMONSTRATIVE	ATTRIBUTIVE	POSSESSIVE
Agent-Action	24, 34, 75			
Action-Object	25, 29, 81			
Agent-Object				
Demonstrative-Entity	5			
Entity-Locative				
Action-Locative	70, 77			
Possessor-Possession				
Attribute-Entity	71			
THREE-TERM				
Agent-Action-Object	19, 82			
Agent-Action-Locative	73, 74			
Action-Object-Locative	58, 89			

© **1993 Thinking Publications** *Duplication permitted for educational use only.*

Name of Child __Sara__

Summary

TWO-TERM PREVALENT SEMANTIC RELATIONS

		Dem	Att	Poss		
3	Agent-Action	0	0	0	=	Total of 0 Expansions
3	Action-Object	0	0	0	=	Total of 0 Expansions
0	Agent-Object					
1	Demonstrative-Entity		0	0	=	Total of 0 Expansions
0	Entity-Locative	0	0	0	=	Total of 0 Expansions
2	Action-Locative					
0	Possessor-Possession	0	0		=	Total of 0 Expansions
1	Attribute-Entity					
10	TOTAL Two-Term Prevalent Semantic Relations					TOTAL of 0 Expansions

= __24.4__ % of Total Multi-Term Utterances   10/41

= __13.9__ % of Total Semantically Coded Utterances   10/72

THREE-TERM PREVALENT SEMANTIC RELATIONS

2	Agent-Action-Object
2	Agent-Action-Locative
2	Action-Object-Locative
6	TOTAL Classic Three-Term Semantic Relations

= __14.6__ % of Total Multi-Term Utterances   6/41

= __8.3__ % of Total Semantically Coded Utterances   6/72

Percent of Total
Semantically
Coded Utterances = __—__ %

© 1993 **Thinking Publications** *Duplication permitted for educational use only.*

Semantic Analysis
Type-Token Ratio

Name of Child *Sara*
Utterances *26—75*

Nouns	Verbs	Adjectives	Adverbs	Prepositions
cup	put /	two	now /	in //
table	sit //		down //	on /
pancakes /	do /		time	to
girl	lays		here	for //
Beret	are		like	at
milk	gonna /		inside //	with
Mamma	eat			
daddy	is ///// //			
children	go /////			
Mark	isn't			
Kristen /	playing /			
Pete	don't			
swingset	know			
swing	can			
teetertotter				
/// (teetot)				
birdseed				
sand				
house ///				
cow /				
people /				
he-mans /				oops
shelter /				also /
kids				
23/35	**14/32**	**1/1**	**6/11**	**8/14**

© **1993 Thinking Publications** *Duplication permitted for educational use only.*

Pronouns	Conjunctions	Negative/Affirmative	Articles	Wh-Words
it ////	cuz	yeah ///	the ///	how
you	and	no	a	where
this ////	but			who
she /				what
they /				
that /				
he				
I				
we /				
9/22	3/3	2/5	2/5	4/4

Total Number of Different:

Nouns	23
Verbs	14
Adjectives	1
Adverbs	6
Prepositions	8
Pronouns	9
Conjunctions	3
Negative/Affirmative	2
Articles	2
Wh-Words	4
TOTAL NUMBER OF DIFFERENT WORDS	72

Total Number of:

Nouns	35
Verbs	32
Adjectives	1
Adverbs	11
Prepositions	14
Pronouns	22
Conjunctions	3
Negative/Affirmative	5
Articles	5
Wh-Words	4
TOTAL NUMBER OF WORDS	132

$$\frac{\text{Total Number of Different Words}}{\text{Total Number of Words}} = \underline{\ .55\ } = \text{Type-Token Ratio (TTR)}$$

© 1993 **Thinking Publications** *Duplication permitted for educational use only.*

APPENDIX D

Syntactic Analysis
Blank Forms and
Example of Completed Analysis
Forms for Sara

Syntactic Analysis
Structural Stage Analysis Grid

Name of Child _____

Utterance Number	Number of Morphemes	Negation	Yes/No Questions	Wh-Questions	Noun Phrase Elaboration	Verb Phrase Elaboration	Complex
1							
2							
3							
4							
5							
6							
7							
8							
9							
10							
11							
12							
13							
14							
15							
16							
17							
18							
19							
20							
21							
22							
23							
24							
25							

Utterance Number	Number of Morphemes	Negation	Yes/No Questions	Wh-Questions	Noun Phrase Elaboration	Verb Phrase Elaboration	Complex
26							
27							
28							
29							
30							
31							
32							
33							
34							
35							
36							
37							
38							
39							
40							
41							
42							
43							
44							
45							
46							
47							
48							
49							
50							
Total							

© 1993 Thinking Publications *Duplication permitted for educational use only.*

Utterance Number	Number of Morphemes	Negation	Yes/No Questions	Wh- Questions	Noun Phrase Elaboration	Verb Phrase Elaboration	Complex
76							
77							
78							
79							
80							
81							
82							
83							
84							
85							
86							
87							
88							
89							
90							
91							
92							
93							
94							
95							
96							
97							
98							
99							
100							
Total							

Utterance Number	Number of Morphemes	Negation	Yes/No Questions	Wh- Questions	Noun Phrase Elaboration	Verb Phrase Elaboration	Complex
51							
52							
53							
54							
55							
56							
57							
58							
59							
60							
61							
62							
63							
64							
65							
66							
67							
68							
69							
70							
71							
72							
73							
74							
75							

© 1993 Thinking Publications Duplication permitted for educational use only.

Syntactic Analysis
Length Distribution Analysis Sheet

Name of Child _____

Length in Morphemes	Tally	Total
1		
2		
3		
4		
5		
6		
7		
8		
9		
10		
11		
12		
13		
14		
15		

Upper Bound Length = _____ morphemes

Lower Bound Length = _____ morphemes

Syntactic Analysis
Grammatical Morpheme Analysis Sheet

Name of Child _____

Grammatical Morpheme	Obligatory Contexts	Use	% Use
1. -ing			
2. plural -s			
3. IN			
4. ON			
5. possessive -s			
6. regular past -ed			
7. irregular past			
8. regular third person singular			
9. articles			
10. contractible copula			
11. contractible auxiliary			
12. uncontractible copula			
13. uncontractible auxiliary			
14. irregular third person singular			

© **1993 Thinking Publications** *Duplication permitted for educational use only.*

Syntactic Analysis
Data Summary

Name of Child _____

Stage	Grammatical Morphemes	Negation	Yes/No Questions	Wh-Questions	Noun Phrase	Verb Phrase	Complex Sentences
Early I							
Late I/ Early II							
II	1. 2. 3.						
III	4. 5.						
Early IV							
Late IV/ Early V							
Late V	6. 7. 8. 9. 10.						
V+	11. 12. 13. 14.						
V++							

© 1993 **Thinking Publications** *Duplication permitted for educational use only.*

Syntactic Analysis
Summary and Interpretation

Name of Child _____

1. Mean Length of Utterance
   in Morphemes (MLU):   _____ morphemes

   Structural Stage by MLU: Stage _____

   Upper Bound Length: _____ morphemes

   Lower Bound Length: _____ morphemes

2. Most Typical Structural Stage

   Grammatical Morphemes: Stage _____

   Negation: Stage _____

   Yes/No Questions: Stage _____

   Wh-Questions: Stage _____

   Noun Phrase Expansion: Stage _____

   Verb Phrase Expansion: Stage _____

   Complex Sentences: Stage _____

3. Most Advanced Structural Stage

   Grammatical Morphemes: Stage _____

   Negation: Stage _____

   Yes/No Questions: Stage _____

   Wh-Questions: Stage _____

   Noun Phrase Expansion: Stage _____

   Verb Phrase Expansion: Stage _____

   Complex Sentences: Stage _____

© 1993 **Thinking Publications** *Duplication permitted for educational use only.*

Syntactic Analysis
Structural Stage Analysis Grid

Name of Child: *Sara*

Utterance Number	Number of Morphemes	Negation	Yes/No Questions	Wh-Questions	Noun Phrase Elaboration	Verb Phrase Elaboration	Complex
1	2	—	—	—	EI–II	—	—
2	3	—	—	—	III	—	—
3	2	—	—	—	III	—	—
4	4	—	—	—	LIV/EV	LV	—
5	4	(—)	—	—	LIV/EV	—	—
6	4	—	—	—	LIV/EV	LV	—
7	4	—	—	—	—	III	EIV
8	1	—	—	—	EI–II	—	—
9	4	EIV	—	—	LIV/EV	III	—
10	5	EIV	—	—	LIV/EV	III	—
11	5	—	—	—	LIV/EV	LV	V+
12	1	—	—	—	EI–II	—	—
13	2	—	—	—	—	EI–II	—
14	1	—	—	—	—	—	—
15	3	—	—	—	LIV/EV	III	—
16	5	—	—	—	III	LV	—
17	5	—	—	—	III	LV	EIV
18	1	—	—	—	—	EI–II	—
19	4	—	—	—	LIV/EV	III	—
20	4	—	—	—	—	III	—
21	3	III	—	—	III	III	(LV)
22	4	—	—	—	III	LV	—
23	4	—	—	—	LIV/EV	III	—
24	3	—	—	—	LIV/EV	EI–II	—
25	4	—	—	—	EI–II	EI–II	—

(annotation: "response to yes/no questions" → Utterance 5 Negation)
(annotation: "Based on IF" → Utterance 21 Complex)

Utterance Number	Number of Morphemes	Negation	Yes/No Questions	Wh-Questions	Noun Phrase Elaboration	Verb Phrase Elaboration	Complex
26	6	—	—	—	III	EI–II	—
27	1	—	—	—	—	—	—
28	1	—	—	—	EI–II	—	—
29	3	—	—	—	EI–II	EI–II	—
30	5	—	—	EIV	III	III	—
31	2	—	—	—	—	EI–II	—
32	5	—	—	—	LIV/EV	LV	—
33	2	—	—	—	EI–II	EI–II	—
34	4	—	—	—	LIV/EV	V+	II
35	2	—	—	—	EI–II	—	—
36	5	—	—	—	LIV/EV	LV	EIV
37	4	—	—	EIV	III	LV	—
38	2	—	—	—	EI–II	—	—
39	6	EIV	—	—	LIV/EV	LIV/EV	V+
40	2	—	—	—	EI–II	—	—
41	1	—	—	—	EI–II	—	—
42	1	—	—	—	—	—	—
43	1	—	—	—	EI–II	—	—
44	5	—	—	—	III	V+	EIV
45	1	—	—	—	III	—	—
46	3	—	—	—	EI–II	LV	—
47	3	—	—	III	III	LV	—
48	1	—	—	—	EI–II	EI–II	—
49	1	—	—	—	—	EI–II	—
50	6	—	—	—	LIV/EV	V+	II
Total	155						

(annotation: "article in prep phrase" → Utterance 26 Noun Phrase Elaboration)

© **1993 Thinking Publications** *Duplication permitted for educational use only.*

Utterance Number	Number of Morphemes	Negation	Yes/No Questions	Wh-Questions	Noun Phrase Elaboration	Verb Phrase Elaboration	Complex
76	5	–	–	–	LIV/EV	LV	V+
77	2	–	–	–	–	EI–II	–
78	1	–	–	–	EI–II	–	–
79	3	–	–	–	III	–	–
80	5	–	–	–	LIV/EV	LV	–
81	3	–	–	–	EI–II	EI–II	–
82	3	–	–	–	LIV/EV	LV	–
83	7	–	–	–	III	LV	–
84	1	–	–	–	–	–	–
85	1	–	–	–	–	–	–
86	6	–	–	–	LIV/EV	–	EIV
87	2	–	–	–	III	–	–
88	–	–	–	–	–	–	–
89	6	–	–	–	III	I–II	–
90	7	–	–	–	LIV/EV	V+	–
91	4	–	–	–	III	–	–
92	5	–	–	–	III	LV	–
93	3	–	–	–	EI–II	–	EIV
94	1	EIV	–	–	III	–	–
95	1	–	–	EIV	III	–	–
96	1	–	–	–	–	–	–
97	4	–	–	–	III	LV	–
98	5	–	–	–	III	–	–
99	3	–	–	–	III	LV	–
100	1	–	–	–	–	–	–
Total	300						

5–0 morphemes

$300 \div 95 = 3.16$ MLU

subjective ALSO (→ utterance 54, Complex: LV)

Utterance Number	Number of Morphemes	Negation	Yes/No Questions	Wh-Questions	Noun Phrase Elaboration	Verb Phrase Elaboration	Complex
51	1	–	–	–	EI–II	–	–
52	–	–	–	–	–	–	–
53	3	–	–	–	III	V+	–
54	6	–	–	–	LIV/EV	LV	LV
55	–	–	–	–	–	–	–
56	–	EIV	–	–	LIV/EV	–	–
57	4	–	–	–	LIV/EV	III	–
58	4	–	–	–	EI–II	EI–II	–
59	1	–	–	–	–	–	–
60	4	–	–	–	III	LV	–
61	1	–	–	–	–	–	–
62	1	–	–	–	–	–	–
63	3	–	–	–	EI–II	–	–
64	3	–	–	–	EI–II	–	–
65	1	–	–	–	–	–	–
66	3	–	–	–	EI–II	–	–
67	5	–	–	–	III	LV	–
68	–	–	–	–	LIV/EV	–	–
69	4	–	–	–	III	–	–
70	4	–	–	–	III	EI–II	–
71	2	–	–	–	EI–II	–	–
72	7	–	–	–	III	III	–
73	3	–	–	–	LIV/EV	III	–
74	3	–	–	–	LIV/EV	III	–
75	2	–	–	–	LIV/EV	III	–

© **1993 Thinking Publications** *Duplication permitted for educational use only.*

Syntactic Analysis
Length Distribution Analysis Sheet

Name of Child *Sara*

Length in Morphemes	Tally	Total
1	//// //// //// //// ////	24
2	//// //// //	12
3	//// //// //// ///	18
4	//// //// //// ////	19
5	//// //// ///	13
6	//// /	6
7	///	3
8		0
9		0
10		0
11		0
12		0
13		0
14		0
15		0

Upper Bound Length = ___7___ morphemes

Lower Bound Length = ___1___ morphemes

5 — 0 morphemes

© **1993 Thinking Publications** *Duplication permitted for educational use only.*

Syntactic Analysis
Grammatical Morpheme Analysis Sheet   Name of Child *Sara*

Grammatical Morpheme	Obligatory Contexts	Use	% Use
1. -ing	*13, 15, 19, 24, 25, 33, 39, 81, 89*	*13, 24, 25, 33, 39, 81, 89*	*78%*
2. plural -s	*1, 35, 40, 72, 89, 91*	*1, 35, 40, 72, 89, 91*	*100%*
3. IN	*26, 70, 79, 91*	*26, 70, 79, 91*	*100%*
4. ON	*29, 50, 89, 92*	*29, 50, 89, 92*	*100%*
5. possessive -s	*69*	*69*	*100%*
6. regular past -ed	*76, 80*	*76, 80*	*100%*
7. irregular past			—
8. regular third person singular	*32, 67, 83, 92*	*32, 67, 83, 92*	*100%*
9. articles	*2, 3, 4, 5, 6, 16, 17, 23, 26, 44, 60, 70, 72, 79, 83, 86, 87, 89, 90, 90, 91, 98*	*2, 3, 4, 5, 6, 16, 17, 23, 26, 44, 60, 70, 72, 79, 83, 86, 87, 89, 90, 90, 91, 98*	*100%*
10. contractible copula	*4, 5, 6, 11, 16, 17, 22, 36, 37, 47, 54, 60, 86, 97*	*4, 6, 11, 16, 17, 22, 36, 37, 47, 54, 60, 97*	*86%*
11. contractible auxiliary	*15, 19, 24, 34, 50*	*34, 50*	*40%*
12. uncontractible copula	*44, 53, 90*	*44, 53, 90*	*100%*
13. uncontractible auxiliary	*39*	*39*	*100%*
14. irregular third person singular			—

© **1993 Thinking Publications** *Duplication permitted for educational use only.*

Syntactic Analysis
Data Summary

Name of Child *Sara*

Stage	Grammatical Morphemes	Negation	Yes/No Questions	Wh-Questions	Noun Phrase	Verb Phrase	Complex Sentences
Early I							
Late I/ Early II							
II	1. *78%* 2. *100%* 3. *100%*				‖‖ ‖‖ ‖‖ ‖‖ ///	‖‖ ‖‖ ////	//
III	4. *100%* 5. *100%*	/		/	‖‖ ‖‖ ‖‖ ‖‖ ////	‖‖ ‖‖ ///	
Early IV		‖‖		///			‖‖ /
Late IV/ Early V					‖‖ ‖‖ ‖‖ ‖‖ ‖‖ /	/	
Late V	6. *100%* 7. *—* 8. *100%* 9. *100%* 10. *86%*					‖‖ ‖‖ ‖‖ ////	//
V+	11. *40%* 12. *100%* 13. *100%* 14. *—*					‖‖	///
V++							

© 1993 Thinking Publications *Duplication permitted for educational use only.*

Syntactic Analysis
Summary and Interpretation

Name of Child *Sara*

$CA = 58\ mos.$

1. Mean Length of Utterance
   in Morphemes (MLU): _____*3.16*_____ morphemes

   Structural Stage by MLU: Stage _____*E/V*_____

   Upper Bound Length: _____*7*_____ morphemes

   Lower Bound Length: _____*1*_____ morphemes

$$\frac{3.16 - 5.32}{1.125} = -1.92$$

2. Most Typical Structural Stage

   Grammatical Morphemes: Stage _____*III*_____

   Negation: Stage _____*E/V*_____

   Yes/No Questions: Stage _____*none present*_____

   Wh-Questions: Stage _____*E/V*_____

   Noun Phrase Expansion: Stage _____*LIV/EV*_____

   Verb Phrase Expansion: Stage _____*LV*_____

   Complex Sentences: Stage _____*E/V*_____

3. Most Advanced Structural Stage

   Grammatical Morphemes: Stage _____*V+*_____

   Negation: Stage _____*E/V*_____

   Yes/No Questions: Stage _____*none present*_____

   Wh-Questions: Stage _____*E/V*_____

   Noun Phrase Expansion: Stage _____*LIV/EV*_____

   Verb Phrase Expansion: Stage _____*V+*_____

   Complex Sentences: Stage _____*V+*_____

© **1993 Thinking Publications** *Duplication permitted for educational use only.*

APPENDIX E

Pragmatic Analysis
Blank Forms

Pragmatic Analysis
Dore's Primitive Speech Acts

Name of Child _____

Act	Utterance Number	Total
Labeling		
Repeating		
Answering		
Requesting Action		
Requesting Answer		
Calling		
Greeting		
Protesting		
Practicing		

© 1993 Thinking Publications *Duplication permitted for educational use only.*

Name of Child _____

Act	Tally	Total
Requests		
Responses to Requests		
Descriptions		
Statements		
Acknowledgments		
Organizational Devices		
Performatives		
Miscellaneous		

© **1993 Thinking Publications** *Duplication permitted for educational use only.*

Pragmatic Analysis
Conversational Moves Analysis Sheet

Name of Child _____

UTT#	Turn Taking		Appropriateness			
	Initiating	Responding	Specificity	Conciseness	Style	
1						
2						
3						
4						
5						
6						
7						
8						
9						
10						
11						
12						
13						
14						
15						
16						
17						
18						
19						
20						
21						
22						
23						
24						
25						

UTT#	Turn Taking		Appropriateness			
	Initiating	Responding	Specificity	Conciseness	Style	
26						
27						
28						
29						
30						
31						
32						
33						
34						
35						
36						
37						
38						
39						
40						
41						
42						
43						
44						
45						
46						
47						
48						
49						
50						

© 1993 Thinking Publications   *Duplication permitted for educational use only.*

Pragmatic Analysis
Conversational Moves Analysis Sheet

Name of Child _____

UTT#	Turn Taking		Appropriateness		
	Initiating	Responding	Specificity	Conciseness	Style
51					
52					
53					
54					
55					
56					
57					
58					
59					
60					
61					
62					
63					
64					
65					
66					
67					
68					
69					
70					
71					
72					
73					
74					
75					

UTT#	Turn Taking		Appropriateness		
	Initiating	Responding	Specificity	Conciseness	Style
76					
77					
78					
79					
80					
81					
82					
83					
84					
85					
86					
87					
88					
89					
90					
91					
92					
93					
94					
95					
96					
97					
98					
99					
100					

© 1993 Thinking Publications Duplication permitted for educational use only.

TURN TAKING

_____ Initiating   =   _____ % of Total Utterances

_____ Responding   =   _____ % of Total Utterances

APPROPRIATENESS JUDGMENTS

Specificity

_____ Lacked Specificity   =   _____ % of Total Utterances

Conciseness

_____ Lacked Conciseness   =   _____ % of Total Utterances

Style

_____ Lacked Stylistic Variation   =   _____ % of Total Utterances

© 1993 **Thinking Publications** *Duplication permitted for educational use only.*

GLOSSARY

ADJECTIVE: a word that describes, identifies, or qualifies a noun, pronoun, or gerund by specifying typically size, color, number, or other attributes.

ADVERB: a word that describes a verb, an adjective, or other adverbs by specifying time, manner, location, duration, or quality.

ANAPHORIC PRONOUNS: pronouns that refer back to information previously stated in the utterance or in previous utterances.

ARTICLE: indefinite (*a*) or definite (*the*).

AUXILIARY VERB: a verb that has no independent existence in a sentence except to support the main verb (e.g., He *is* going home); auxiliary verbs are typically called helping verbs because they help the main verb by adding mood, aspect, or voice; simple auxiliaries include *be, have, shall, will,* and sometimes *get*; the acquisition of the auxiliary *be* is the only auxiliary that is considered one of Brown's (1973) 14 grammatical morphemes.

CATENATIVE VERB: semi-auxiliary verb forms (e.g., gonna, wanna, hafta) without an auxiliary that result from a syllabic reduction of the main verb and an infinitive verb form (i.e., gonna go = going to go); children tend to demonstrate a "partiality for particular catenatives" in the early stages of linguistic production and only later use a full range of semi-auxiliaries (e.g., I gonna go vs. I'm gonna go) (Brown, 1973, p. 318).

CLAUSE: a group of words that includes a subject and a predicate; main clauses may stand alone as a sentence; subordinate clauses are incomplete and must be used with main clauses to express related ideas.

COMPLEX SENTENCE: a sentence that contains more than one verb phrase; the additional verb phrase may be a full sentence proposition (compound sentence) or assumed within a clause.

CONJUNCTION: words that are used to join words, phrases, or clauses; coordinating conjunctions join sentence elements of equivalent value (single words, phrases, or clauses) and include *and, but, for, or, nor, either, neither, yet, so,* and *so that;* subordinating conjunctions are used to join two clauses, a main one and a dependent one, and include *although, because, since, while, until, whenever, as, as if,* and others which place a condition on a sentence.

CONTINGENT SPEECH: speaking turns that are linked to preceding turns through topic (e.g., I like dogs.—Me, too) and/or other conversational conventions (e.g., How ya doing?—Pretty good. And you?).

CONTRACTIBLE AUXILIARY: the contractible form of the verb *be* as an auxiliary (e.g., She is riding a bike. → She's riding a bike). Keep in mind that this grammatical morpheme deals with the *contractible* auxiliary, not the *contracted* auxiliary, and that the child does not have to contract the auxiliary to count this form.

CONTRACTIBLE COPULA: the contractible form of the verb *be* as a main verb (e.g., She is hungry. → She's hungry). Keep in mind that this grammatical morpheme deals with the *contractible* copula, not the *contracted* copula, and that the child does not have to contract the copula to count this form.

COPULA: the form of a verb, typically used as an auxiliary verb, that is used as a main verb; also referred to as a linking verb, the copula relates the subject of a sentence to the complement (e.g., She *is* happy. He *was* hungry); in relation to Brown's (1973) stages, only the copular form of the verb *to be* is significant.

DEIXIS: the process of using the perspective of the speaker as the reference; the use of spatial, temporal, and/or interpersonal features to mark relationships; deictic pronouns include *this, that, me, you;* deictic verbs include *come, go, bring, take.*

DEMONSTRATIVE PRONOUN: a pronoun that points out that which it modifies either as an adjective to the subject of the sentence (e.g., *That* ball is big) or as the subject of the sentence itself (e.g., *That* is a big ball); singular demonstrative pronouns include *this* and *that;* plural forms include *these* and *those.*

DISCOURSE: a unit of language sample analysis larger than the utterance encompassing, at the very least, adjacency pairs (e.g., request-response), and including several speaker changes that are linked by a common topic.

ELICITED SPEECH: speech that uses some part of previous utterances either through imitation (e.g., The doggie is _____. — The doggie is big) or through fill-in-the-blank (e.g., This is a _____. —Doggie).

ELLIPSIS: a conversational convention that shortens an utterance based on information from a preceding utterance (e.g., Who likes raisins?—I do [instead of *I like raisins*]).

EMBEDDED CLAUSE: a clause that is subordinated into a full sentence; see subordinate clause.

FORMAL ASSESSMENT PROCEDURE: a test, format, or inventory that has been standardized on specific populations of individuals.

GERUND: a verb ending in *-ing* that functions as a noun in a sentence (e.g., *Jogging* is good for your health).

GERUND CLAUSE: actually a phrase; a gerund and its modifiers; a gerund phrase can function as the subject of a verb (e.g., *Counting sheep* puts me to sleep), the object of a verb (e.g., I fall asleep *counting sheep*), or the object of a preposition (e.g., The monotony *of counting sheep* puts me to sleep).

GRAMMATICAL MORPHEME: a morpheme that adds to the grammatical structure of a word or phrase; one of 14 free and bound morphemes studied by Brown (1973), primarily because of the obligatory context each possesses.

ILLOCUTIONARY FORCE: the intended interpretation of an utterance or speech act; the illocutionary force must be combined with a proposition for the speech act to be conveyed.

IMITATIVE SPEECH: speech that repeats all or part of previous utterances (e.g., This is a doggie.—Doggie).

INFINITIVE: a form of the verb that consists of *to* plus a verb (e.g., to eat); infinitives typically are used as nouns and thus function as subjects or objects of verbs; infinitives can be used as adjectives (e.g., He ran out of places *to hide*) or adverbs (She was unable *to go*).

INFINITIVE CLAUSE: actually an infinitive phrase; an infinitive plus its modifiers and subject or object (e.g., I wanted *to eat the biggest cookie*).

INFINITIVE CLAUSE WITH SUBJECTS DIFFERENT FROM THAT OF THE MAIN SENTENCE: an infinitive form of a verb that has a subject that is not the subject of the main verb (e.g., in the sentence, *I wanted the train to go chug-chug,* the subject of the sentence is *I* but the subject of the infinitive is *the train).*

INFORMAL ASSESSMENT PROCEDURE: a descriptive analysis procedure based on the techniques used in collecting and interpreting data from research designs.

IRREGULAR PAST TENSE OF THE VERB: the form of an irregular verb indicating that an action has already taken place; there is no consistent device for marking the past tense of irregular verbs; (e.g., She *hit* the ball. She *ran* to first base. She *struck* out).

IRREGULAR THIRD PERSON SINGULAR PRESENT TENSE: the irregular form of the third person singular (*I* = first person singular, *you* = second person singular, *he/she/it* = third person singular) form of the present tense of a verb (e.g., She *has* a cold. He *does* the dishes after dinner).

LANGUAGE COMPREHENSION: the process of understanding language.

LANGUAGE PRODUCTION: the process of expressing language.

MEAN LENGTH OF UTTERANCE (MLU): average number of morphemes per utterance.

MODAL AUXILIARY: an auxiliary verb that carries its own meaning and influences the meaning of the main verb; common modal auxiliaries include *can, could, do, get, may, might, must, should,* and *would;* typical meanings include ability (*can*) intent (*will*), obligation (*must*), permission (*may*), and possibility (*might*).

MORPHEME: the smallest unit of meaning in a language, typically root words, but also all prefixes and suffixes in a language.

MULTIPLE EMBEDDINGS: sentences that contain more than one type of embedding; may include sentences with relative clauses and infinitives or semi-auxiliaries (e.g., I think we need to pour some water in it) and infinitives plus relative clauses (e.g., We looked all over to find jellies what's my size).

MULTI-TERM UTTERANCE: an utterance that contains more than one semantic role or grammatical category (e.g., Agent-Action-Object); there is not a one-to-one relationship between semantic roles or grammatical categories and words in an utterance (e.g., *The boy kicked the ball* has five words and three terms: Agent-Action-Object).

NARRATIVE: a story or description of actual or fictional events; may consist of one of four basic types: recounts, event casts, accounts, or stories.

NEGATIVE SENTENCE: a sentence that contains *no* or *not* within the sentence proposition (e.g., He *is not* sleeping; She wants *no* part of this).

NONCONTINGENT SPEECH: speaking turns that are not linked to preceding utterances.

NOUN: the name of a person, place, or thing; nouns can be common (e.g., girl, tree, house, rock) or proper (Bridget, Mama, Sara).

NOUN PHRASE: a noun, or phrase functioning as a noun, that fulfills the role of subject or object of a verb in a sentence; the only obligatory component of this sentence constituent is a noun or pronoun.

OBJECT NOUN PHRASE: a phrase that functions as the object of the verb (or predicate) of a sentence; the form of object noun phrases changes developmentally (e.g., eat *cookie;* I ate the *chocolate chip cookie*).

OBJECT NOUN PHRASE COMPLEMENT: a part of the predicate, or verb phrase, that serves to complement by stating in a different way the object of the verb, or object noun phrase (e.g., She made his room a *mess*).

OBLIGATORY CONTEXT: the grammatical obligation of a structure for meaning to be clear; in relation to Brown's (1973) 14 grammatical morphemes, use was judged to be obligatory, rather than optional, so that absence of the morpheme would indicate nonacquisition, not choice.

PERFECT TENSES: pairs of simple tenses (e.g., I *have written* four letters to the President) and progressive tenses (e.g., I *have been writing* every week) of verbs indicating that action was, is, or will be completed before a given time.

PHRASE: a group of words that functions as a single part of speech but does not have a subject and a verb; phrases may be used as a noun (*The red bird* flew away), a verb (*I could have eaten* more cookies), an adjective (The cat *with brown stripes* ran away), or an adverb (The sun came out *in the afternoon*).

PRAGMATICS: the study of language use independent of language structure; rules and principles which relate the structure of language to its use; a level of linguistic analysis.

PREDICATE OF A SENTENCE: the explanation of the action, condition, or effect of the subject of a sentence; the verb phrase of the sentence.

PREPOSITION: a word that shows how a noun or pronoun is related to another word in a sentence; most are simple (consist of one word: *at, in, over, of, to, under, up, from, with*) and introduce a phrase (e.g., *at the store; in the box*); may be considered a verb particle; in relation to Brown's (1973) 14 grammatical morphemes, only the prepositions *in* and *on* are considered.

PRESENT PROGRESSIVE *-ING:* the present tense form of a verb with an *-ing* ending indicating ongoing action; the present tense, progressive aspect of a verb (e.g., *going*) that when used in a sentence requires the use of an auxiliary verb (e.g., She is *kicking* the ball).

PRONOUN: a word that takes the place of a noun including *I, you, she, them, his,* and *ours,* among others; order of acquisition in production by Brown's (1973) Stages = I: *I, mine*; II: *my, it, me*; III: *you, your, she, them, he, yours, we, her*; IV: *they, us, him, hers, his*; V: *its, our, ours, myself, yourself, their, theirs*; VI: *herself, himself, itself, ourselves, yourselves, themselves*.

PROPOSITION OR PROPOSITIONAL FORCE: the conceptual information contained within an utterance or speech act; the proposition of a speech act is the speaker's meaning; the proposition must be combined with an intention for the speech act to be conveyed.

PROPOSITIONAL CONTENT: the meaning of a speech act expressed most simply as the noun-verb relationship.

REFERENT: a word that stands for a real thing (e.g., the word *ball* is the referent for a real ball; the word *bounces* stands for the activity of bouncing).

REGULAR PAST TENSE OF THE VERB *-ED*: the form of a regular verb indicating that an action has already taken place; the past tense form of a regular verb requires the addition of *-ed* to the verb (e.g., She *kicked* the ball).

REGULAR THIRD PERSON SINGULAR TENSE: the regular form of the third person singular (*I* = first person singular, *you* = second person singular, *he/she/it* = third person singular) form of the present tense of a verb; the regular third person singular present tense requires the addition of *-s* to the verb (e.g., She *hits* the ball).

RELATIVE CLAUSE: a subordinate clause that is introduced by a relative pronoun (i.e., *who, which, that,* and sometimes *what*) (e.g., My shoes have these holes *what your toes come out*); see subordinate clause.

SEMANTIC RELATION: a combination of two or more individual semantic roles and/or grammatical categories; typically, semantic relations express meanings in addition to the meanings expressed by individual words (i.e., the semantic relation *Agent-Action* expresses the relationship between the noun and verb in addition to the meaning expressed by the noun and verb).

SEMANTICS: the study of language content; rules and principles for the expression and understanding of meaning; a level of linguistic analysis.

SEMI-AUXILIARY: the words *gonna, wanna, hafta* used with a verb that appears to be the main verb of a sentence (e.g., He *gonna* go); the term *semi-auxiliary* is really incorrect in that semi-auxiliaries are actually semi-infinitives because they are reduced forms of infinitives that appear to function as auxiliaries in sentences (e.g., *gonna* is a reduction of *going to* in relation to a verb).

SEMI-AUXILIARY COMPLEMENT: a noun phrase which is the complement of the infinitive within the semi-auxiliary verb phrase (e.g., I wanna *pour the water*).

SENTENCE: a subject, or noun phrase, and a predicate, or verb phrase, that together express a complete thought; can be either simple (i.e., contains only one verb phrase) or complex (i.e., contains more than one verb phrase); in sentence notation, S = sentence and S → NP + VP.

SIMPLE INFINITIVE: the form of a verb consisting of *to* plus the verb; see infinitive.

SIMPLE INFINITIVE CLAUSE: the form of a verb consisting of *to* plus the verb used in a sentence without other sentence constituents (e.g., I wanted *to go*).

SPEECH ACT: a linguistic unit of communication consisting of a proposition and illocutionary force or meaning and intention; also considered when analyzing speech acts is the listener's interpretation of the speaker's meaning and intention.

SPONTANEOUS SPEECH: speech that does not repeat part of preceding utterances.

SUBJECT NOUN PHRASE: a phrase that functions as the subject of the verb (or predicate) of a sentence; the form of subject noun phrases changes developmentally (e.g., *boy* go; *The little boy* is going to school).

SUBJECT OF A SENTENCE: the person, thing, or idea, expressed as a single noun, pronoun, or noun phrase, being described in a sentence.

SUBORDINATE CLAUSE: a group of words consisting at least of a noun and a verb that cannot stand alone because it is introduced by a subordinating conjunction (e.g., *although, because, since, while, until, whenever, as, as if*) or a relative pronoun (i.e., *who, which, that,* and sometimes *what*).

SYNTAX: the study of language forms; rules and principles for combining grammatical elements and words into utterances and sentences; a level of linguistic analysis.

TOPIC: an aspect of conversation that holds conversation together; topic may be viewed as old or new in relation to previous utterances; may be manipulated using a variety of linguistic devices.

TYPE-TOKEN RATIO (TTR): a measure of vocabulary diversity obtained by dividing the number of different words in a sample of 50 utterances by the total number of words.

UNCONTRACTIBLE AUXILIARY: the uncontractible form of the verb *be* as an auxiliary verb; uncontractible forms are uncontractible because they cannot be pronounced as a contraction (e.g., The mouse *is* sleeping), cannot be pronounced as a contraction without losing tense or number information (e.g., They *were* sleeping), or cannot be reduced further because it is elliptical (e.g., Who is going to the picnic?—I *am*). Keep in mind that this grammatical morpheme deals with the *uncontractible* auxiliary, not the *uncontracted* auxiliary, and caution should be used in identifying uncontractible forms, not uncontracted forms.

UNCONTRACTIBLE COPULA: the uncontractible form of the verb *be* as a main verb; uncontractible forms are uncontractible because they cannot be pronounced as a contraction (e.g., The mouse *is* dead), cannot be pronounced as a contraction without losing tense or number information (e.g., She *was* sick), or cannot be reduced further because it is elliptical (e.g., Who is hungry?—I *am*). Keep in mind that this grammatical morpheme deals with the *uncontractible* copula, not the *uncontracted* copula, and caution should be used in identifying uncontractible forms not uncontracted forms.

UNMARKED INFINITIVE CLAUSE: infinitive clauses in which the *to* is not stated but is implied from the sentence structure (e.g., Help me [*to*] pick these up).

VERB: a word that depicts action or state of being; verbs typically function as the predicate of a sentence and explain the action, condition, or effect of the subject of that sentence.

VERB PARTICLE: a relational word that is associated with a verb (e.g., *up, down, off, on*); verb particles can be differentiated from prepositions by transposing the word in question to the right of the object noun and judging grammaticality (e.g., She *put on* the hat → She *put* the hat *on* = verb particle; She danced *on* the table → She danced the table *on* = preposition).

VERB PHRASE: the verb plus any additional words or phrases that are needed to complete the verb; the only obligatory component of this sentence constituent is a verb; object noun phrases are considered to be part of the verb phrase.

WH-QUESTION: a question form that requests specific information characterized by one of the following wh-words: *what, what-doing, where, why, when,* and *how.*

WH-CLAUSE: a subordinate clause that is introduced by a wh-word and provides adjectival information (e.g., I know *where he is*); typical wh-words that introduce wh-clauses and not relative clauses include *where, when, why, how,* and sometimes *what.*

WH-INFINITIVE CLAUSE: an infinitive that is introduced by a wh-word, therefore subordinated to the main verb (e.g., You know *how to make this;* Show me *what to do*).

YES/NO QUESTION: a question form that requires a yes or no response (e.g., More?; Do you want a cookie?).

SOURCES

Huddleston, R. (1988). *Introduction to the grammar of English.* New York, NY: Cambridge University Press.

Mosher, J.R. (1968). *English grammar.* Lincoln, NE: Cliff's Notes.

Owens, R.E. (1992). *Language development: An introduction.* Columbus, OH: Merrill Publishing.

Quirk, R., Greenbaum, S., Leech, G., and Svartvik, J. (1972). *A grammar of contemporary English.* New York, NY: Seminar Press.

Shertzer, M. (1986). *The elements of grammar.* New York, NY: Macmillan Publishing.

REFERENCES

Anderson, E.S. (1977). *Learning to speak with style: A study of the sociolinguistic skills of young children.* Unpublished doctoral dissertation, Stanford University, Stanford, CA.

Bates, E. (1976). *Language and context.* New York, NY: Academic Press.

Bedrosian, J.L. (1985). *An approach to developing conversational competence.* In D.N. Ripich and F.M. Spinelli (Eds.), *School discourse problems* (pp. 231–255). San Diego, CA: College Hill Press.

Beilin, H. (1975). *Studies in the cognitive basis of language development.* New York, NY: Academic Press.

Benedict, H. (1979). Early lexical development: Comprehension and production. *Journal of Child Language, 10,* 321–335.

Beveridge, M., and Conti-Ramsden, G. (1987). *Children with language disabilities.* Milton Keynes, England: Open University Press.

Bishop, D., and Edmundson, A. (1987). Language-impaired 4-year-olds: Distinguishing transient from persistent impairment. *Journal of Speech and Hearing Disorders, 52,* 156–173.

Bloom, L. (1973). *One word at a time: The use of single-word utterances before syntax.* The Hague: Mouton.

Bloom, L., and Lahey, M. (1978). *Language development and language disorders.* New York, NY: John Wiley and Sons.

Bloom, L., Lightbown, P., and Hood, L. (1975). Structure and variation in child language. *Monographs of the Society for Research in Child Development, 40*(2).

Bloom, L., Rocissano, L., and Hood, L. (1976). Adult-child discourse: Developmental interaction between information processing and linguistic knowledge. *Cognitive Psychology, 8,* 521–552.

Boehm, A. (1986). *Boehm test of basic concepts—revised.* New York, NY: The Psychological Corporation.

Bray, C., and Wiig, E. (1985). *Let's talk inventory for children.* San Antonio, TX: Psychological Corporation.

Brinton, B. (1990). Peer commentary on "Clinical pragmatics: Expectations and realizations" by Tanya Gallagher. *Journal of Speech-Language Pathology and Audiology, 14*(1), 7–8.

Brinton, B., and Fujuki, M. (1984). Development of topic manipulation skills in discourse. *Journal of Speech and Hearing Research, 27,* 350–358.

Brinton, B., and Fujuki, M. (1989). *Conversational management with language-impaired children: Pragmatic assessment and intervention.* Rockville, MD: Aspen Publishers.

Brinton, B., Fujuki, M., and Loeb, D., and Winkler, E. (1986). The development of conversational repair strategies in response to requests for clarification. *Journal of Speech and Hearing Research, 29,* 75–81.

Brown, R. (1973). *A first language: The early stages.* Cambridge, MA: Harvard University Press.

Brown, R., and Bellugi, U. (1964). Three processes in the child's acquisition of syntax. *Harvard Educational Review, 34,* 133–151.

Carpenter, L. (1991, November). *Narrative discourse in language minority and language learning disabled children.* Paper presented at the Annual Convention of the American Speech-Language-Hearing Association, Atlanta, GA.

Carrow-Woolfolk, E. (1985). *Test for auditory comprehension of language—revised.* Allen, TX: DLM Teaching Resources.

Cazden, C. (1968). The acquisition of noun and verb inflections. *Child Development, 39,* 433–438.

Chapman, R. (1978). Personal communication. In J. Miller (Ed.), (1981), *Assessing language production in children: Experimental procedures.* Baltimore, MD: University Park Press.

Chapman, R. (1981). Exploring children's communicative intents. In J. Miller (Ed.), *Assessing language production in children: Experimental procedures.* Baltimore, MD: University Park Press.

Chapman, R., Paul, R., and Wanska, S. (1981). *Syntactic structures in simple sentences.* Unpublished raw data.

Clancy, P., Jacobsen, T., and Silva, M. (1976, April). The acquisition of conjunction: A cross-linguistic study. In Department of Linguistics, *Papers and Reports on Child Language Development.* Paper presented at the Eighth Annual Forum on Child Language Research, Stanford University, Stanford, CA.

Coggins, T., and Carpenter, R. (1981). The communicative intention inventory: A system for observing and coding children's early intentional communication. *Applied Psycholinguistics, 2,* 235–251.

Cook-Gumperz, J., and Corsaro, W. (1977). Social-ecological constraints on children's communication strategies. *Sociology, 11,* 411–434.

Craig, H. (1991). Pragmatic characteristics of the child with specific language impairment: An interactionist perspective. In T. Gallagher (Ed.), *Pragmatics of language: Clinical practice issues* (pp. 163–198). San Diego, CA: Singular Publishing Group.

Crystal, D. (1982). Profile in semantics (PRISM+). In, *Profiling linguistic disability* (pp. 139–213). London, England: Edward Arnold Publishers.

Crystal, D., Fletcher, P., and Garman, M. (1976). *The grammatical analysis of language disability: A procedure for assessment and remediation.* London: Edward Arnold.

Crystal, D., Fletcher, P., and Garman, M. (1991). *The grammatical analysis of language disability: A procedure for assessment and remediation.* San Diego, CA: Singular Publishing Group.

Damico, J. (1991). Clinical discourse analysis: A functional approach to language assessment. In C. Simon (Ed.), *Communication skills and classroom success: Assessment and therapy methodologies for language and learning disabled students* (pp. 165–206). Eau Claire, WI: Thinking Publications.

de Villiers, J., and de Villiers, P. (1973). A cross-sectional study of the acquisition of grammatical morphemes. *Journal of Psycholinguistic Research, 2,* 267–278.

de Villiers, J., and de Villiers, P. (1978). *Language acquisition.* Cambridge, MA: Harvard University Press.

Dore, J. (1974). A pragmatic description of early language development. *Journal of Psycholinguistic Research, 4,* 343–350.

Dore, J. (1978). Variation in preschool children's conversational performances. In K. Nelson (Ed.), *Children's language: Vol. I* (pp. 397–444). New York, NY: Gardner Press.

Dunn, T., and Dunn, L. (1981). *Peabody picture vocabulary test.* Circle Pines, MN: American Guidance Service.

Ervin-Tripp, S. (1970). Discourse agreement: How children answer questions. In J.R. Hayes (Ed.), *Cognition and the development of language* (pp. 79–107). New York, NY: John Wiley and Sons.

Fey, M. (1986). *Language intervention with young children.* San Diego, CA: College Hill Press.

Fey, M. (1987, January). Personal communication.

Fey, M., and Leonard, L. (1983). Pragmatic skills of children with specific language impairment. In T. Gallagher and C. Prutting (Eds.), *Pragmatic assessment and intervention issues in language* (pp. 65–82). San Diego, CA: College Hill Press.

Gallagher, T. (1983). Pre-assessment: A procedure for accommodating language use variability. In T. Gallagher and C. Prutting (Eds.), *Pragmatic assessment and intervention issues in language* (pp. 11–41). San Diego, CA: College-Hill Press.

Gallagher, T. (1991). Language and social skills: Implications for clinical assessment and intervention with school-age children. In T. Gallagher (Ed.), *Pragmatics of language: Clinical practice issues* (pp. 11–41). San Diego, CA: Singular Publishing Group.

Gleason, J. Berko (1973). Code switching in children's language. In T.E. Moore (Ed.), *Cognitive development and the acquisition of language* (pp. 159–167). New York, NY: Academic Press.

Gleitman, L., Gleitman, H., and Shipley, E. (1972). The emergence of the child as grammarian. *Cognition, 1,* 137–164.

Golinkoff, R., and Ames, G. (1979). A comparison of fathers' and mothers' speech with their children. *Child Development, 50,* 28–32.

Greenfield, P., and Smith, J. (1976). *The structure of communication in early language development.* New York, NY: Academic Press.

Grice, H.P. (1975). Logic and conversation. In P. Cole and J. Morgan (Eds.), *Syntax and semantics. Volume 3: Speech acts* (pp. 41–58). New York, NY: Academic Press.

Griffith, P.L., Ripich, D.N., and Dastoli, S.L. (1986). Story structure, cohesion and propositions in story recalls by learning-disabled and nondisabled children. *Journal of Psycholinguistic Research, 15*(6), 539–555.

Hall, W., and Cole, M. (1978). On participants' shaping of discourse through their understanding of the task. In K. Nelson (Ed.), *Children's language: Vol. I* (pp. 445–465). New York, NY: Gardner Press.

Halliday, M. (1975). Learning how to mean. In E. Lenneberg and E. Lenneberg (Eds.), *Foundations of language development: A multidisciplinary approach* (Vol. 1). New York, NY: Academic Press.

Horgan, D. (1979, May). Nouns: Love 'em or leave 'em. Address to the New York Academy of Sciences. New York, NY.

Hresko, W., Reid, D., and Hammill, D. (1981). *Test of early language development.* Austin, TX: Pro-Ed.

Huddleston, R. (1988). *Introduction to the grammar of English.* New York, NY: Cambridge University Press.

Huttenlocher, J. (1974). The origins of language comprehension. In R.L. Solso (Ed.), *Theories in cognitive psychology.* New York, NY: Halsted.

Ingram, D. (1972). The development of phrase structure rules. *Language Learning, 22,* 65–77.

Ingram, D. (1981) *Assessing communication behavior: Procedures for the phonological analysis of children's language* (Vol. 2). Baltimore, MD: University Park Press.

Keenan, E., and Schieffelin, B. (1976). Topic as a discourse notion: A study of topic in the conversation of children and adults. In C. Li (Ed.), *Subject and topic* (pp. 337–383). New York, NY: Academic Press.

Klima, E., and Bellugi, U. (1966). Syntactic regularities in the speech of children. In J. Lyons and R. Wales (Eds.), *Psycholinguistic papers* (pp. 183–208). Edinburgh, England: Edinburgh University Press.

Kramer, C., James, S., and Saxman, J. (1979). A comparison of language samples elicited at home and in the clinic. *Journal of Speech and Hearing Disorders, 44*(3), 321–330.

Lee, L. (1966). Developmental sentence types: A method for comparing normal and deviant syntactic development. *Journal of Speech and Hearing Disorders, 31,* 311–330.

Lee, L. (1974). *Developmental sentence analysis.* Evanston, IL: Northwestern University Press.

Leonard, L. (1976). *Meaning in child language.* New York, NY: Greene and Stratton.

Leonard, L., and Fey, M. (1991). Facilitating grammatical development: The contribution of pragmatics. In T. Gallagher (Ed.), *Pragmatics of language: Clinical practice issues* (pp. 333–355). San Diego, CA: Singular Publishing Group.

Liles, B. (1985a). Cohesion in the narratives of normal and language-disordered children. *Journal of Speech and Hearing Research, 28,* 123–133.

Liles, B. (1985b). Production and comprehension of narrative discourse in normal and language-disordered children. *Journal of Communication Disorders, 18,* 409–427.

Liles, B. (1987). Episode organization and cohesion conjunctions in narratives of children with and without language disorder. *Journal of Speech and Hearing Research, 30,* 185–196.

Limber, J. (1973). The genesis of complex sentences. In T. Moore (Ed.), *Cognitive development and the acquisition of language* (pp. 169–185). New York, NY: Academic Press.

Long, S., and Fey, M. (1989). *Computerized language profiling version 6.1.* Computer software. Ithaca, NY: Ithaca College.

Longhurst, T., and File, J. (1977). A comparison of developmental sentence scores from head start children collected in four conditions. *Language, Speech, and Hearing Services in Schools, 8,* 54–64.

MacDonald, J. (1978). *Environmental language inventory.* Columbus, Ohio: Charles E. Merrill.

Mayer, M. (1973). *Froggie on his own.* New York, NY: Dial Books for Young Readers.

McLean, J., and Snyder-McLean, L. (1978). *Transactional approach to early language training.* Columbus, Ohio: Charles E. Merrill.

McNeill, D. (1970). *The acquisition of language: The study of developmental psycholinguistics.* New York, NY: Harper and Row.

McTear, M. (1985). *Children's conversation.* Oxford, England: Blackwell Publishing.

McTear, M., and Conti-Ramsden, G. (1991). *Pragmatic disability in children.* San Diego, CA: Singular Publishing Group.

Martlew, M. (1980). Mothers' control strategies in dyadic mother/child conversations. *Journal of Psycholinguistic Research, 9*(4), 327–346.

Martlew, M., Connolly, K., and McCleod, C. (1978). Language use, role, and context in a five-year-old. *Journal of Child Language, 5,* 81–99.

Merritt, D.D. and Liles, B.Z. (1987). Story grammar ability in children with and without language disorder: Story generation, story retelling, and story comprehension. *Journal of Speech and Hearing Research, 30,* 539–552.

Miller, J. (1981). *Assessing language production in children: Experimental procedures.* Baltimore, MD: University Park Press.

Miller, J. (1991). Quantifying productive language disorder. In J. Miller (Ed.), *Research on child language disorders: A decade of progress* (pp. 211–220). Austin, TX: PRO-ED.

Miller, J., and Chapman, R. (1981). The relation between age and mean length of utterance in morphemes. *Journal of Speech and Hearing Research, 24,* 154–161.

Miller, J., and Chapman, R. (1983). *Systematic analysis of language transcripts.* Madison, WI: Language Analysis Laboratory, Waisman Center, University of Wisconsin.

Miller, J., and Chapman, R. (1991). *SALT: A computer program for the systematic analysis of language transcripts.* Madison, WI: Language Analysis Laboratory, Waisman Center, University of Wisconsin.

Miller, J., and Yoder, D. (1984). *Miller-Yoder language comprehension test.* Baltimore, MD: University Park Press.

Mordecai, D., Palin, M., and Palmer, C. (1982). *Lingquest 1: Language sample analysis.* Napa, CA: Lingquist Software.

Mosher, J.R. (1968). *English grammar.* Lincoln, NE: Cliff's Notes.

Nelson, K. (1973). Structure and strategy in learning to talk. *Monographs of the Society for Research in Child Development, 38*(1–2, Serial No. 149).

Nisswandt, B. (1983). *The effects of situational variability on the grammatical speech forms of three-year-olds.* Unpublished masters' thesis, University of Wisconsin, Eau Claire.

Norris, J., and Damico, J. (1990). Whole language in theory and practice: Implications for language intervention. *Language, Speech, and Hearing Services in Schools, 21*, 212–220.

Olswang, L., and Carpenter, R. (1978). Elicitor effects on the language obtained from young language-impaired children. *Journal of Speech and Hearing Disorders, 43*, 76–88.

Owens, R. (1991). *Language disorders: A functional approach to assessment and intervention.* New York, NY: Macmillan.

Owens, R. (1992). *Language development: An introduction.* Columbus, OH: Merrill.

Paul, R. (1981). Analyzing complex sentence development. In J. Miller (Ed.), *Assessing language production in children.* Baltimore, MD: University Park Press.

Penn, C. (1988). The profiling of syntax and pragmatics in aphasia. *Clinical Linguistics and Phonetics, 2*, 179–207.

Phillips, J. (1973). Syntax and vocabulary of mother's speech to young children: Age and sex comparisons. *Child Development, 44*, 182–185.

Prutting, C., and Kirchner, D. (1983). Applied pragmatics. In T. Gallagher and C. Prutting (Eds.), *Pragmatic assessment and intervention issues in language* (pp. 29–64). San Diego, CA: College-Hill Press.

Prutting, C., and Kirchner, D. (1987). A clinical appraisal of pragmatic aspects of language. *Journal of Speech and Hearing Disorders, 52*, 105–119.

Pye, C. (1987). *Pye analysis of language.* Computer software. Lawrence, KS: University of Kansas.

Quirk, R., Greenbaum, S., Leech, G., and Svartvik, J. (1972). *A grammar of contemporary English.* New York, NY: Seminar Press.

Renfrew, C. (1969). *The bus story: A test of continuous speech.* (Available from the author at North Place, Old Headington, Oxford, England.)

Retherford, K. (1992). *Guide applied: Production characteristics of language impaired children.* Eau Claire, WI: Thinking Publications.

Retherford Stickler, K. (1980). *Appropriateness judgements.* Unpublished materials, University of Wisconsin, Eau Claire.

Retherford, K., Schwartz, B., and Chapman, R. (1977, September). *The changing relationship between semantic relations in mother and child speech.* Paper presented at the Second Annual Boston University Conference on Language Acquisition.

Retherford, K., Schwartz, B., and Chapman, R. (1981). Semantic roles in mother and child speech: Who tunes into whom? *Journal of Child Language, 8*, 583–608.

Rizzo, J., and Stephens, M. (1981). Performance of children with normal and impaired oral language production on a set of auditory comprehension tests. *Journal of Speech and Hearing Disorders, 46*, 150–159.

Roth, F.P. (1986). Oral narrative abilities of learning-disabled students. *Topics in Language Disorders, 7*(1), 21–30.

Roth, F., and Spekman, N. (1984). Assessing the pragmatic abilities of children: Part I. Organizational framework and assessment parameters. *Journal of Speech and Hearing Disorders, 49*, 2–11.

Sachs, J., and Devin, J. (1976). Young children's use of age-appropriate speech styles in social interaction and role playing. *Journal of Child Language, 3*, 81–98.

Schlesinger, I. (1971). Learning grammar: From pivot to realization rule. In R. Huxley and E. Ingram (Eds.), *Language acquisition: Models and methods* (pp. 79–89). New York, NY: Academic Press.

Schwartz, A. (1985). Microcomputer-assisted assessment of linguistic and phonological processes. *Topics in Language Disorders, 6*(1), 26–40.

Scott, C., and Taylor, A. (1978). A comparison of home and clinic gathered language samples. *Journal of Speech and Hearing Disorders, 43*(4), 482–495.

Searle, J. (1969). *Speech acts.* Cambridge, MA: Cambridge University Press.

Shatz, M., and Gelman, R. (1973). The development of communication skills: Modifications in the speech of young children as a function of listener. *Monographs of the Society for Research in Child Development, 38*(1–2, Serial No. 149).

Shertzer, M. (1986). *The elements of grammar.* New York, NY: Macmillan.

Shulman, B. (1985). *Test of pragmatic skills.* Tucson, AZ: Communication Skill Builders.

Smedley, M. (1989). Semantic-pragmatic language disorder: A description with some practical suggestions for teachers. *Child Language Teaching and Therapy, 5,* 174–190.

Smith, P., and Daglish, L. (1977). Sex differences in parent and infant behavior in the home. *Child Development, 48*(4), 1250–1254.

Stalnaker, L., and Craighead, N. (1982). An examination of language samples obtained under three experimental conditions. *Language, Speech, and Hearing Services in Schools, 13*(2), 121–128.

Stein, N., and Glenn, C. (1979). An analysis of story comprehension in elementary school children. In R. Freedle (Ed.), *New directions in discourse processing* (Vol. 2). Norwood, NJ: Ablex.

Templin, M. (1957). *Certain language skills in children: Their development and relationships.* Minneapolis, MN: University of Minnesota Press.

Tyack, D., and Gottsleben, R. (1974). *Language sampling, analysis, and training: A handbook for teachers and clinicians.* Palo Alto, CA: Consulting Psychological Press.

Tyack, D., and Ingram, D. (1977). Children's production and comprehension of questions. *Journal of Child Language, 4*(2), 211–224.

Weiner, F. (1984). *Computerized language sample analysis.* State College, PA: Parrot Software.

Weiner, F. (1988). *Parrot easy language sample analysis (PELSA).* State College, PA: Parrot Software.

Wetherby, A., and Prizant, B. (1992). Profiling young children's communicative competence. In S. Warren and J. Reichle (Eds.), *Causes and effects in communication and language intervention* (pp. 217–253). Baltimore, MD: Paul H. Brookes.

Wiig, E. (1982). *Let's talk inventory for adolescents.* Columbus, OH: Charles E. Merrill.

Wilkinson, L., Hiebert, E., and Rembold, K. (1981). Parents' and peers' communication to toddlers. *Journal of Speech and Hearing Research, 24,* 383–388.

Zimmerman, I., Steiner, V., and Pond, R. (1992). *Preschool language scale—3.* New York, NY: The Psychological Corporation.

Use the Companion Book to *Guide*!

Guide Applied:
Production Characteristics of Language Impaired Children

Guide Applied provides the language sample practice needed to develop expertise in transcribing, analyzing, and interpreting language samples of children with language impairments.

Four language samples are provided on audio tape; each sample containing 100 child utterances was professionally recorded. Two of the four samples are analyzed and explained in a step-by-step sequence provided by the author. The remaining two samples can be transcribed and compared against the author's results. These results are available in an **Answer Key** which may be obtained by university professors and professionals upon written request.

This resource is a top choice for teaching language transcription to university students. University professors considering **Guide Applied** for a course can order a *complimentary* examination copy by faxing a request on university letterhead or by returning the following order form. (Sorry, no phone requests accepted.)

✂

Please Send Me a *Complimentary Examination Copy* of
Guide Applied: *Production Characteristics of Language Impaired Children*
by Kristine S. Retherford, Ph.D.

Ship to:

Name _____   Title _____

Institution _____

Address _____

City _____   State/Province _____ Zip _____

Daytime Phone (_____) _____   FAX (_____) _____

Course Name _____   Enrollment _____

When Taught _____   Decision Date _____

Current Text _____

**THINKING
PUBLICATIONS®**
A Division of McKinley Companies, Inc.

P.O. Box 163 • Eau Claire, WI 54702-0163
715-832-2488 • **1-800-225-GROW** • FAX 715-832-9082